Sustainable Living For Dummies®

Ten Fossil-Fuel Busters

- **Let the sun heat your water.** Install a solar hot water system to cut your electricity use by up to one third.
- **Work with nature in the home.** Turn lights off during the day, use cold water to wash your clothes, and dry clothes on a rack or line rather than in a dryer.
- **Apply elbow grease.** Do the dishes by hand, sweep paths instead of pulling out the blower, and try hand tools in the kitchen and garden.
- **Reject plastic.** Take shopping bags with you everywhere. Buy a picnic set instead of throwaway cups, plates and cutlery. Don't buy plastic toys and doodahs.
- **Use public transport.** Catch the bus, or take the train when you can. Plan ahead so you can work around the timetable.
- **Get on your bike.** Buy a bicycle and ride it. It's good for your health, a great way to see the neighbourhood, and sometimes faster than sitting in peak-hour traffic.
- **Leave the car at home.** Walk or cycle to the shops, or go for a stroll in the evening. Visit friends who live nearby on foot.
- **Shop locally.** Buy small amounts of food when you need it. You may pay more per item, but you'll save money on wasted food, parking and petrol.
- **Read the ratings.** Whenever you're buying an appliance, look at the energy ratings and buy the most efficient appliance that will do the job.
- **Generate power at home.** If you can afford to, install solar panels or a domestic windmill. These devices can also earn you an income.

Key Ways to Reduce Your Rubbish

- **Avoid packaged food.** Buy fresh food and pop it into your own shopping bags. This is healthier and helps reduce your rubbish pile.
- **Carry your own shopping bags.** Billions of plastic bags are given away in Australia each year. Ninety per cent of them end up in the stormwater system and then the sea, and kill animals by strangulation or internal blockages. Carry your own shopping bags everywhere.
- **Buy quality goods that last.** It's usually cheaper in the long run and means you have less junk to throw away.
- **Get friendly with your local secondhand shops.** Give away your old clothes, furniture, books and music. Hunt for bargains on their racks and shelves.
- **Fix things as they wear out or break.** Don't let things deteriorate until you have to throw them out. If you can't fix them yourself, find a local repair shop or call a handyman.
- **Compost your organic waste.** Your garden will love the extra nutrients, you'll love the fresh flowers and food. The planet will benefit from less waste processing.
- **Recycle all paper and cardboard.** Nearly all councils in Australia recycle paper. Some even recycle milk cartons.
- **Buy only recyclable plastics.** When you must buy plastic, check the recycling number (see Chapter 8). Most councils recycle plastics type 1, 2 and 3.

For Dummies®: Bestselling Book Series for Beginners

Sustainable Living For Dummies®

Top Tips for Temperature Control

- **Use your windows to control the temperature.** Open your windows when the outside temperature is pleasant; shut the house up when it is not.
- **Use window coverings.** Curtains, blinds and awnings keep out the summer heat, and keep in warmth during winter.
- **Block air gaps.** Use 'sausages' to seal the gaps under doors, and hangings to divide rooms with permanent openings. Seal gaps around powerpoints and lights.
- **Dress appropriately.** Put on a woolly jumper instead of flicking on the heater.
- **Get the garden working.** Plant deciduous trees to shade walls that get full sun. Your house will be noticeably cooler in summer and warmer in winter.
- **Improve air flow in the roof.** Vents and whirligigs in the roof will shift hot air out of the roof cavity, cooling the house. You may want to shut them for winter.
- **Install ceiling fans.** Inexpensive to buy and cheaper to run than air-conditioners, ceiling fans keep the air moving to cool you in summer, and stop warm air lurking uselessly near the ceiling in winter.
- **Insulate, insulate, insulate.** Insulate the ceilings and the walls to save money and energy. Double-glaze windows where you can.
- **Buy energy-efficient appliances.** Check the ratings on any heating or cooling appliances before you buy them. Install them properly for maximum efficiency.
- **Use appliances sparingly.** Set heaters and air-conditioners on the minimum effective setting. It's usually more efficient to run them for longer at low settings than to use them at maximum settings for a short time.

Specialist Disposal Services

- **Vehicle oil:** Rather than contaminate the environment, find your nearest used oil recycling facility. Visit www.oilrecycling.gov.au.
- **Mobile phones:** Up to 90 per cent of the materials in mobile phones, and in batteries, can be recycled. Visit www.mobilemuster.com.au or call 1800 730 070.
- **Medicines:** For household safety and to reduce the impact of drug molecules in the environment, take them to your chemist to dispose of. For more details visit, www.returnmed.com.au.
- **Printer cartridges:** Toner dust and injket printer inks are heavy-duty pollutants. You can recycle them at many retail outlets. Or, check out www.recyclingnearyou.com.au for more information.

For Dummies®: Bestselling Book Series for Beginners

Sustainable Living

FOR

DUMMIES®

Sustainable Living For Dummies is a must-read edition for people in homes and businesses who genuinely want to follow the 'Life. Be in it.' view that it's time to 'live more of your life'. Not only will you be more in touch with the impact of your day-to-day life choices by adopting a sustainable living stance, but the whole planet stands to be more viable. This book is not only a practical first step towards sustainable prosperity, it's the next step that we all can take to move towards a more enjoyable life.

Dr Jane Shelton
Chief Executive Officer
'Life. Be in it.' International

Sustainable Living

FOR

DUMMIES®

by **Michael Grosvenor**

Wiley Publishing Australia Pty Ltd

Sustainable Living For Dummies®

published by
Wiley Publishing Australia Pty Ltd
42 McDougall Street
Milton, Qld 4064
www.dummies.com

Copyright © 2007 Wiley Publishing Australia Pty Ltd

The moral rights of the author have been asserted.

National Library of Australia
Cataloguing-in-Publication data

Grosvenor, Michael, 1966–
    Sustainable living for dummies.

    Australian ed.
    Includes index.
    ISBN 978 1 74031 157 1(pbk).

    1. Conservation of natural resources. 2. Organic
    living. 3. Household ecology. 4. Natural foods.
    5. Organic gardening. 6. Water conservation.
    I. Title.

333.72

Cover image: © Photodisc

Wiley Bicentennial Logo: Richard J. Pacifico

Printed in Australia by
McPherson's Printing Group

10 9 8 7 6 5 4 3 2

About the Author

Michael Grosvenor is a leading urban planning professional and freelance writer on sustainability. Through his work and writing, Michael promotes the benefits of making sustainable lifestyle choices. Michael has particular expertise in transport and advises the private sector and government on policies that promote increased public transport, walking and cycling facilities. Michael is a strong advocate for the important role that public transport plays in our cities and towns.

Michael is the director of his own consultancy and holds Masters degrees in Urban Affairs and Applied Social Research and a Degree in Town Planning. He is also a member of the Planning Institute of Australia and provides advice to the Institute on integrated land use and transport planning issues.

Michael has also lived and studied in New York City, in the United States, but currently enjoys an inner-city lifestyle in Sydney, Australia.

Dedication

To my best friend and partner, Justine — thank you for your encouragement and support.

Author's Acknowledgments

My desire to talk to the general public about sustainable living motivated me to write this book. I'm often preaching to the converted in my consulting work. The environmentalists, planners, architects, social scientists, engineers and geographers I work with find ourselves saying the same things to each other, and we're often scribbling messages and ideas on whiteboards that no-one else gets to see.

Writing a book for an audience interested in living sustainably has been very rewarding. Hence, I am extremely grateful to Lesley Beaumont at Wiley Publishing Australia for supporting my idea for this book in the first instance and then giving the go-ahead for its publication.

This book covers a lot of ground — way too much ground for one person to have the required expertise on every topic. I have been able to carry out the necessary research for this book thanks to the thousands of committed professionals out there who have tested, researched and published their findings about the problems facing the planet. This book could not have been written without their passion.

I thoroughly enjoyed working with editor extraordinaire Maryanne Phillips and thank her for her brilliant guidance and direction. I'd also like to thank Giovanni Ebono for his excellent editorial contributions and ideas.

Publisher's Acknowledgments

We're proud of this book; please register your comments through our Online Registration Form located at www.dummies.com.

Some of the people who helped bring this book to market include the following:

Acquisitions, Editorial and Media Development

Project Editor: Maryanne Phillips

Senior Acquisitions Editor: Lesley Beaumont

Technical Reviewer: Peter Warrington

Copy editor: Giovanni Ebono

Editorial Manager: Gabrielle Packman

Image Credits: © Good Environmental Choice Australia: page 62 • NAEEEP: pages 71 and 72, reproduced by permission of NAEEEP, www.energyrating.gov.au • Hush Energy: page 78, O'Connor Wind Energy Pty Ltd • Solahart Industries Pty Ltd: page 81 • Commonwealth Copyright Administration: page 97, Department of Environment & Heritage Water Efficiency Labelling and Standards (WELS) Scheme; page 271, Department of Transport and Regional Services. Both images © Commonwealth of Australia, reproduced by permission • BioNatural Australia Pty Ltd: page 119, www.bionatural.com.au • BlueScope Steel Limited: page 142, © BlueScope Water • © Biological Farmers of Australia Co-Op Ltd: page 182 • NASAA: page 183 (top), reproduced with permission of the NASAA • © Organic Growers of Australia: page 183 (lower) • © IFAT: page 200 (top) • Homeworkers Code of Practice: page 200 (lower), reproduced by permission of Homeworkers Code of Practice Committee • © Ecotourism Australia: page 289.

Production

Layout and Graphics: Wiley Composition Services, Wiley Art Studio

Cartoons: Glenn Lumsden

Proofreaders: Liz Goodman, Marguerite Thomas

Indexer: Max McMaster, Master Indexing

Contents at a Glance

Table of Contents

• •

Introduction

● ●

Welcome to *Sustainable Living For Dummies*. This book is designed to help you adopt a lifestyle that helps heal the planet instead of harming it. Living sustainably can also make you healthier, happier and probably wealthier. Eating more sustainably, engaging with your local community and finding new 'greener' ways to work and travel are not just good for the planet, they're good for you.

When you're at the beginning of a long journey, whether you're planning to lose weight, save money for an overseas holiday or start a new project, the rewards can seem a long way off. But with sustainable living, every change you make can have an immediate impact on reducing the pressure on the planet. It really is a win-win-win situation: For you, your community and the planet.

Your decision to embark on this journey could not come at a more important time. Scientists suggest communities may only have about another decade before the planet throws up its hands in resignation. Climate change, water shortages, energy crises, food shortages, new diseases — the list of problems caused by people's consumption habits is alarming, to say the least. Thankfully, more and more people are doing their bit to halt the slide.

This book is not about changing your whole life and living like a monk, though. On the contrary, this book offers practical advice to show you how to live, work and travel in a more eco-friendly fashion. I'm glad you're interested in finding out more. Welcome aboard — you won't regret it.

About This Book

More than likely you've picked up this book because you know the planet is in trouble. Therefore, throughout this book I provide tips, suggestions and examples to show you how best you can help out. In fact, this book deals with nearly every part of your life. I even poke around your bedroom and bathroom and tag along with you on your way to work.

I'd love you to sit down and read the book from end to end. After all, I think it's a great read. But realistically, you'll probably dip in and out of it to find the tips you need — I cover a lot of ground. Some parts are about making green choices, and focus on environmental actions. Other parts focus on fair trading and community involvement. And, of course, a big part of this book deals with healthy living, the food you eat and the place you live. Each of these themes has the same broad goal: To live in harmony with the planet.

I'm not expecting you to adopt every single one of the actions contained in this book. Far from it. I know from personal experience it is a life-long task to do so. There's no shame in starting small: Adopting any one of the hundreds of tips in this book is a great start.

Perhaps most significantly, this book is not just about actions you take in the kitchen, the garden and the laundry. It's about your choices as a consumer, an employee and a voter. Where you live, what you live in and where you work all have an influence on the health of the planet. I am confident that this book can give you an even better understanding of the choices available to you and how making these choices will make a real difference.

How to Use This Book

Sustainable Living For Dummies covers each topic in its own chapter. How many books provide you with detailed advice about fuel consumption in one chapter, then where to buy locally produced organic food in the next!

Some of you know enough about some topics not to want to listen to me. You may be more interested in taking action around the home, rather than at work. Whatever the case, skim the contents and go straight to the chapters that interest you most.

If you've come to this book as a sustainability novice and want a bit of background on the topic, then your best bet is to go straight to Part I and begin your journey there. You can then move through subsequent parts at your own speed with a much better feel for why each action is worthwhile.

How This Book is Organised

Sustainable Living For Dummies is divided into seven parts, with each part focusing on a different aspect integral to people's lifestyles.

Part I: Your Environment, Your Responsibility

This part defines what sustainability actually means. Find out why the planet is in trouble and why living sustainably is an important way to help out. It also talks about how you can influence governments to do more good than harm.

Part II: Home Sweet (Sustainable) Home

This part uncovers negative lifestyle habits that can't be sustained and what you can do to turn them around. It covers where you live, what you live in, how to renovate and power your home and how to tend your garden. But wait . . . there's more. This part also provides you with useful tips for becoming more energy efficient and less wasteful around the home.

Part III: Use It Again, Sam

The three r's — reducing, reusing and recycling — play a critical role in a sustainable community. The chapters in this part contain tips that help lower the amount of waste created and also reduce the amount of natural resources you consume when you buy new products.

Part IV: Sustainable Shopping

Let's go shopping. This part guides you to the most sustainable building materials, electrical appliances, recycling equipment, clothes and food. You name it, I provide you with help on how to find it.

Part V: Working More Sustainably

You can do a suprising number of things around the office to minimise your company's impact on the planet. In these chapters I explain how you can help make your workplace paperless — well, less paper-intensive — and more energy efficient.

Part VI: Travelling the Sustainable Way

These chapters encourage you to use the car less and consider alternatives such as public transport, riding a bike or simply walking. It also gives you the good oil on the innovations being made in developing cars that run on cleaner fuels, and how to holiday the eco-friendly way.

Part VII: The Part of Tens

In keeping with a long *For Dummies* tradition, this part is a compendium of short chapters that give you ready references and useful facts. I provide you with a list of the most sustainable actions you can take today, my list of most useful Internet sites, recent innovations to help you live more sustainably and tips for enabling your kids to grow up with a sustainable mindset.

Special Icons

No, I don't mean case studies; I mean inside stories about real, live people who have incorporated sustainable practices into their lifestyle. Councils, businesses and community organisations get a look-in, too.

This icon flags handy Web sites.

Warning icons are serious stuff. If you want to save the planet without crippling your lifestyle, read warnings carefully and take heed.

Don't forget these little pearls of wisdom. Remember, remember, remember . . .

This icon flags relatively in-depth detail. You may want to skim over these, or undertake further research on the technical area being discussed. Believe me, they can be fascinating.

Tips are the little things you can do to make your (sustainable) life more achievable. These brain waves offer you handy shortcuts.

Part I
Your Environment, Your Responsibility

Glenn Lumsden

'You use your half of the air the way you want, and I'll use mine the way I want.'

In this part . . .

Most people agree that humans are polluting and using natural resources faster than the environment is able to regenerate them. And when the environment has nothing more to give, the social and economic welfare of communities suffer. The balance needs to be restored — and fast!

Sustainability is not just about protecting the environment and becoming a greenie. Yes, adopting greener habits is the key, but sustainability also includes enriching the social fabric of the community you live in as well as ensuring continued economic prosperity. All these factors make living sustainably worthwhile.

This part gets to the heart of the matter and explains why sustainable living is such a good idea, and introduces lifestyle choices and habits you can adopt to help get the planet's balance back on an even keel.

Chapter 1

The Whys and Wherefores of Sustainable Living

• •

In This Chapter

▶ Understanding what living sustainably is all about

▶ Checking out the warning signs

▶ Adopting a sustainable lifestyle

• •

Have you seen the recent headlines? *Arctic meltdown just decades away. Global warming fuelled 2005 hurricanes. Natural disasters more common. Earth hottest in 2,000 years. Global warming to take economic toll.* What's going on?

Perhaps you already understand that these problems are caused by burning fossil fuels and by other human activities. Maybe you still need convincing. Or, perhaps you've already jumped aboard the Good Ship Sustainability and want to know more — every day, I talk to people excited about making the leap. So, in this chapter I outline both the problems that have been created by global warming and mass consumption, and the great benefits you're likely to gain by discovering more ways to live sustainably.

The basic premise of this book is that you live *sustainably* when the things that you buy, eat and use do not damage the planet. For example, it's not sustainable to eat more fish than can breed each year. If you do, the supply will eventually run out. The same applies to every resource that you use.

When you limit your consumption to a level that enables the earth to regenerate itself, you can live sustainably. Pure and simple. No magic wand required — just take your foot off the pedal to reduce the pressure you put on the planet as you go about your daily life.

Satisfaction Guaranteed

As with most things you do with a conscience, you have plenty to gain if you adopt a more sustainable lifestyle. The big advantage here is that you can save two (or more) birds with one stone. (Note that no feathered animals were harmed during the production of this book.) Living sustainably doesn't kill your lifestyle, it enriches it — on so many levels.

Living a sustainable lifestyle has been one heck of a satisfying achievement for me. Although I had been recommending sustainable policies professionally for many years, it was only through my wife's encouragements that I started seriously practising what I preach.

As an urban planning consultant, I travel far and wide for meetings and site visits. And I do it all on public transport. This is easy when my clients' offices are located adjacent to the rail network — it gets a little bit harder when they're located well away from it.

One of my major clients happens to be located in the middle of nowhere. I had to do some homework to work out which bus company serviced the area and what bus I could catch from the nearest railway station. But when I figured it out and successfully caught the train and bus to my client's office, it turned out that I was the only one she knew who used public transport to get there.

After talking to a few people in her office about this, I found out the following week that some of them had trialled getting to work by public transport. And they reported to me they found it so worthwhile, even from a financial perspective, that they thought they would take it up permanently. I can't tell you how satisfied this made me feel. Just like how satisfied my wife must have felt when I started sorting out the paper and plastics from our garbage and started adopting energy-efficient actions around the home.

Sustainability simplified

When I ask people to define what they think sustainability is, I often get a mixture of answers. The cynic usually suggests sustainability is something promoted by left-wing greenies. Others more concerned about the environment define sustainability as not screwing up the planet for the next generation.

Sustainable living is as much about healthy lifestyle choices, supporting the community you live in and enhancing the long-term strength of the economy as it is about environmental consciousness. That's why the word *sustainable* is better than the word *green,* which primarily concentrates on environmental protection, or *ecological* and *eco,* which focus on protecting the interrelationship between organisms (including humans) and their environment.

A Google search can shed more light on the many definitions and explanations that people use to describe sustainability. Here are some examples that I like:

- To keep in existence, to nourish, maintain or prolong.
- A process or state that can be maintained indefinitely.
- Sustainable living provides for the needs of the world's current population without damaging the ability of future generations to provide for themselves.
- When a process is sustainable, it can be carried out over and over without negative environmental effects or impossibly high costs to anyone involved.
- Meeting the needs of the present without compromising the ability of future generations to meet their own needs.

- Sustainability is an economic, social and environmental concept. It's intended to be a means of configuring civilisation and human activity so that society and its members are able to meet their needs and express their greatest potential in the present while preserving biodiversity and natural ecosystems, and planning and acting to maintain these ideals indefinitely. Sustainability affects every level of organisation, from the local neighbourhood to the entire planet.

The proof is in the pudding

You don't have to look far to see proof that sustainable actions work. In the last decade, Australians became more energy and water-efficient in the home, and began recycling and reducing waste.

Here's how these actions have made a difference:

- ✔ **Greenhouse gas emissions:** The Australian Greenhouse Office (www.greenhouse.gov.au) states that annual greenhouse gas emissions will only be 8 per cent higher in 2010 than they were in 1990. This is mainly because government agencies, businesses and homes are using alternative energy sources and becoming more energy-efficient. 'Business as usual' emissions growth — that is, no behaviour or policy changes — would have resulted in a 23 per cent growth by 2010. Of course, an 8 per cent increase is still not sustainable, but it's a start.

- ✔ **Water use:** In the 12 years between 1990 and 2002, average annual water consumption in New South Wales fell some 33 per cent. This is the result of heavy investment by governments in installing water-saving devices in new homes, and in encouraging people to reduce their water consumption.

- ✔ **Waste:** The government agency Resource NSW indicates that overall waste production in New South Wales has decreased by 7 per cent since the year 2000.

Even better results could be achieved if more people adopted a sustainable lifestyle.

Top Reasons to Heed the Warning Signs

Obviously, when you don't take care of something, it eventually becomes unreliable. And if you don't do something to service or repair it, it's likely to break down. I don't think there can be any debate that humans have not been taking care of the planet very well. In fact, the debate has recently shifted to whether the damage is reversible.

My personal rave

Humans have taken the planet for granted for too long. We expect the planet to deal with the waste that's generated from human activities in order to satisfy our insatiable demand for comfort and convenience. But tell-tale warning signs suggest that the planet can only take so much. We need to start repairing the damage.

It's time to face the facts. You and I, as members of the human race, clearly have a destructive impact on the earth (and our bodies). We've made the planet warmer, created intense natural catastrophes, used up much of the earth's natural energy supplies, created new viruses and even poisoned communities to death. We have managed high levels of economic growth in only part of the world and yet even this growth has resulted in planet-wide catastrophes. Of course, the planet will recover one day, but civilisation may not. The lifestyle that you lead is not only at fault, it's also at risk.

Some people say global warming is a myth, and that burning fossil fuels to power the world's energy demands is not affecting weather patterns. For the sake of economic growth, these people believe that you can just keep on digging for those fossil fuels — there's more where they come from — or technology will deliver a solution. Other people believe that water will never run out or, if supplies do run dry, that the water in the oceans can be used. The scariest point of view is that it's somebody else's, or another country's, problem.

The globe is warming up

Global warming is behind the most serious environmental problems. Scientists blame global warning for the rising sea levels, unnatural weather patterns and changing ecosystems (see the related sidebar 'Marching to extinction' for more details). Burning and refining fossil fuels for electrical energy and transport is the main culprit. When processed, these fossil fuels emit greenhouse-forming gases, such as carbon dioxide, into the atmosphere, which create a blanket that traps heat between it and the earth.

In Chapter 2, I explain in more detail why the earth is warming at an alarming rate — much faster than at any stage in history. The polar ice caps have started melting and sea levels are rising. If the polar caps continue to melt at current rates, coastlines will diminish and some smaller island countries may cease to exist.

Natural catastrophes are on the rise

The incidence and power of weather-related catastrophes are increasing. Scientists agree that these events are directly related to the rising temperatures in oceans caused by global warming, and that the world is likely to experience more catastrophic hurricanes, like those that begin in the Atlantic Ocean and hit the United States, and floods that devastate densely populated regions in south-east Asia and Europe.

Water — in short supply

Water, water — when will it rain? One effect of increased global temperatures has been to make arid areas even more arid and droughts last much longer. This has increased pressure on water supplies, and is exacerbated by the extraordinary amount of water used in homes, at work, in factories and on farms.

The traditional approach of damming natural waterways, creating new reservoirs and concreting streams and rivers is not enough anymore. Water sources are drying up, so the problem authorities now face is finding other ways to supply people with the water they need. I cover the supply problems and how to manage your water usage more effectively in more detail in Chapters 5 and 7.

The energy crisis is 'booming'

Electrical energy powers millions of homes and businesses around the world. Currently, the cheapest and most reliable way of providing electricity to cities and towns is to burn fossil fuels, such as coal, in power plants. Transport also consumes energy produced by refining another fossil fuel, this time, oil. And burning fossil fuels also creates greenhouse gases (as I mention in the section 'The globe is warming up' earlier in this chapter).

It doesn't have to be this way. Alternative energy sources that produce little or no greenhouse emissions are now available and, as demand increases, becoming more affordable. As well as switching to alternative sources of energy, some simple lifestyle changes can greatly reduce your energy consumption. See Chapters 4 and 5 for more information.

Using fossil fuels is a major environmental problem, but there's another aspect to this crisis. Demand for fossil fuels has been so high that the planet is running out of them. This imminent depletion may force world leaders to look more seriously at alternative, cleaner sources of energy.

Marching to extinction

Effects attributed to global warming may be irreversible. For example, some of the planet's oldest and most valuable ecosystems, including the Amazon rainforest in South America, the Everglades in the United States and the Great Barrier Reef off the Australian coastline, have already suffered some permanent damage. Animals, plants, fish, birds and insects are affected by changes to their environments, which means that many species will become extinct if these habitats are destroyed.

Ecosystems are not only affected by global warming, though. Increased urban sprawl, land clearing and tourism can also change or damage them.

Waste (out of sight, out of mind)

One tragic example of how humans have taken the planet for granted is the disposal of waste. Historically, your waste has been burned or sent to a landfill site hidden away on the edge of your city or town. (Fancy just dumping it in the ground, hoping it would all go away!)

Thankfully, many countries have stopped burning waste in big incinerators to reduce air pollution and greenhouse gases. The alternative, though, has been to send *more* waste to landfills. Now, many large urban areas are running out of suitable landfill sites. As well as running out of space, governments have to deal with the contamination of land where landfills are located.

Your health is at risk

Cars, trucks and factories don't only emit greenhouse-forming gases. Other gases and particles they release into the atmosphere induce respiratory infections and illnesses. A massive health bill is accruing for countries that don't control the emissions they produce.

Then there are the nasty byproducts of chemical production. Industries that manufacture medicines, plastics, textiles, detergents, paints and pesticides previously released these toxins into the air, rivers, streams or wherever they could hide the mess. Most wealthy nations have strict controls over this now. The downside is that many companies have moved operations to countries in the developing world that have little or no environmental regulation.

Despite recent tightening of regulations in Western nations, previous neglect still continues to cause health problems in urban areas; for example, soil and groundwater contamination is evident in areas near old industrial sites.

Sprawling cities, urban wastelands

Throughout this book, I suggest that the high consumption of electrical energy and fuel for car use is a function of the way people have decided to live: The type of houses people live in, the appliances people have in their homes and the sprawling nature of cities and towns all consume vast quantities of energy.

But if more people could live close to public transport and within walking distance of community services and facilities, they wouldn't need to use cars so often. And if people's homes and workplaces were designed to be more energy-efficient, less electrical energy would be consumed.

The impact of global trading

The relocation of Western manufacturing plants to developing countries is clearly not sustainable. They relocate to take advantage of cheaper resources and labour, to achieve greater profits. Many of your household valuables, including appliances, clothes and homewares, are now produced in developing countries by multinational corporations.

There are serious social impacts from this get-rich-quick strategy. People accept extremely low wages and work in sweat shops, for example, because they are offered no real alternatives, and so unwittingly assist the company to achieve much higher profits that it repatriates to the West — the rich get richer and the poor get poorer. This huge inequity seems to be taken for granted in the name of economic progress.

Global trading has also had major impacts on local economies in the cities and towns of developed nations through the loss of industries that once specialised in manufacturing these goods. Significant social issues confront regions with large numbers of unemployed people.

Affluenza

It's clear that the problems I mention in the preceding section are created by the production of goods (as cheaply as possible) to meet a perceived demand.

But *why* do people continue to crave fuel that emits greenhouse-forming gases, products made from plastics that poison the planet, food that has travelled thousands of kilometres, and use water like it comes from a bottomless well? It's simple — it's a lifestyle thing.

The desire for more convenience and comfort — or simply for more — is natural. The problem is, it's out of control. Without any brakes, economic growth has become exponential. Social institutions, morals, educational values and health matters have all taken second place to the economy.

In the long run, this is good for no-one. You might be better off working less, enjoying more time with your family and eating simpler food than consuming as much of the world's resources as possible.

Unhealthy pleasures

Mass consumption of food has led to mass-production of the way food is processed. Chemical additives, antibiotics, artificial hormones, genetic engineering and industrial farming methods have all evolved as a result of the need to get food to the table quickly and cheaply. Unfortunately, guaranteeing people's long-term health has not necessarily been a consideration in this process.

The predictions are dire

Scientists point out that the short-term implications of continuing to be blasé about the earth are dire. Here's a snapshot of what they're saying:

- Rising sea levels (resulting from warmer seas melting the polar ice caps) will result in the loss of land, with smaller islands disappearing first and then possibly whole coastal regions.

- The globe is in for more extreme weather events that may simply wipe out large communities on the receiving end.

- Increased flooding due to rising sea levels will wipe out prime low-lying agricultural land, which places greater pressure on the remaining areas to adopt unhealthy mass-production methods.

- Increased mass-production of food will lead to lower-quality foods and have major health implications for the population.

- Changing ecosystems could result in new types of viruses invading populated areas.

- Existing arid areas will become more arid, reducing water supply to urban areas and limiting agricultural production in rural areas. In developing nations, this will result in even greater rates of poverty than currently exist.

Top Reasons to Live Sustainably

This planet needs time out to recover from the onslaught it's received over the last 100 years or so. One option might be to get off — the earth, that is. The United Nations could organise an extended holiday for all humans to another planet, in which time the earth could get back to normal programming. (I pity the other planet selected, though.)

The other option, which I think the United Nation may favour, involves considerable more effort: Everyone makes behavioural changes and leads a more sustainable lifestyle — a lifestyle that provides a better balance between what's taken from the earth and what the earth can give back. Living sustainably provides lots of personal benefits for you, too.

The environment gets a chance to recover

The natural systems that have sustained life on earth to this point are remarkable. They evolved over billions of years. They're perfectly capable of healing themselves — if left alone — even during bizarre periods of human history. For example, during both World Wars in the 20th century, fish stocks in the North Atlantic recovered dramatically, simply because it was too dangerous for fishing fleets to head out to sea and capture fish.

Although many people believe that some environmental catastrophes caused by human activity may be irreversible (as I mention in the sidebar 'Marching to extinction' earlier in this chapter), an increasing number of examples show that a once-natural environment can quickly recover, if its deterioration is checked in time.

If you'd love to be inspired by what people are doing to repair the environment, visit the National Landcare program Web site (www.landcareonline.com). This program funds groups around the country to reclaim and rehabilitate areas suffering from serious environmental problems. Funding examples include reclaiming land ruined by siltation, fixing rivers and streams that appeared to be devastated by toxic algae blooms, and restoring forests that contain unique ecosystems.

Saving the environment can save you money, too

It just so happens that individuals who adopt sustainable lifestyles save money. You start consuming less. Here are some examples:

- Turning off lights reduces your electricity bill, and shortening your shower time and recycling your greywater reduces your water bill. (See Chapters 5 and 7 for more information.)
- Recycling and reusing your homewares and clothes can save you a stack of money compared to the cost of buying new gear. (Turn to Chapters 9 and 11.)
- Growing your own fruit and veggies in your own sustainable garden is much cheaper than buying them from a shop. (Check out Chapter 6 for more details.)
- Walking, cycling and using public transport is much cheaper than running a car. (See Chapter 15 to find out why.)

Living sustainably keeps the doctor away

Most of the sustainable actions and suggestions in this book are also healthy. The following are a few examples that come to mind:

- Buying organic fresh food goes a long way to guaranteeing that your body is not being infiltrated with pesticides, preservatives and other chemical additives.
- Reducing your car use ensures that you walk more often — this is a great way to get exercise if you rely on machines to do most other physical work. Relying less on a car also helps reduce smog and pollution levels, which contribute to diseases like asthma.
- Outfitting and decorating your home with natural products reduces the amount of volatile organic compounds (VOCs), which bombard your lungs every breathing second you're inside. At the same time, you can make stylish, artistic, comfortable and unique choices among the broad range of new sustainable options for home decor.

The future is brighter for local communities

Communities benefit when people start shopping and working locally. So does the environment.

Usually, people are happier when they live in communities and can share common experiences. For example, sharing food you have grown yourself, shopping locally and selling or giving away items that you don't need any more, all create connections between you and your neighbours.

Economic growth that minimises its environmental impact almost always empowers and enriches local communities — a win–win for everyone.

Being sustainable means being profitable

A business that makes a positive contribution to the environment and the community can ensure long-term financial profits. More businesses now invest in resources that are not going to run out or damage the community they're located within. Some short-term financial pain for long-term profit and gain. Yep, another win–win.

This economic realisation — a much better term than *economic rationalisation*, don't you think! — will take hold faster if you support businesses that are ethical and responsible. You can do this by:

✔ Buying products from businesses in sustainable industries or that are adopting sustainable practices. This includes food producers and manufacturers. See Chapter 10 for more details.

✔ Investing your money in ethical investment portfolios.

✔ Boycotting companies that continue to compromise the earth's long-term future. This includes identifying those companies that *greenwash* (that is, spend money on token environmental and social initiatives while continuing major unsustainable activities).

For more ways to identify and support companies that are being good to the environment, see Chapter 14.

Leaving a legacy for future generations

After all is said and done, future generations will determine if today's lifestyle is sustainable. If your current consumption habits leave nothing for future generations to enjoy, then your habits can clearly not be sustained. I'm not talking about a long-term future — like *Star Trek*, involving creatures from other planets. No, I'm talking about the immediate future: Your children and their children.

You can make a difference if you consume only what you need, stop throwing away so much stuff, do things more naturally and invest locally. For some simple guidelines before launching into other chapters in this book, see the sidebars 'Pinpointing your environmental priorities' and 'Developing sustainable habits is easy'.

Pinpointing your environmental priorities

Some of the tips and suggestions in this book are easier to adopt than others. Some of them depend on where you live, the type of house you live in, your philosophies, your budget and even your job. It usually comes down to where you can make the biggest differences. One consideration is getting the biggest bang for your sustainability buck.

Each chapter attempts to broadly cover as many lifestyles as possible, but some actions will suit you better than others. For example, I live in an apartment, so some of the backyard gardening tips are not as relevant to me as a suburban dweller. Similarly, some people are more able to reduce their car use than others, depending on their location, job and family circumstances.

Every action in this book can't be adopted by everyone. But your greatest achievement will be to take your first new action. That one action will hopefully show you how easy it is to do something for the planet without degrading the quality of your life. I'm confident that you'll get so much out of adopting that one action that you'll soon take on more.

Developing sustainable habits is easy

How do you go from just one simple action to a weekly routine of sustainable actions? The key to sustainable living is to make it a habit. I don't know about you, but I'm a creature of habit. And like me, if you can get some sustainable actions into your daily routine somehow, then it'll be just like you've lived that way all your life.

Here's an example of how the first day of your new sustainable life might play out. Imagine:

- 7.00 am: You get out of bed to have a shower. With your new shower timer, you reduce your shower time from 15 minutes down to 5 minutes, just for starters.

- 7.15 am: You get dressed, putting on some of your new comfortable yet stylish organic cotton clothes, and then go to the kitchen to make some breakfast using organic oats for your cereal and bread from your local bakery. The butter is from grass-fed cows and tastes creamy and delicious. You brew yourself some organic free-trade coffee and wash your breakfast down with some freshly squeezed organic orange juice in a recycled-glass tumbler.

- 7.45 am: You walk to work (if you're living within a reasonable distance in a multi-use type of urban centre) or take the local bus to the nearest train station so that you can catch the express train, which ensures that you'll get to work on time and with zero stress.

- 9.00 am: At work, you use as little paper as possible. That paper you do use is of a recycled variety (and worth checking to see if it is and ask why not, if it isn't). When disposing of paper, you make sure it goes in a recycling bin. You also make sure any lights that don't need to be on aren't on, and turn off your computer when you're away from your desk for any length of time (or set it to go into sleep mode when not used after a certain number of minutes).

- Midday: For lunch, you either open the food that you brought to the office, prepared the night before and stored in a durable container that can be washed, or you buy an unpackaged lunch, perhaps from a local organic cafe.

- 5.00 pm: On your way home from work, drop into the shops to buy yourself some organic food to cook for dinner.

- 7.00 pm: Cook your organic chicken or vegetable stir-fry for dinner on your natural gas cook-top, and compost any 'waste' from preparation. After eating by the romantic glow of candlelight from all-natural beeswax candles, wash up all the heavy pans and dishes in the sink with biodegradable detergent. The remaining plates, cups and saucers (especially if you have enough family members to generate a lot of these) can be washed in your energy-efficient 5-star dishwasher with biodegradable dishwashing detergent when the machine is full.

- 8.00 pm: You watch a little TV or listen to some music on your energy-star appliances. Or turn off the electric devices and play an old-fashioned, non-electronic game with the children — the one you traded some of your organic tomatoes for with the neighbour when their kids outgrew it.

✔ 10.00 pm: Before going to bed, you make sure that all the lights and electrical appliances are turned off. You open a screened window or two for cross-ventilation and a light, fresh breeze.

✔ 10.30 am: Once under your organic cotton sheets and comforter, you doze off to sleep knowing you have done your daily bit for the planet and your local community.

There you go — simple tasks that can make a big difference. But there is much more you can do to make a difference, as you will see when you start on your sustainable living journey.

Chapter 2

The Environment, Society and You

In This Chapter

▶ Facing up to over-consumption

▶ Examining what's happening to the environment

▶ Understanding the political agenda

▶ Balancing community and business interests

▶ Finding your place in the sustainable living movement

*L*ike most people, I want to live a satisfying and healthy life that protects me from the worst excesses of the global economy. It's good to know that I'm not alone. I'm part of a worldwide movement seeking solutions for a planet that's in poor shape.

On the largest scale, the problem is simple. People consume resources faster than the earth can provide them and are damaging the environment quicker than it can regenerate itself. You can liken this to borrowing money from your best friend for years, and doing nothing to pay it back.

Many commentators believe that the earth will run out of natural resources some time this century if current rates of consumption continue. However, a growing number of people believe that if longer-term policies are put in place to support and enhance sustainable industries, a profitable, *sustainable* economy can evolve.

This chapter helps you understand how the choices you make each day affect the environment. I also look at what's happening to the planet as a whole, explore the political landscape and check out what communities are doing to reverse the negative trends.

Diagnosing Affluenza

Ah yes, the Australian dream: To own a home on a quarter-acre block in a quiet suburb, with a picket fence out the front, a Hills hoist clothesline out the back, a Victa lawnmower to keep the lawn looking lovely and one or two vehicles to park in the garage. To many people, this dream represents so much more: Independence, wealth, security and happiness. It also represents the benefits of an economic system built on growth, investment and consumption — concepts that have shaped this urbanised, industrialised, free-market country.

Some academics say that this Australian dream — similar to the American dream — has been replaced by a concept called *affluenza*, defined by Clive Hamilton in Australia and John de Graaf in the United States as an affliction that has become rampant within Western culture. According to Hamilton and de Graaf, affluenza infects people living comfortable, middle-class lives by making them feel they're actually deprived and require a bigger home and more goods and gadgets to be happy. Better appliances, larger houses, big plasma TVs, a more powerful and fancier car . . . perhaps you're caught in the same trap?

Social welfare commentators and the media also link affluenza to record rates of credit card debt and bankruptcies, as well as longer working hours and high rates of personal depression. More relevant to this chapter, affluenza is behind the record rates of natural resource use, waste and emissions that pollute the environment and cause health problems.

An out-of-balance world

As far as natural resources go, the Western world pretty much takes the cake — and eats the icing, too. These statistics highlight the extent of the West's consumption:

- Around 20 per cent of the world's population consumes over 70 per cent of the earth's natural resources, and owns over 80 per cent of its wealth. The global elite live in the United States, Canada, Western Europe, Saudi Arabia, Australia and Japan.

- The United States alone, home to only 6 per cent of the world's population, consumes 30 per cent of the world's natural resources.

- The world produces enough grain to supply every single individual on the planet with over 2,500 calories per day, yet starvation still plagues many people living in developing nations.

✔ Twenty per cent of the world's population (people in the elite countries), is responsible for over 50 per cent of greenhouse pollutants and 90 per cent of the ozone-depleting gases emitted into the earth's atmosphere.

I think these figures show that the world is out of balance: People in the Western nations, and that includes you, are using an unequal proportion of the world's natural resources. For more statistics like these, check out the anti-consumerism campaigner Enough Web site at `www.enough.org.uk`.

Calculating your ecological footprint

Everything you do and consume each day impacts on the environment. A useful way to understand how you're affecting the environment is to measure your *ecological footprint* — calculate the amount of land area that's actually required to support your consumption of natural resources.

The average ecological footprint in Australia is 7.6 global hectares per person, per year. Think of this as a way of describing the amount of land required to farm your food, mine your energy sources, make and transport your goods and services, and deal with your waste.

The Earth Day Network — an organisation based in the United States that brings together a global community of citizens concerned about the environment — estimates that per person, only 1.8 biologically productive global hectares remain on the planet (see the following section 'The Environmental State of Play: Past and Present' to find out why). This means that the average Australian is consuming much more than the earth can sustain. (Note that a global hectare is one hectare of 'useable' or 'productive' land or water, such as found in cities, rural areas, forests and even oceans, but does not include deserts and other unusable and unproductive spaces.)

You can measure your own ecological footprint on The Earth Day Network's Web site at `www.myfootprint.org`. The site prompts you to type in information about how you live, then tells you how many hectares of earth you're using to satisfy your lifestyle.

Don't be surprised if your ecological footprint stretches to the horizon, because when I used the Earth Day Network on two Australian friends recently, both discovered that they're living beyond their ecological means. One is a single young person living in an apartment in Sydney, who eats local produce and catches public transport most of the time. The other is a middle-aged man with a family of five living in a detached outer suburban home in Brisbane who drives his car everywhere.

The Earth Day Network estimated that my single young friend — with the more sustainable practices of the two — has an ecological footprint of only 2.3 global hectares, which is well below the Australian average, but still higher than what's estimated the earth can now supply. However, my outer suburban Brisbane friend has an ecological footprint right on the average of 7.6 global hectares per person, largely because he spends more on food to feed his family and uses large quantities of fuel to drive his car.

The Environmental State of Play: Past and Present

The increasing demand for natural resources, which underpins many of the environmental issues I discuss in this chapter, is the inevitable result of consumerism. Right now, people still want more goods and services, and they want them faster and more conveniently.

The trouble is, the natural world can't keep up. Resources are in short supply. These examples highlight what the world is running out of:

- **Land resources.** The amount of land available for agriculture has diminished and is now less than half of what's required to feed the world by Western standards. This loss of farming land is largely a result of urbanisation, land clearing and the loss of arable land to deserts.

- **Water resources.** Rapid population growth and wasteful consumption are combining to rapidly deplete available water supplies. The world's total rainfall is enough to provide the world's current population with adequate fresh water if shared equally. However, rain falls in specific regions, leaving other areas water-deficient.

- **Energy resources.** Energy use has been growing faster than the world's population. The Organisation of Petroleum Exporting Countries estimates that oil supplies (used mainly for electricity and transport) will run dry in about 50 years' time if current rates of consumption and population growth continue. The World Wildlife Fund backs up this deadline. Moreover, the Association for the Study of Peak Oil (www.peakoil.net/uhdsg) is concerned that the remaining oil supplies will be difficult and expensive to extract. As demand outstrips supply, oil prices will continue to rise sharply.

- **Biological resources.** Studies by scientists indicate that humans depend on the presence of approximately 10 million other species to support the food-production process. These species, which exist within the food-chain process to produce, protect or enhance what you eat, are ever diminishing as human lifestyles impact on fragile ecosystems.

Wasn't last winter warm? The truth about climate change

How many times have you thought that the passing summer seemed hotter than the last one? Or maybe you thought last winter was mild. Is your mind playing tricks on you as you get older, or is the weather actually getting warmer — and if so, why?

Global warming has been a hot topic of debate scientifically and politically for some time now. The debate is not so much centred on whether the world is getting warmer — scientists readily show that it is — but whether global warming is going to actually cause irreversible damage to the earth and create problems for those who live on it.

Scientists at the United Nation's Intergovernmental Panel on Climate Change believe the following changes highlight the extent of global warming so far:

- The average global surface temperature has increased by approximately 0.6 degrees Celsius since the late 1800s.
- The warming rate since 1976 has been 0.17 degrees Celsius a decade.
- Alpine and continental glaciers have reduced in size as a result of warming during the 1900s. Since the 1970s, it has been estimated that 400,000 square miles of Arctic sea ice has disappeared (an area the combined size of Texas and California).
- Comparison of satellite pictures between the 1960s and today suggests that the planet has lost 10 per cent of its snow cover and that the Northern Hemisphere lakes and rivers are now covered by ice for two weeks less each year than they were a century ago.

Global warming is caused by human activities that add too much carbon dioxide and nitrous oxide to the atmosphere, which form *greenhouse* heat-trapping gases. Burning fossil fuels for energy is the main culprit (see the sidebar 'Fossil fuel facts' for more details). Global warming is exacerbated by the rampant reduction of forests, which would normally otherwise take up carbon dioxide from the atmosphere as part of the photosynthesis process.

Can global warming be ignored?

Fortunately, climate change is not going to destroy the planet, or all life in one go, but it has the potential to severely disrupt civilisation.

Technological advancements allow forecasters to predict when extreme events are likely to occur, but withstanding the impact of these events seriously challenges communities across the globe. Even in the United States and in Australia, communities wait for events to happen and then react to minimise the damage. Consider, for example, how 'ready' people were when Hurricane Katrina hit New Orleans in late August 2005, or when Tropical Cyclone Larry slammed into the Innisfail region in Queensland in March 2006.

The United Nation's Intergovernmental Panel on Climate Change states that the 0.6-degree average increase in global temperatures will trigger more extreme scenarios in the future:

- Huge forest fires close to urban areas because of extreme heat
- Infectious disease epidemics created in tropical areas
- Years of drought in arid regions
- Coastal erosion (and building collapses) caused by intense rain
- Flash floods due to monsoons and freak storms

Hang on a second — did I just say that these events would happen in the future? Of course, you and I've watched these types of events occur on TV (or worse, at first hand) with scary regularity over the last five years.

Fossil fuel facts

Fossil fuels are energy-rich substances that contain hydrocarbons, formed from long-buried plants and microorganisms. Petroleum, coal and natural gas contain this energy captured from the sun by plants over billions of years ago. Fossil fuels have been influential in powering the growth of modern society, providing energy for transport, industry and domestic power, and are used in plastics, fertilisers and pesticides. Here's how much the world relies on them:

- Currently, fossil fuels are used to meet 80 per cent of the world's energy consumption needs (in the United States, usage is slightly higher, at 85 per cent).

- By 2002, the world had consumed 29 billion barrels of petroleum, 5 billion metric tonnes of coal, and 2.6 trillion cubic metres of natural gas.

- In 2004, the average price for oil was US$38 a barrel; in 2005 it reached US$46; and in 2006 it nudged US$60 a barrel — a great indicator that demand is outweighing supply.

- The world's main coal reserves are located in the backyards of most of the major electricity consumers — for example, the United States, China, Russia and Australia — making coal cheaper and more accessible for these countries and their neighbours.

- Oil reserves, first discovered 150 years ago, have dwindled everywhere, and what's left is becoming more expensive and difficult to extract (even in the Middle East).

Global warming warning signs

The following areas of the globe regularly feel the effects of climate change:

- ✔ **Asia.** Every year, Bangladesh and India experience major flood events across huge areas of heavily populated, low-lying land. Climate change has made them more susceptible to flooding due to sea levels rising, the increasing intensities of rainfall, and the lowering of water tables due to over-irrigation.

- ✔ **Africa.** Africa suffers what is known as *low food security* — a nice way of saying that starvation is a part of everyday life in many countries across the continent. Increased drought conditions do nothing to improve the situation. Inland lakes and rivers that provide much of the continent's protein, through fish, have just about dried up.

- ✔ **Australia and the Pacific.** Two issues have become key in this region. First, nearly every year serious bushfires threaten several of Australia's major cities and towns (thanks to hotter conditions and decreases in rainfall). Second, rising sea levels combined with more storm events are jeopardising the future of many Pacific Islands; and soon, several more islands may join the queue of those that have already drowned (Tebua, Tarawa and Abanuea). Islands identified as being in danger include Kiribati, Tuvalu and the atolls that form the Marshall Islands.

- ✔ **Europe.** Yearly flooding events are now the norm in many parts of Europe, due to the rapid melting of snow in alpine regions when warmer temperatures arrive. Some floods have also been caused by freak rainfall events. Who can forget the dramatic pictures of floods rampaging through the picture-perfect streets of Prague in 2002? Dramatic wildfires and heatwaves are now a regular summer occurrence across southern Europe.

- ✔ **Latin America.** The Amazonian rainforest, which is home to unique species of frogs, mammals and an enormous range of plant life, is in trouble — not only because of urban and industrial encroachment but also because of increasingly dry weather.

- ✔ **North America.** Hurricane Katrina, which devastated the low-lying city of New Orleans on 29 August 2005, was a result of the combined impact of increasing sea levels and a massive storm surge. Other regions in the United States and Canada have to cope with completely different scenarios, such as yearly bushfires in California and Oregon, water-quantity problems in Arizona and California, and the ever-thinning ice cover in the sub-arctic and arctic regions of northern Canada. (Climate change is now firmly on the political agenda in North America.)

Who's taking advantage of the little guy?

Many of the goods that you buy draw on natural resources in developing countries. Some of these resources are then manufactured in factories that emit pollution in countries with less stringent environmental controls.

Unfortunately, many of these manufacturers are Western companies. The big advantage for them is that they can utilise a cheaper labour force, which helps maximise profits, and can avoid having to deal with minimising their environmental impacts.

These days, companies can manufacture goods less expensively in developing countries because of *free trade* agreements, made in the name of globalisation. In general terms, a large Western economy makes an agreement with a developing nation to allow its companies to buy facilities and to employ local populations at a much cheaper rate than they could domestically.

Clothing, food, cars and even services linked to banking and IT are produced in developing countries for the Western world.

What you can't see can harm you

You may not be able to see them, but the gases that are produced by burning fossil fuels, and the toxic chemicals that are used to manufacture products, pollute the environment and can create serious health problems in people. They're in the air you breathe. Some are also in the ground and in waterways, and then absorbed by the food you eat.

All you need is the air that you breathe

Carbon dioxide and nitrous oxide gases are major contributors to the greenhouse effect that causes global warming (refer to 'Wasn't last winter warm? The truth about climate change' earlier in this chapter for more details).

Other dangerous gases (or matter) in the environment include:

- ✔ **Ozone.** Good ozone is the layer that exists between 10 and 50 kilometres above the earth's surface and protects you against the sun's ultraviolet rays. However, bad ozone is formed when pollutants emitted by cars, factories and refineries react chemically in the presence of sunlight.

- ✔ **Particle pollution.** Most fine particle pollutants are only visible through a microscope, but together can form the smog you see on windless days.

- ✔ **Carbon monoxide.** Carbon monoxide is odourless and colourless, which makes it hard to detect. This gas forms when the carbon in fuels doesn't completely burn. Cars contribute a high proportion of carbon monoxide, especially in winter when the combustion process doesn't work quite as well. Industry and bushfires also contribute to carbon monoxide emissions.

- ✔ **Sulfur dioxide.** Although colourless, sulfur dioxide smells like rotten-egg gas, so you'll know when you're breathing it. This reactive gas is produced when coal and oil are burned in power plants and industrial boilers. The smell is the main reason that people stay away from industrial areas using these fuels. (Besides being offensive to your nose, this stuff is also offensive to your lungs and heart.)

For more details about greenhouse gases produced by high rates of car use and how they affect your health, see Chapter 15.

 When you next watch your local news service on TV, pay close attention to the weather report and the *air-quality index*. This index measures the extent of major gases and particles in the air on a given day. In Sydney, for example, the New South Wales Department of Environment and Conservation produces the Regional Pollution Index (RPI), which measures the levels of ozone and nitrous dioxide (low, medium and high) in the air. Another index, the *visibility index*, measures particle pollution in the air.

The seeping giant

Toxic chemical pollution doesn't break down, is usually hidden, and can do real damage to the environment (and you) long after it has been dumped. The biggest users of toxic chemicals are industries that manufacture products like medicines, plastics, textiles, detergents, paints and pesticides.

 Some of the major toxic problems include:

- ✔ **Metals.** Toxic metals that don't break down in the environment and aren't destroyed at any temperature include lead and mercury. Lead is the most prevalent industrial toxin released into the environment. It's also released into the atmosphere through petroleum and paint. Lead is responsible for many environmental-related health problems. Low levels of lead and mercury can cause mental retardation, learning disabilities and stunted growth in children.

- ✔ **Dioxins.** A byproduct of making PolyVinylChloride (PVC) plastics, industrial bleaching and incineration, dioxins create diseases of the immune system, reproductive and developmental disorders, as well as cancers.

✔ **Organochlorine pesticides.** These nasties are used as pesticides in farming and gardening and can end up in soils, the water table, and rivers and streams. They include DDT, dieldrin, heptachlor, chlordane and mirex. They are still used in Australia today but have been banned in many other countries. They cause cancer and are toxic to the immune system.

✔ **Brominated flame retardants.** Retardants are used in plastics for computer casings, white goods, car interiors, carpets and polyurethane foams in furniture and bedding. They can end up in the dust of homes and offices and may cause cancer and reproductive problems.

✔ **Perfluorochemicals.** These acids are used in the manufacture of everyday items such as clothing, stain resistants and cosmetics, and are linked to cancer and liver damage.

When the damage caused by poisons such as these have become obvious, government regulations have forced industries to be more careful about how they get rid of their toxic waste. Better late than never, I suppose — governments will jump on board the sustainability bandwagon when people demand action.

Zoning in on at-risk areas

One of the major outcomes of globalisation is the rampant growth of urban areas and the rise of *megacities* in developing nations. Researchers estimate that in the not-too-distant future, ten cities will emerge with populations of over 20 million (currently only four exist — New York, Tokyo, Seoul and Mexico City). The new entrants include Beijing, in China; Cairo, in Egypt; Jakarta, in Indonesia; Mumbai and Delhi, in India; Lagos, in Nigeria; and Sao Paulo, in Brazil.

This new megacities are evolving because relatively poor rural populations are flocking to the big cities where global investment is taking place. The result is vast conurbations of under-employed poor people living in substandard housing. Local and global agencies find it impossible to overcome the resulting social, health and environmental issues.

Megacities are also perfect incubators for modern-day viruses that kill large numbers of people, including the yet-to-be-defeated AIDS virus and the recent menace, bird flu.

Scanning the Political Climate: Where Do the Politicians Stand?

Like other governments around the world, the Australian federal government is focused on economics. This means that Australia's position on sustainability and the environment is indifferent, to say the least. This focus on economics is good if you seek tax cuts and reduced government spending, but not so good if you're like me and want your government to support sustainable policies.

Why the Greens are on the rise

Historically, progressive parties, such as the Labor Party in Australia (and the Democrats in the United States), positioned themselves as the guardians of the environment. They promised to protect the environment, workers' rights and social infrastructures (such as education) as part of their plan for a better society.

Conservative parties, like the Australian Liberal Party, believe that economic interests come first and that everyone is better off if the economy is well managed. Phrases such as the 'trickle down effect' and 'market forces will deliver what consumers demand' summarise their position.

The Kyoto Protocol

At the Kyoto conference, held in Kyoto in Japan in 1997, developed countries sat down to agree on specific targets for cutting their emissions of greenhouse gases. The general framework defined there became known as the Kyoto Protocol. The key agreement was that industrialised countries (not including India and China) would reduce their greenhouse gas emissions to 5.2 per cent below 1990 levels, for the period 2008–2012. This agreement was the result of a major trade-off and, even then, the United States and Australia did not sign. Since 1997, even the Canadian and UK governments have back-pedalled on their commitments.

These positions have been blurred as the traditionally progressive parties have attempted to display their economic prowess. This means that in most industrialised nations, both conservative and progressive governments now put economic considerations first, even though major environmental problems, increasing gaps between the rich and poor, and evidence of a lack of morality by major corporations continue to ring alarm bells.

Some people may tell you that they have become disillusioned with the major political parties. They want to see something done about the major environmental problems, increasing gaps between rich and poor, and evidence of a lack of morality by major corporations. For example, the Australian Greens party is riding a wave of support for its focus on the environment. In the United States, the Progressive Democrats of America, the Green Party of the United States and other progressive groups pursue similar agendas.

- ✔ The Australian Greens holds four seats in the federal Senate, and has major influence in more than ten municipal councils. Its share of the primary vote is around 10 per cent across the nation and above 30 per cent in some electorates.

- ✔ Major opposition parties have read the tea leaves. The Australian Labor Party says that if in power it would sign the Kyoto Protocol. It has recruited renowned activists like Peter Garrett, who is now the Labor member for Kingsford Smith in Sydney.

- ✔ The Conservative Party in the United Kingdom is leading the call for revolutionary change to power generation and controlling carbon emissions.

Why the environment is a political hot potato

The United States justified not signing the Kyoto Protocol agreement to reduce greenhouse gases (see the related sidebar 'The Kyoto Protocol' for more details), because doing so would raise energy costs, slow the economy and put Americans out of work. Australia adopted a similar position. Both countries say that technological advancements will solve environmental and social problems.

Herein lies the problem: Many Western governments are not willing to bear the short-term economic costs of reversing the damage to the environment or creating greater social equity. Most Western leaders only have a three-year or four-year period before they start campaigning for re-election; adopting long-term policies that adversely impact on the economy within this short-term framework may jeopardise their chances for another term.

Maybe you're thinking that it would be easier for politicians to get on board if every nation adopted a one-in all-in approach, right? Well, not quite. That's the problem with Kyoto. The largest economies have the most to lose. Most developed nations are so used to consuming 20 or 30 times their fair share of the world's resources that the effort required to achieve some sort of equilibrium is too difficult to face.

 The bottom line is, politicians need voters — that means you. The best way to get your sustainable message across is to hound your local members of Parliament. Start by checking out some Web sites devoted to political activism. For example, GetUp! at www.getup.org.au runs campaigns on a variety of issues and provides tools so that you can lobby politicians directly. You can also promote your own issues by contacting your local representative. Visit the main government Web site at www.gov.au for links to all Australian government agencies.

For more information about environmental groups, see 'Supporting the local agenda' later in this chapter.

Supporting the Ecology and the Economy

Traditionally, governments and business in Australia have separated society, economy and environment into unrelated parts of the political equation. For example, increased investment in construction and development has largely been driven by a perspective on economic growth, despite the damaging environmental and social impacts. The *bottom line* value of a project or a business is simply a measure of financial costs and benefits with no consideration of the environmental and social impacts.

The good news is that an increasing number of companies consider the *triple bottom line*. This refers to all three components in the cost–benefit analysis — the financial, the environmental and the social (I cover triple bottom line reporting in more detail in Chapter 14, and show you that an increasing number of companies are adopting sustainable practices while maintaining profitability).

Acting locally

Many environmental issues are global in nature but impact locally, and this is where all the good work is happening. An increasing number of local councils around Australia are leading the way in approving sustainable development and encouraging sustainable practices. Many of these decisions result from community pressure and lobbying of councils to adopt more sustainable policies.

In recent years, the Australian Local Government National Awards have highlighted where sustainable actions are taking place:

- **Community Power, Darebin (Melbourne), 2004.** Darebin Council, with the help of neighbouring councils, engaged an existing electricity retailer to deliver *triple bottom-line* objectives: Namely cost-competitive prices, greenhouse gas reductions, and fair and reasonable contract conditions.

- **Kogarah Town Square, Sydney, 2003.** Australia's largest solar-powered medium-density development consists of 194 apartments, commercial/retail space, library and underground car park. The solar power produced by the development saves about 145 tonnes of carbon dioxide emissions each year. This development is also a leading example of urban water collection, treatment and reuse. Up to 85 per cent of rainwater and stormwater is collected onsite and reused, resulting in a 40 per cent reduction in the use of potable (drinking) water.

- **Northern Adelaide Cities for Climate Protection, 2000.** The various cities north of Adelaide signed a memorandum of understanding to develop strategic greenhouse policies and strategies. A project officer was then appointed to compile an energy and emissions inventory; forecast likely emissions; establish greenhouse gas reduction targets; and develop local action plans.

- **Destination Subiaco: Driving the Change, Perth, 2001.** Subiaco City Council has committed to changing the high car use behaviour of its community by promoting public transport and other transport alternatives. The council has brought together stakeholders to develop infrastructure, planning and policy initiatives. These include establishing Perth's first intra-suburban bus service and a campaign to reduce traffic and parking congestion during sporting events at Subiaco Oval.

- **The Virtual Green Home, Brisbane City Council, 2004.** This house is an innovative educational tool developed to encourage Brisbane residents to embrace sustainable behaviours. People are encouraged to visit a sample home and garden. An interactive 3D display features objects in the home where visitors find key messages and information about sustainable living.

Hundreds more examples of sustainable projects and policies are being undertaken at the local level as community support for living sustainably grows stronger.

Cooperating and working together

Plenty of national, state and local support networks can help you with your sustainable ideas and actions or even just offer advice about how you can get involved.

Consider the following:

- **Local councils.** Your council is a great place to start your sustainable living search. Most councils provide plenty of information on sustainable practices and the environment, and usually provide you with the contact details of local community groups. To find out more about what different councils might be doing to encourage sustainable living, go to the Australian Local Government Association Web site (www.alga.asn.au). Every council in Australia with a Web site is listed here.

- **Australian Greenhouse Office.** The Australian federal government set up the Australian Greenhouse Office some time back to drive funding for greenhouse policy initiatives throughout Australia. The Web site provides an excellent overview of local sustainable projects that individuals and groups have participated in. Check out www.greenhouse.gov.au/local for more details.

- **Sustainable Living Foundation.** The Sustainable Living Foundation is an Australian non-profit organisation that assists government, community groups and businesses in meeting their sustainability objectives. The foundation specialises in assisting community groups with their sustainable projects. The foundation's Web site (at www.slf.org.au) includes a sustainable living events calendar to show what is happening around Australia and a shopping directory to help you make sustainable purchasing choices.

Preventive Medicine for Mother Earth

From little things, big things grow . . .

As an individual, you can help prevent more damage being done to the environment. You can start at any level.

Riding the wave — actions that change behaviour

You'd be amazed how many sustainable actions you've probably adopted — or now accept as part of life. These were all initiated by people who wanted to do something positive for the environment:

- **Clean Up Australia Day.** A day that involves a big clean-up, and focuses everyone's attention on how rubbish is discarded. You can join in as well, and help clear rubbish on a beach, in a park or beside a road. Check the campaign's Web site at www.cleanup.com.au.

- **Say No to Plastic Bags.** A variety of campaigns have made people aware of the amount of plastic bags that are clogging waterways, drains, beaches and natural environments. Many people now use green or calico bags when shopping. For more details, visit the government-sponsored No Plastic Bags Web site at www.noplasticbags.org.au.

- **Wise About Water.** The recent water-saving campaign in New South Wales and the Australian Capital Territory has made people very conscious about how they use water, especially in their gardens. Many people now think twice about watering their gardens needlessly or running the tap endlessly. You can find out about the Wise About Water campaign on the Nursery and Garden Industry Web site at www.ngia.com.au.

- **Life. Be in it.** The 'Life. Be in it.' campaign sprang to life approximately 30 years ago to encourage people to get off their lounges (just like the cartoon character Norm) to 'live more of your life' and 'make life worthwhile' by participating in outdoor activities. Today, 'Life. Be in it.' is a community corporation that works with a range of education and health organisations to continue to encourage people to be more active. Check out the Web site at www.lifebeinit.org.

Supporting the local agenda

You can do plenty to support your local environment and community, and empower those around you to adopt a similar sustainable approach. Some actions you may like to try include:

- Checking your local council's Web site and your local paper to find out how to participate in any consultation activities that are taking place on major projects, policies or strategies. These days, most councils strongly encourage citizens to participate in the decision-making process by commenting on projects that may affect the community.

✔ Attending council meetings to witness the democratic process in action. These meetings can give you a more holistic appreciation of the range of issues that inform political decisions. I can tell you from first-hand experience that these meetings are often the best show in town — the debate on the issue you're interested in is often passionate and heated. These council meetings are open to the public and usually held once a month.

✔ Supporting local businesses by shopping in your own neighbourhood and town, rather than hopping in a car to travel to the nearest big mall. When you buy locally, you're protecting the economic viability of the place where you live.

✔ Volunteering or supporting a local community action group that has similar interests to you, such as a cyclist's user group or a group representing a sustainable lifestyle.

If you're interested in finding out about some of the higher-profile environmental organisations seeking volunteer assistance, I recommend that you check out the Web sites of Friends of the Earth (www.foe.org.au) and the Australian Conservation Foundation (www.acfonline.org.au).

✔ Writing letters to the editors of newspapers, magazines, Internet Web sites, your council and your local political member. The Get Up! Web site, which I also mention in the section 'Why the environment is a political hot potato' earlier in this chapter, coordinates petitions and rallies in support of important political and social causes. For example, the site recently ran a campaign to encourage the government to do more about climate change. Check out www.getup.org.au for more information.

When a lot of people take individual action, politicians responsible for policy making are encouraged to do the right thing — that is, if the politicians want to be re-elected at the next election.

Short-term actions for long-term gains

The phrase *short-term action for long-term gain* is usually used to encourage people to budget more wisely to ensure their financial future. I like it, and think that the same principle applies to the environment — sustainable budgeting now will ensure a better life for future generations.

Many of the tips and suggestions I provide throughout this book are simple, achievable changes that you can make without compromising your lifestyle. You can help turn the tide to ensure the planet can sustain future generations.

Part II
Home Sweet (Sustainable) Home

Glenn Lumsden

'Kids, we promise to do something about global warming when the water level reaches the television.'

In this part . . .

Consider this part your lifestyle makeover.

First, I look at where you live and explain why some housing locations are more sustainable than others, and how to assess the region you live in or you're planning to move to. I also provide you with advice about how best to build or renovate using the most sustainable materials you can get your hands on.

Inside the home, I show you how to be more energy efficient — after all, reducing your power bill is not just about saving money. I look at the appliances you outfit your home with, using alternative energy sources, and then take you from room to room and show you some 'green' practices that you and members of your family can adopt.

Finally, I head outside to the garden, the *Australian* garden, that major source of urban water consumption and haven for pests (which are not so bad until you start using poisonous chemicals to get rid of them). But whether you're pottering away on the balcony of your apartment or in the backyard of your house, you can create a natural, healthy garden that becomes a positive contributor to the ecosystem where you live.

Chapter 3

Location and Design Matters

Anything worth doing well needs a good plan. If you're seriously considering moving, renovating or building, you have a unique opportunity to choose where to live and what to live in, and do something positive for the planet.

In this chapter, I explore why the location of a house or apartment is such an important sustainability issue. For example, where you live can reduce your dependence on a car or allow you to use more efficient or renewable energy resources. I also show you some of the unique design factors that contribute to the energy-efficiency of a home (and save you money, too) and check out sustainable building materials — eco-friendly products that cause minimal harm to the environment.

What's Wrong with Living in a McMansion, Anyway?

Homes in areas such as the newest suburbs on the outskirts of Australian cities, bought off-the-plan by middle-income earners, are sometimes called McMansions by town planners. A McMansion offers these modern trappings: A huge house that dominates the block of land that it's built on, a grand entrance, multiple bedrooms with ensuites, multiple garages, multiple playrooms, and even multiple eating areas.

Doesn't this description remind you of ordering a burger, fries and a drink at a fast-food joint and being asked whether you want to 'super-size' your order?

You're tempted to say yes because you're getting more food for a little more money. Get the picture?

Living in a McMansion in a sprawling urban area requires you to travel some distance to get from your home to just about anywhere. You may also have to deal with the following:

✔ No footpaths and few trees. Long winding roads dominate the landscape.

✔ Shops and other community services are so far away you can't walk to them. (As a consequence, there's little sign of life on the streets and no sense of community.)

✔ No rail services and minimal bus services.

✔ Higher crime rates, because these dormitory suburbs are often deserted during the day.

✔ A housing design that incorporates large roof areas and driveways that send most of the rainwater straight down the stormwater drain. Inside, large, poorly designed rooms waste energy on heating and cooling.

✔ Community health problems borne out of a dependence on the car — lack of exercise can lead to obesity and other diseases. (I cover these health problems in more detail in Chapter 15.)

Some people — like the old and the sick — can feel isolated living in these types of communities. This social isolation particularly worries many health practitioners because it can lead to boredom, depression and even suicide.

A mansion on a large block of land, set among rows and rows of other large houses in outer suburban areas, is called *low-density housing*, as is the traditional free-standing dwelling on a quarter-acre block in more established residential streets. Low-density housing requires lots of land; when cars first entered the picture, carving up more and more land for this type of housing became more important than providing good public transport and community services.

By comparison, *high-density housing* uses less space, and includes apartments, townhouses and villas. High-density housing is typically located in 'accessible' regions — areas close to services and transport routes, which encourages less car use.

Town planning: The new direction

Town planners in Australia are actively encouraging the development of more compact and vibrant communities that are complete towns on the edges of cities. Many call this approach *new urbanism* — an architectural and design-led concept born in the United States that encourages new, self-contained communities linked by public transport, and walking and cycling infrastructures. Others think of this as a return to the way suburban communities were first developed in the middle part of the last century along newly constructed railway corridors in larger cities and towns (for some examples, see 'Why old suburbs are new again' in the following section).

Reversing the unsustainable sprawl in outer urban areas requires:

✔ Developing housing close to village centres, shops, services and transport systems, with facilities and services built at the same time as the housing.

✔ Designing suburbs with houses, apartments and townhouses mixed together, encouraging community and outdoor activities and reducing the need for transport.

✔ Developing road and footpath networks that enable bus and train services to reach the majority of the population, providing opportunities for people to be less reliant on the family car.

These solutions involve a combination of town planning to ensure that you can live near the services you require, and good building design to ensure that your home is ecologically friendly.

Why old suburbs are new again

Many sustainable examples of urban development are suburbs that have existed in our cities and towns for decades — older, traditional suburbs that were once frowned upon — but are now considered desirable, relatively affordable and sustainable housing locations.

Here are some examples around Australia:

✔ **Parramatta in western Sydney.** Now a thriving centre with a reinvigorated restaurant strip, new apartments overlooking the revived Parramatta River, good public transport, walking and cycling links, and a good mix of housing types to suit all budgets.

✔ **Port Melbourne.** This once overlooked part of industrial Melbourne has been revitalised and features new residential apartments and townhouses located around new light-rail services.

✔ **East Perth.** A prototype, transit-oriented development where a mix of housing choices have been provided within easy walking distance of the railway line.

✔ **Milton in western Brisbane.** A traditional working-class suburb that integrates new housing with retail and commercial buildings, close to the railway line.

Yes, these days, many government agencies encourage developers to provide housing around established centres with railway stations in preference to developing subdivisions further out on the edge of the urban area. The huge increase in the number of apartments in most big cities is a direct result of an increasing number of people willing to trade away living space for a better location near good public transport links.

For more information about why urban redevelopments in inner-city areas are sustainable, see the section 'Defining what makes a suburb or town sustainable' later in this chapter.

Location, Sustainable Location

You've probably heard the real estate theory that says the value of a property is highly dependent on these three important things: Location, location and location. Well, the location of your home not only affects its value, but your lifestyle as well.

For example, a location can influence the following:

✔ The type of housing on offer, and how much energy the home requires to allow you to maintain a comfortable lifestyle.

✔ How you travel to work, to shops, to community facilities and to visit family and friends.

✔ The kind of exercise you do, and whether you stay fit and healthy.

✔ How you socialise and become part of your community.

✔ The type of energy and water sources you can use — determined by government services, local councils and other authorities.

Catering for young and old

Children and the elderly are especially more likely to thrive in communities that include the following facilities:

✔ Safe, well-lit and direct walking and cycling paths that lead to schools, libraries and shops.

✔ Nearby public transport facilities, such as bus stops and railway stations, that provide easy access to child-care centres, community services and aged-care facilities.

✔ Plenty of nearby open space, park and recreation areas, including community gardens and sporting venues.

✔ Established community activities that make use of that public space.

Defining what makes a suburb or town sustainable

Sustainable housing locations offer the following:

- **Transport facilities.** *Transit-oriented housing developments* adjacent to public transport reduce your need to travel to work and the shops in your petrol-chugging car. A sustainable area also has good quality footpaths, open spaces, cycle paths, and low levels of traffic.

- **Local services.** In a sustainable housing location, essential services such as schools, churches, leisure activities, public open spaces and shops are within walking distance. These areas are especially appropriate for people who don't drive, particularly children and the elderly (see the sidebar 'Catering for young and old' for more details).

- **Local community.** In a sustainable community, many people of all ages are walking the street: The shops and services are open and the streets and paths are clean. A good mix of housing styles and types also attract to the area a variety of people from different age groups, cultural backgrounds and financial positions, creating a vibrant community.

- **Sustainable regulations.** Some councils or local authorities actively encourage residents to install solar panels, domestic windmills, rainwater tanks, recycled water systems and composting toilets at home, and support community gardens in public areas. Others do not. (For more details, see the following section 'Checking the regulations'.)

The best sustainable locations allow as many people as possible to access a public transport network and to walk or cycle to nearby shops, services and facilities. These locations include:

- The inner-city areas of capital cities
- Regional centres where shops and jobs are concentrated

Public transport only works cost-effectively when a lot of people live in a relatively small geographic area (and use the services regularly).

Even country towns, where most of the township lives within walking distance of the main street and its shops and services, provide much greater accessibility to services and facilities than most large, sprawling suburban areas.

Checking the regulations

Getting the location right is all well and good, but if your local council doesn't offer a recycling service or doesn't encourage sustainable development, your plans to live more sustainably could be seriously limited. For example, does the local council have ties with an energy provider to allow you to use renewable energy instead of the fossil fuel kind? Are you allowed to install a water tank? My point is this: Local council policies matter as much as the human geography of a region.

To assess how 'green' the policies are that govern an area, visit the local council's Web site and check the following:

- ✔ **The state of the environment.** Most councils now produce a yearly State of the Environment report that shows how the local area is performing in relation to key environmental issues, such as water efficiency, stormwater pollution, energy efficiency, transport, air quality, greenhouse gas emissions, waste avoidance and recycling and noise.

- ✔ **Community services.** Does the council list the range of community facilities it provides in its area? You should be able to find out the location and number of child-care centres, community activity venues, services for senior citizens, disability services and youth services. Sustainable residential areas have most of these services located near your home.

- ✔ **Development.** A key function of councils is to develop the strategies and plans that guide future development in an area. Have a look at the council's four-year management plan and check its aims, objectives and the major focus for future development. If the council places an emphasis on economic growth and more development, with little reference to environmental protection, then be suspicious.

- ✔ **Sustainable principles.** Check the council's support for rainwater collection, waste water treatment, community gardens and the like. Councils supporting sustainable principles are more likely to talk about promoting the environment, accessibility, vitality and social fabric, and should have policies on street planting, community gardens, water and energy systems to match.

Seeking the sunny side of the street

Some streets are better placed than others, and each property has its own advantages and disadvantages. Here are some things to consider that can directly impact on your sustainable dream home:

- One of the primary influences on your energy use is the way the sun falls on your garden and your home. In Australia, the sun is to the north in the winter, so the northern side of your house is where you would place solar hot water services, electricity panels and vegetable gardens. If the house is shaded to the north, this could be problematic.

- Prevailing winds will also influence your plans for cooling the house and keeping it warm, your planting program and whether you can produce electricity from wind energy or not.

- In areas where heat is a major consideration, the westerly aspect deserves special consideration. Will you be able to shade the western side of the house in summer?

- The slope of your land, and the height of the bathroom and kitchen floor will impact on your ability to recycle waste water. If you plan to run water from the house into your vegetable garden, consider where to place the two in relation to each other.

- Your immediate neighbours could also have a significant influence on whether you're allowed to install a composting toilet, put up a domestic windmill or even keep hens. It may be worth doing a little investigation into local community attitudes to be sure you can act on your plans.

Many of these factors are design considerations that you can take into account when you're ready to move, renovate or build. I deal with each in more detail in the sections 'Drawing up your grand plan' and 'Designing for energy efficiency' later in this chapter.

Sustainable housing location checklist

The best way to determine whether your home is in a sustainable location is to answer the questions in Figure 3-1 and see how many of the boxes you can tick. The more ticks, the more sustainable the location.

Location Checklist

❏   Is your house within 800 metres of a local shopping area?

❏   Is your house within 800 metres of a railway station?

❏   Is your house within 400 metres of a regularly serviced bus stop?

❏   Are there paved footpaths in front of your house or apartment?

❏   Are there any cycle paths or lanes nearby?

❏   Are there community gardens or open spaces in your suburb?

❏   Does the local council allow residents in the area to install rainwater tanks?

❏   Are community facilities close by?

❏   Can you sell electricity that you generate to an electricity supplier?

❏   Is your local shopping centre busy?

❏   Is there a good housing mix (apartments, town houses, villas and single dwellings) in your street or in your suburb?

❏   Does the location of the house and land lend itself to the design you have in mind?

Figure 3-1:
The sustainable housing location checklist.

Designing Your Sustainable Dream Home

Perhaps you've decided to renovate your existing home, build a new one from scratch or move to a new home or apartment in a brand-new location. Whatever the case, you've got some key design elements to consider before spending your hard-earned dollars to achieve a more sustainable home.

Drawing up your grand plan

Good sustainable design begins with factoring in what you want your new home or renovation to achieve, then making a plan to ensure it happens.

Whether you're house hunting, building or renovating, the key aspects of sustainable housing design and construction include:

✔ Power sources that rely on a minimal amount of electrical energy, such as solar power. (For information about solar energy, see Chapter 4.)

✔ Building design that enhances natural ventilation, cooling and heating. This includes the position of the dwelling so that it takes advantage of natural sunlight and breezes, and adding insulation to reduce your artificial heating and cooling bill.

✔ Facilities for recycling — indoor and outdoor.

✔ Plumbing facilities that enable the use of *greywater* from your washing machine (and even the bathroom and kitchen).

✔ Low-maintenance gardens and yards — enough space to grow Australian native plants for shade (these don't need much watering) or to raise some vegetables and to compost, but small enough to reduce reliance on chemicals and water use. (Check out Chapter 6 for information about landscaping and gardening.)

✔ Outdoor tanks that enable you to catch rainwater.

✔ Building materials that are natural, developed from renewable resources and non-toxic.

The materials you use to build or renovate your home are the stuff your dream sustainable home is made of. I cover building materials in more detail in the sections 'Building From the Ground Up: Construction Materials' and 'Finishing with Flair' later in this chapter.

If you're building a new home or renovating, ask an architect or builder to design your new home or renovation so that it's as naturally energy-efficient as possible. Show the architect or the builder your wishlist to ensure that he considers all the elements you want before you approve a formal set of plans and construction takes place.

Designing for energy efficiency

Did you know that 15 per cent of all the energy used in Australian cities is consumed inside homes, and the fastest-growing usage of electricity is for domestic air-conditioning? Many homes are not designed well enough to enable adequate ventilation, and a large number of homes run powerful energy-inefficient air-conditioners to cool rooms as quickly as possible.

An energy-efficient house reduces the need for electrical or gas-powered energy sources by using sustainable energy alternatives, especially for heating and cooling. You can achieve this by

- ✔ **Capturing the sun.** I mention this in preceding sections in this chapter, and it's so effective that I'm saying it again: Ensure that the living areas are located on the northern side of the home, with as many windows as possible on the northern walls to capture the sun's rays in the winter. You can also use solar heating to warm parts of the home.

- ✔ **Insulating.** The insulation in the internal building structure, the type of windows you use and the way you decorate rooms all play a part in insulating your home to reduce your need to resort to turning on the air-conditioner or heaters.

- ✔ **Shading.** The position of outdoor vegetation can shade your home in summer. Installing awnings and screens on windows facing north and west also helps keep the temperature down in summer, reducing the need for air-conditioning.

The wall that faces the sun most often, usually the northern wall in Australia, can be insulated, or it can make use of *thermal mass*. Whereas insulation blocks the flow of heat, thermal mass absorbs it, then releases it later. For example, materials like concrete and brick absorb rather than reflect heat, so they have a high level of thermal mass because they allow heat to travel through them. By using thermal mass on the northern wall, or on the southern side of north-facing rooms with large windows, you can take advantage of sunny winter days and cool summer evenings to reduce your heating and cooling requirements. The correct use of thermal mass requires specialist understanding, so make sure your architect or an adviser explains these concepts to you. Get a second opinion just to be sure.

See also Chapter 4 for more information on outfitting your home with energy-efficient appliances.

Obviously, the way that you live at home also affects the amount of energy you use. In Chapter 5, I provide some practical advice on how to adopt a sustainable lifestyle.

Building From the Ground Up: Construction Materials

Whether you're building a home or fixing an existing building to make it as eco-friendly as possible, the materials you use are an important component of your overall ecological footprint (refer to Chapter 2 to find out how to calculate your footprint).

Building materials have an impact on the environment during their production, either because their production damages the environment or uses large amounts of energy. Some are harmful to you at home because of the pollution they release into the air you breathe inside the house. Some are more helpful than others in reducing the impact of your lifestyle.

Most homes are built using a combination of timber, concrete and brick, or alternatives that mimic them. Putting aside time to understand their environmental advantages and disadvantages is worthwhile, though, because none of them makes for a straightforward choice. Many products with better environmental characteristics in the home are energy intensive to produce (for more information, see the sidebar 'All materials are not equal').

Concrete and brick

Concrete and brick are considered heavyweight construction materials most suited to climates with a high variation in daily temperatures, like most of inland Australia. Concrete (for foundations and walls) and brick (for veneers to cover the structure) help insulate against heat in summer and retain the heat in winter. Some companies market them as sustainable due to their insulating qualities (thereby reducing the need for artificial heating and cooling).

However, using commercial concrete and brick has some downsides. These include:

- Most brick and concrete is quarried from the earth and then heavily processed (in the case of concrete, using the hard-setting and reliable Portland cement). The burning in a large kiln of brick and concrete has significant air-quality impacts. It's safe to say that most commercial brick and concrete products have high levels of embodied energy. See the sidebar 'All materials are not equal' for more details.

- Transporting large quantities of sand, soil and stone from a quarry to a processing plant and then the processed product from the plant to a building site is an energy-consuming task.

- Brick structures usually require a deep construction footing on the building site and also disturb the natural site environment compared to other construction materials.

Bricks made from mud provide you with a better alternative to build sustainably. If you can find a local supplier that makes basic mud bricks — by mixing earth with water and placing the mixture into moulds, then drying the bricks in the open air (adobe bricks) or burning them in a kiln with little or no processing — then you're getting close to the perfect sustainable building product.

All materials are not equal

All the materials that are used to help you live your life, like the construction materials used to build or renovate your home, the furniture and appliances you buy for inside your home and even the packaging and containers used to store your food, contain a 'hidden' or 'embodied' level of energy. When you think about how the materials in products were captured, processed and transported, you begin to appreciate how much energy goes into getting products ready for consumption.

Most references to embodied energy are related to the building industry. Finished products with high levels of *embodied energy* would normally emit high levels of damaging emissions during processing and consume a large amount of fossil fuel for production and transport purposes. The more highly processed a material is, the higher its *embodied energy*. And if there is a high level of *embodied energy* within the materials you use

for your homes, then the chances are they are also going to have an unhealthy impact inside your home.

Wool insulation, for example, requires much less energy to produce than fibreglass batts. Wool batts are spun from sheep's wool whereas fibreglass batts are created from a production process that includes the use of chemicals, resins, dyes and oils. Another example is furniture made from plastics, which have a much higher embodied energy rating than furniture made from recycled or plantation-grown timber.

To get a feel for the different levels of embodied energy of building products, visit the Australian Greenhouse Office's Technical Manual. The manual lists the amount of embodied energy calculated for a variety of materials (go to www.greenhouse.gov.au/yourhome/technical/fs31.htm).

The most sustainable concrete products on the market are autoclaved, aerated concrete (AAC) and flyash concrete (which uses flyash to replace the greenhouse gas-producing Portland cement). If you have seen the type of concrete that looks like it has air holes in it, like an Aero chocolate bar, then it's probably AAC. It consists of silica sand (one of the more abundant natural resources on the planet), cement, lime and gypsum. The ingredients are mixed and slurried to form a gooey cake-like mix that is dried in a mould. When dry, the finished product is greatly increased in size, with air forming up to 80 per cent of the hardened product. As a result, compared to other concrete products, less materials are used and the production process is entirely natural, making it another one of the more sustainable building products on the market.

Timber

Yeah, trees are 'green', but cutting them down for their timber is a particularly important sustainability issue. Although wood is renewable, it's one of the natural resources used at a much faster rate than it can grow.

Of course, reducing the amount of trees on earth affects air quality and is a major influence on global warming.

The use of timber as a lightweight construction material has been particularly beneficial in Australia's warmer climate. It's effective in maintaining cooler inside temperatures in sustainably designed homes.

As more lightweight building materials evolve, the key is to use timber as minimally as possible. An increasingly popular design concept used in building construction is called Optimum Value Engineering (OVE). In simple terms, OVE attempts to minimise the amount of overall lumber (cut timber) required in constructing the building framework by using thicker planks, thereby increasing the space between frames that can be used and reducing the number of frames required.

When you have to use timber, ensure that it has come from a managed plantation that was established to regenerate cleared land, and that only releases timber at the same rate it's produced (grown to harvest stage). Unfortunately, at this stage, no Australian timber or wood certification process is in place to ensure that businesses are selling 'managed' timber for use in housing.

To help you out, the Rainforest Information Centre, a not-for-profit organisation based in northern New South Wales, provides the following guide for choosing timber. In order of preference, seek out:

✔ Recycled timber or non-timber materials wherever possible.

✔ Plantation timber direct from a 'well-managed' plantation. The types of timbers available from such plantations include:

- Mixed species timber, which more closely approximates the natural growing community that timber would come from, rather than a heavily produced, unsustainable, single-species plantation.

- Plantation hoop pine or plantation eucalypt (such as karri and yellow box), which are some of the few Australian rainforest timbers to be successfully grown in plantations.

- Plantation-sourced composite timber products, which include particle boards, fibreboards, composite beams, laminated timbers, finger-jointed timbers, plywood and veneers.

✔ Certified timber from a 'well-managed' forest. This means the wood comes from a 'regrowth forest' rather than a plantation, making it less desirable.

Any other timber options are likely to fall into the unsustainable timber basket. However, innovative, sustainable timber alternatives are being developed today, such as composite wood and plastic made from reclaimed hardwood sawdust and reclaimed/recycled plastic.

Timber alternatives

An increasing number of timber alternatives (other than recycling old timber itself) are now available, including products used to provide the framework for new houses and apartments. These include:

- **Recycled steel frames.** Although steel, like concrete, has a relatively high embedded energy component, it's recyclable. Most light-framed steel beams are made from at least approximately 25 per cent recycled steel and are, themselves, 100 per cent recyclable. A good company to contact regarding the advantages of using recycled metal is Simsmetal (visit www.simsmetal.com.au).

- **Bamboo.** This product is now being recognised in the Western world as one of the most sustainable alternatives to timber. Of course, many other parts of the world, particularly Asia, have known its construction benefits for years. If designed and produced correctly, bamboo can rival steel for strength and tension. Bamboo is considered sustainable by the likes of the Australian Rainforest Information Centre because it's a fully renewable resource and is fast growing and land-efficient. For more information on the qualities of bamboo, go to the Australian Bamboo Network Web site at www.ctl.com.au.

- **Plant-based plastics.** Traditional plastics are made from fossil fuels and use a wide range of toxic chemicals in their manufacture. New plant-based plastics use nothing other than water and mechanical energy. They're useful for furniture and non-load bearing surfaces and offer the structural qualities of wood with the finish of high-grade plastics. A leading example is Zelfo at www.zelfo.com.au.

- **Plastic lumber.** I know I'm beginning to sound like a broken record, but this point keeps on coming up: Although plastic products have a high level of embodied energy and create pollution, there are several companies recycling the plastic used for food, drink and cleaning product containers into a timber alternative. Several companies now specialise in the provision of timber look-a-like plastic decking, fencing, furniture and other structural alternatives. Check out Advanced Plastic Recycling (at www.a-p-r.com.au) for all you want to know about the applications of plastic lumber.

- **Recycled paper.** Most recycled paper products are converted into, um, paper. More recently, however, some companies have started to develop recycled paper timber alternatives, especially for less intensive and smaller applications such as doors and table tops. Although not as extensively available as the other alternatives listed in this section, you can start your search by checking American recycled product companies that sell recycled paper timber alternatives, such as Canopy (www.canopyhome.com) and Homasote (www.homasote.com).

Sustainable building checklist

To find out whether a building material falls into the sustainable category, check the list in Figure 3-2 and see if you can put a tick beside the eco-friendly factors.

Building Materials Checklist

❏   Is the wood sustainably harvested timber?

❏   Is there maximum use of recycled materials?

❏   Are the resources renewable?

❏   Are non-toxic chemicals used in production?

❏   Does the product avoid materials that come from a heavily resourced energy process?

❏   Are the raw materials used in the product locally or at least regionally based?

❏   Are there any wasteful byproducts?

❏   Does the material use renewable energy in production?

❏   Is the amount of water used in production minimised?

❏   Is the use of packaging minimised?

❏   Is the shipping distance minimised?

❏   Can the product be installed by traditional methods (less machinery and more elbow grease)?

❏   Can the material be reused again?

Figure 3-2:
The sustainable building materials checklist.

Finishing with Flair

The basic construction materials determine the overall environmental impact of the house, but did you know that the materials you use to finish your home can also affect the air that you breathe as well as the environment where they're manufactured?

You may be surprised to know how much pollution is released by the materials and furnishings you use to build and decorate your home. These combine with pollutants that are transported inside — the bacteria, dust mites, mould and mildew that flourish in the mess you make; and the pollution emitted by the cleaning products that you use to clean up around the home to create a cocktail of chemicals. Given this environmental problem, it's no wonder rates of asthma, influenza and other viruses increase every year, especially in children. (For more information about the dangerous gases released by products in the home, see the related sidebar 'Going home can damage your health'.)

You don't need to turn into Jack Nicholson's compulsive–obsessive character in the film *As Good as it Gets* to keep yourself healthy inside your home. Here are some simple solutions that can greatly reduce indoor pollution and improve the health of your home:

- Design your home or renovation to maximise natural air flow throughout the home and ensure that any fumes, gases or particles created are transported away.

- Don't use toxic materials to build, renovate, decorate and clean your home. Instead, decorate your home with natural furnishings, and use natural cleaning products to reduce the pollution in the first place. For more details, see Chapter 5.

The walls

The walls of many modern homes are constructed of gypsum and encased with paper or made from plain fibreboard planks. These days, you can even get wall panelling made from recycled materials, such as paper pulp and even recycled gypsum.

Roofing

One of the first things people see when they fly into Sydney are red roofs sitting atop a sprawling sea of houses. Terracotta tiles have been the traditional roofing choice for much of urban Australia. Unfortunately, these tiles go through quite an intensive production process, involving the extraction of clay, firing of moulded tiles in a kiln and the application of a chemically laden sealant and glazing. Terracotta tiles have also been found to break during severe storms that generate hail and wind, which has encouraged people to look for cost-saving alternatives.

Going home can damage your health

The health and greenhouse gas problems created by household building and furnishing products can be broken down into the following categories:

✔ **Gases:** One of the most invisible yet health-affecting gases released in the home is formaldehyde. This preservative is found in timber and wall panelling resins and coatings, clothing and furniture colourings, paints, carpets, upholstery, curtains and disinfectants. The other major toxic gas released within the home is carbon monoxide from poorly ventilated gas appliances and fireplaces.

✔ **Metals:** Many older places were built and decorated with extremely toxic lead-based paints and arsenic in treated timber and wall panellings. These become a particular issue in renovations, when stripping and removal of paints and timber release dangerous amounts of these metals into the atmosphere.

✔ **Mineral particles:** These are the most visible and possibly damaging pollutants within a home and are generated by materials built with known killer particles such as asbestos (wall and floor panels and roofing insulation) and fibreglass (roofing insulation).

The gases and metals that are released in the invisible vapours from these materials are also called VOCs (Volatile Organic Compounds). VOCs are readily absorbed through the skin, lungs and stomach and can lead to dizziness, nausea and general sickness. More serious doses of VOCs can affect the central nervous system and have been linked to skin conditions and diseases of the lung, liver and reproductive system.

Some of the more reliable and cost-effective sustainable roofing alternatives on the market include:

✔ Steel or aluminium sheets sourced from recycled material.

✔ Concrete tiles that have been developed with flyash and recycled materials.

✔ Asphalt shingles, which have been popular in the United States, with some asphalt sourced naturally. Unfortunately, asphalt shingles appear to have a much shorter life than most other roofing alternatives.

✔ Timber shingles from renewable timber sources.

✔ Thatch roofing from straw with cement or mud/earth rendering to hide the straw. Although only really effective in dry climates, straw is considered a renewable resource that grows plentifully in many regions.

When looking into the most effective roof for your home, you may want to consider your ability to fit photovoltaic panels to provide your electrical energy and solar hot water to supply your water heating needs inside your home (for more details, see Chapter 4).

Flooring

The floors in most homes are usually timber or concrete (to find out more about these materials, refer to the sections, 'Concrete and brick' and 'Timber' earlier in this chapter). Exposed timber floorboards usually end up with a polyurethane-type protection, which introduces unhealthy VOCs (volatile organic compounds) into the home environment. Concrete floors are usually covered with carpets, and although many carpets can be made from recycled materials, carpets end up housing much of the dust, mites and bacteria (to name a few) in the home.

The range of alternative sustainable flooring materials today is quite varied and extensive. These include:

- Bamboo, which has the same application and advantages of any timber (it looks just the same) but comes from a more renewable source. BIO Paint sells clear finish varnish to protect bamboo flooring (for more information, see the section 'Paints' later in this chapter).

- Cork, which is produced from the bark of cork trees in the Mediterranean region of Europe. The bark grows back approximately every seven years, making it relatively renewable without damaging the tree. For Australians, however, the transport costs of imported cork makes it less sustainable than bamboo.

- Linoleum, marmoleum and artoleum, which are floor-covering alternatives to tiles and carpet. The sustainable versions are generally made with a natural oil-like linseed, which is oxidised to form granules that are pressed and dried with natural colours and dyes.

- Recycled carpets, which are produced from a variety of recycled materials such as plastics and rubber (don't forget, though, that carpets can introduce bugs and VOCs into the home).

Insulation

Insulation is a key design element in any energy efficient home. Insulating your ceilings, floors and walls can play a major role in your ability to stay cool in summer and warm in winter — without turning on electrical appliances (I discuss the pros and cons of artificial heating methods in more detail in Chapter 4).

You can use bulk or reflective insulation in your ceiling, floors and walls. Window thickness can act as an insulator, too. Here's the lowdown:

- ✔ **Bulk insulation.** This stuff traps much of the heat that transfers into and out of the home. Insulation batts and blankets made out of glass 'wool' are the most common form of household bulk insulation. Some of the more sustainable bulk insulation includes cellulose made of recycled paper pulp (which is pumped into cavities), rockwool (melted volcanic rock that forms a 'wool'), natural wool and recycled polyester threads that are non-toxic. Most of these insulation types are generally supplied to larger-scale industrial or commercial buildings.

  Most residential bulk insulation is made from glass and fibreglass products, which can add to the mineral particle pollution found in the home, especially as they're being laid.

- ✔ **Reflective insulation.** Sheets of reflective foil (usually aluminium) stuck to panels of paper or plastic. As the name suggests, these panels help reflect the heat generated outside or keep the heat generated inside. It also reduces humidity collecting in the insulation. Reflective insulation is usually used in walls in addition to bulk insulation. Given that aluminium is the most common form of reflective insulation and that aluminium is a highly processed metal, this is a classic embodied-energy versus ongoing-energy-savings dilemma. Because it reduces your electrical heating and cooling requirements with no negative health impact, reflective insulation remains on most sustainable architects' list of useful products.

- ✔ **Windows.** Glass thickness, the sizes of your windows and the number of windows in a home (plus their furnishings) all play a role in insulating your home. The type of glass in your windows has a major impact in keeping heat in or out. For example, double-glazed windows and doors are commonplace in the colder regions of the world. The Window Energy Rating System (WERS) rates a window from 0 to 5 in being able to block the sun. Go to www.wers.net for more information on what to look out for when buying windows.

It may be difficult to find insulation alternatives to the 'glass wool' variety of insulation batts found in Australian stores. If your only option is to buy glass or fiberglass insulation, check for those that have been produced using recycled materials.

The following two Web sites help you get a better feel for the type of insulation you need to heat you up or cool your place down:

- ✔ **Choice Australia** (www.choice.com.au)**:** Choice Australia is the independent advisory service on consumer products and provides a calculator to determine your insulation requirements. Go to the Web site and click on Products then Heating/Cooling to find the heating and cooling calculators.

✔ **Insulco** (www.insulco.com.au): This Australian insulation batts company calculates the types of batt you require based on where you live (which takes into account your climate) and the size of the area you want to insulate. Check with the company to see if they can provide you with batts that use sustainable materials.

Paints

Most eco-sensitive paints are water-based (acrylic) and contain fewer chemical additives and toxic materials than the more standard type of paints, aren't tested on animals, and come in recycled packaging. Some paints can even be produced using recycled materials.

The most sustainable paint brand on the market in Australia is BIO Paint (www.bioproducts.com.au). Most products in the range are interior paints and varnishes made from natural materials, such as plant oils, essential oils, natural pigments, mineral fillers and water. And because the products are free of lead chromates, they don't emit VOCs into the home.

Two other natural paint and varnish brands on the market are imported from overseas: Livos and Auro. You can find more information about these products at www.livos.co.uk and www.auro.co.uk.

Independent ratings

The independent Australian Environmental Labelling Association (AELA) maintains a product register of certified building products that meet environmental, quality and social performance standards. The AELA develops scientific measures for the environmental performance of products throughout the market. A product's performance against these benchmarks determines whether the product is awarded the Australian *Good Environmental Choice* eco-label. So look out for the label shown here on the products you use for your home.

Another Web site worth checking out to see the range of sustainable building products available for constructing or renovating your home is the Australian Greenhouse Office's technical manual (visit www.greenhouse.gov.au/yourhome/technical/fs30.htm to get your copy).

The Australian Greenhouse Office also provides the nitty gritty on embodied energy at www.greenhouse.gov.au/yourhome/technical/fs31.htm. The page helps you work through the different levels of embodied energy in each of the materials you may be considering to use to build or renovate your home.

If you're ready to do some painting and you can't get hold of an eco-sensitive paint brand, choose water-based paints in preference to oil-based paints. Oil-based paints contain the most dangerous levels of VOCs. The Good Environmental Choice Australia Web site also endorses safer paints. Visit www.aela.org.au/LabelUse.htm for more details.

Chapter 4

The Energy-Efficient Household

You don't have to buy or build a brand new 'green' house to become more energy-efficient — you can do plenty to reduce the amount of power you use by paying attention to which of your appliances consume the most electricity. Understanding this helps you prioritise your energy budget.

In this chapter I show you that heating and cooling appliances are among the biggest users of energy in your house, but with insulation you can significantly reduce how often you need to use them. Many people are surprised to discover that hot water is also a major energy hog. A solar hot-water service is a relatively cheap way to reduce your energy consumption in a big way.

As well as controlling how much energy you consume, you can contribute to the health of the planet by being careful about where you get your energy from. I explain why conventional energy sources are unsustainable and provide you with alternatives that are much kinder on our planet. This includes buying green power or generating your own power.

Holistic Approaches to Heating and Cooling

How do you heat and cool your home? Perhaps you take the edge off the heat in summer by putting on your air-conditioner for a little while. Or maybe you turn on electric heaters in the winter to keep the temperature pleasant in the rooms you use most often.

Power usage, at home

The Australian Greenhouse Office points out that the average Australian home uses electrical energy the following ways:

✔ Heating and cooling: 39 per cent

✔ Water heating: 27 per cent

✔ General electrical appliances (the TV, dishwasher, washing machine, hairdryer and so on): 12 per cent

✔ Refrigeration: 9 per cent

✔ Lighting: 5 per cent

✔ Cooking: 4 per cent

✔ Standby energy use (used by electronic equipment like the DVD when shut down by remote control): 4 per cent

The appliances you use to heat and cool your home may be costing you more than you realise, though (see the sidebar 'Power usage, at home' to find out how much the average Australian household relies on electrical energy to heat and cool the home). In the following sections, I explain how you can avoid reacting to extremes of temperature with extreme energy usage.

Most artificial heaters and coolers use some sort of electrical energy. Here's a run-down on how they work:

✔ **Reverse-cycle air-conditioners.** To lower temperatures, these appliances use coolants that produce greenhouse gases, just like a refrigerator does (to find out more about how refrigerators work, see Chapter 5). However, the newer type of air-conditioners, called *inverters*, manage electricity more effectively to cool a room, which means they're cheaper to run and produce less greenhouse gas. (Check out Chapter 12 for more information about what to look for when buying an air-conditioner.)

If you already have air-conditioning installed in your home, employ some strategies to minimise how often you use it. For example, try only using the air-conditioner for small amounts of time to lower the temperature in your home, and make sure your home is insulated to maintain the temperature. Needless to say, don't leave the air-con on when you go out, or when doors or windows are open.

✔ **Evaporative coolers.** These units don't use coolants that emit damaging greenhouse gases, but they do use more electricity than smaller electric fans and ceiling fans. Also, evaporative coolers don't work well in humid climates because they can't deal with the moisture in the air. Evaporative coolers suit dry climates, like the outback of Australia.

✔ **Ceiling fans.** Often overlooked in the rush to buy cold air, ceiling fans are the traditional artefacts of a hot climate lifestyle; they keep the air moving and prevent heat from building up. Overhead fans, combined with properly shaded windows, won't bring the temperature in your home down to 22 degrees Celsius when it's 40 in the shade outside, but they can create a pleasant and relaxing environment.

✔ **Electric radiant heaters.** Most electric heaters only heat the objects in front of them; they're not very good at heating the air in a room.

Better alternatives to electric radiant heaters are fan or convection heaters, which circulate the heat throughout the room. Even better are gas heaters. See the sidebar 'Heating with gas' for more details.

✔ **Fireplaces that use wood.** The good news is that you don't need electricity to stoke the wood in a fireplace (although some fake fireplaces are powered by electricity). The bad news is that wood fires produce high levels of air pollution because they release gases as the wood burns (just like a bushfire does). They're also an inefficient heating method because much of the heat goes up the chimney (although you can address this by installing a slow-combustion model that redirects the heat from the chimney back into the room).

Insulation is the key

Insulation is a big sustainable deal. A well-insulated home can maintain the inside temperature throughout the day and night. Insulation reduces your need for electrical heating and air-conditioning. If your place is insulated, you only need to use heaters and coolers when temperatures are above or below average for a small amount of time to get the temperature back to a comfortable level.

Even old homes or apartments that weren't designed to be energy efficient can be greatly improved with insulation by keeping the heat out in summer and keeping the warmth in during winter. And if you're renting your house or apartment, working with the landlord to install insulation may save you money in the medium term by reducing your electricity bill.

Insulation is one of the key design elements to look for when you're buying or building an energy-efficient home or improving your existing home. Chapter 3 discusses the types of insulating material available in more detail.

Beating the heat

The Australian summer can be a stinker. Sometimes you may wonder how people once survived 40-degree days without the help of air-conditioners and electric fans. Even average outside summer temperatures can make life quite stuffy inside.

Glass windows can let a lot of heat into your home. In fact, covering your windows to protect your rooms from the summer sun is the most effective way of keeping the heat out. Installing awnings and screens and even planting vegetation in the line between the sun and the window will work wonders. Here are some other simple things that you can do to ensure that you keep much of the heat generated outside from getting inside.

- ✔ **Verandahs, eaves and awnings.** The traditional colonial homestead was surrounded by verandahs on all sides. This was not just the mark of an outdoors lifestyle; the shade provided by those verandahs and the movement of cool air past the external walls of the house kept these homes much cooler in summer. By contrast, large houses on relatively small suburban blocks with small eaves provide almost no shade, which can turn these houses into ovens on hot days.

  If you're building or renovating, ensure that your eaves protect your windows and walls from the summer sun, but allow the low winter sun to stream in through the windows. Alternatively, use awnings or other screens to achieve the same effect.

- ✔ **Shutters.** From the icy plains of northern Europe to the deserts of northern Africa, shutters have traditionally protected homes from the vagaries of the weather. Strangely, they're almost absent from suburban home design these days.

- ✔ **Curtains and blinds.** Although considered old fashioned by many people, window coverings have a major role to play in keeping the heat out. Importantly, the *pelmet box* traditionally used to hide the top of the curtain traps hot air between the curtain and the window and prevents it circulating into the rest of the room.

If you're building or renovating, one of the most important design factors to include to make your home energy efficient is this: Create air flow through the house. Ensure windows are placed in the face of the common cooling breezes, which in an Australian summer usually come from a southerly direction. To take advantage of any breezes that come in, rooms should connect to allow air to flow from one end of the home to the other.

Placing rotating vents, or whirligigs, in the roof is another very cheap way to keep a house cool in summer. These devices can reduce the temperature inside a roof cavity by ten degrees or more, and take the strain off your insulation and internal cooling systems.

Heating with gas

Gas heaters with reverse-cycle heat pumps produce approximately one-third the amount of greenhouse emissions of standard electric heating equivalents. Gas heaters also warm a room very quickly, making them more efficient (and much cheaper to run) than electrical heaters.

Two styles of natural or LPG gas heaters are on the market: Portable heaters and fixed heaters.

With both styles of heaters, you need to ensure that you have enough good air flow to maintain indoor air quality, but not too much to affect the efficiency of the heaters. To overcome some of these problems, you can now get low-combustion heaters, which produce lower emissions and require less air flow.

For more information about gas, see also the sidebar 'The wonder of gas' later in this chapter.

Staying warm

In Australia, most areas get a lot of exposure in the winter to that great big heater in the sky. As a result, keeping warmth inside the home is a lot easier than cooling it down. Many other countries in the world, especially in the northern hemisphere, rarely get to see the sun during the winter months and don't get much of an opportunity to utilise the sun to offset their heating needs.

The following low-energy techniques take advantage of the sun's ability to heat your home:

- **Let the sun shine in.** When the temperatures start to drop, lift the shades on those windows that face the sun. The sun can then stream in and heat up the room.

- **Keep the warmth in.** You've warmed up your room, now you've got to keep it in.

  - Make sure your doors and windows are well sealed so that cold air doesn't get in and the warm air inside doesn't get out.

  - Furnishings like rugs, carpets and curtains are very good at ensuring that the heat stays in a room well into the night instead of escaping through the floor, ceilings and windows.

  - Insulation that keeps the heat out can also keep the heat in. For more information about insulation, refer to the section 'Insulation is the key' earlier in this chapter.

Using Energy-Efficient Appliances

The household appliances you use, including refrigerators and microwaves, washing machines and entertainment systems, account for about a quarter of household energy consumption in Australia (for more details, refer to the sidebar 'Power usage, at home' earlier in this chapter).

Obviously, reducing your reliance on these appliances is one way to cut your energy consumption. For example, you can hang your clothes on a clothesline instead of putting them in the dryer, or you can wash the dishes in a double sink instead of using a dishwasher. However, if you find the concept of living without these appliances too inconvenient to take seriously, buy the most energy-efficient appliances you can find when you're shopping for new electrical goods, and choose gas over electricity in the kitchen.

Calculate your energy efficiency

Many electrical energy suppliers and renewable energy traders provide online calculators to help you calculate your energy efficiency. For example, electricity and gas provider Origin Energy and renewable energy trader Climate Friendly offer excellent step-by-step calculators that you can use to see the impact of your electrical consumption patterns. The results also show you how much it'll cost you to offset your carbon dioxide emissions with renewable sources.

To test how these work, I used the energy-efficiency calculator on the Origin Energy Web site (www.originenergy.com.au/efficiency/#calc_intro) to compare the cost of different levels of electrical usage and how much greenhouse gases were emitted. I compared the annual use of electricity for a household living in a two-bedroom apartment with 4-star appliances against a similar household using 2-star appliances.

Entering average data for use of electricity in all rooms of the 2-star appliance home yielded a total yearly electricity bill of $634, with 5.64 tonnes of carbon dioxide generated. By comparison, the household using 4-star appliances attracted an annual bill of $568 and generated 5.04 tonnes of carbon dioxide.

By the way, 5.04 tonnes of carbon dioxide is the same amount that 1.92 cars driving on the road (averaging 15,000 kilometres per year or 41 kilometres a day) emit into the air per year. Notice the cost savings that took place in the energy-efficient household.

These calculations show that you can easily cut in half the amount of electrical energy you use.

To calculate your energy usage, visit Origin Energy or the Climate Friendly Web site at www.climatefriendly.com.au. Look for the energy-efficiency calculator to get started.

It's all in the ratings

You may have already seen the energy rating labels displayed on electrical whitegoods at your favourite department store. This mandatory labelling system, developed by the Australian Greenhouse Office and called the Australian Appliance Energy Rating Scheme (ERS), is designed to help you better understand the energy efficiency of the products you're buying. The greater the number of stars displayed on the labels, as shown in Figure 4-1, the less electricity the appliances use compared to similar products on the market. Appliances that have both hot and cold settings, such as a reverse-cycle air-conditioner, show two bands of star ratings on its label (see the image at right in Figure 4-1). Remember also that appliances with higher star ratings emit less greenhouse gases, too.

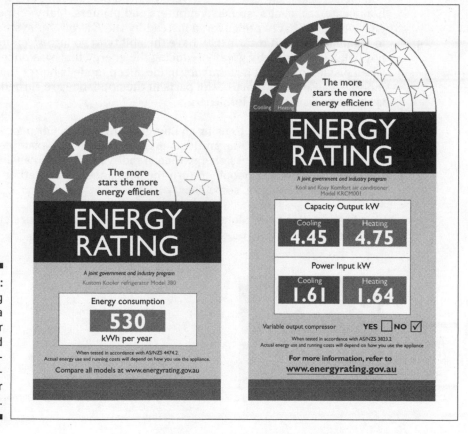

Figure 4-1: Energy rating labels for a refrigerator (at left) and a reverse-cycle air-conditioner (at right).

Energy rating labels also contain a number that may be difficult to decipher at first glance. This number is, in fact, an estimate of the energy an appliance will consume in kilowatts (kW) under standard conditions over a given time. The number actually provides a more accurate way of comparing the energy efficiency of similar models.

You can look up the energy-efficiency ratings of various brands of air-conditioners, clothes dryers, washing machines, refrigerators and freezers online at www.energyrating.gov.au. I also compare the energy-efficiency ratings on popular brands of appliances in Chapter 12.

Becoming an Energy Star

Some electrical products aren't covered by the ERS system, including TVs, home entertainment systems, computers and printers. Many of these electrical must-haves are covered instead by the *Energy Star* system (shown in Figure 4-2), which means they have the ability to go into *sleep* mode when not being used, thereby greatly reducing the energy that was once spent when just left on or put into *standby* mode. Sleep mode is better than standby mode because many more of the parts in the appliance are turned off and it is therefore using much less energy.

There are pros and cons to using an Energy Star product. For people who just leave things on, Energy Star products do save energy: For example, sleep mode uses 75 per cent less energy than standby mode. Then again, you may believe in encouraging people to turn the appliance off altogether because sleep mode still requires some energy.

Turning something completely off at the power point saves more energy than both sleep and standby modes.

Figure 4-2:
The Energy
Star label.

Don't believe anyone who tells you that turning an appliance off and on again uses more energy than leaving the appliance in sleep or standby mode. Remember, *off* is the most energy-efficient mode for any electrical appliance. By itself, standby mode accounts for 4 per cent of domestic energy consumption.

Cooking with gas

Although a fossil fuel resource, natural gas is more energy-efficient than electricity. The most popular household natural gas appliances in homes are ovens and cooktops. The more efficient performer of the two is the cooktop. A gas cooktop produces half the greenhouse gases of a standard electric cooktop, and uses less energy, too. (For more information about how gas stacks up against electricity, check out the related sidebar 'The wonder of gas'.)

The wonder of gas

Luckily, Australia has large reserves of natural gas. Using natural gas in the home has many advantages over using electricity. Piping gas direct to you is more efficient than converting it to electricity and then sending that to your house in wires. Natural gas (methane) is also a more efficient fuel than other fossil fuels because you use less of it to get the same result. The other big advantage is that natural gas produces only one-third the greenhouse gas emissions than that of coal-powered electricity.

Natural gas is also better than liquid petroleum gas (LPG), the other main commercial gas product on the market. Although both have similar rates of greenhouse gas emissions, LPG needs to be transported in tankers or trucks, which are major greenhouse gas contributors, too. By comparison, natural gas is delivered by pipe direct to your home.

If natural gas is available in your area, I recommend you use it. You can use natural gas in your home for:

- Cooking, in ovens or on cooktops.

- Boosting the heat in your solar hot water system.

- Heating your home, using portable or fixed heaters — when rugging up doesn't do the trick. For more information, refer to the sidebar 'Heating with gas' earlier in this chapter.

- Stoking your barbecue.

For more details about how other gas products stack up against different sources of energy in terms of their impact on the environment, see Chapter 16.

A gas oven also usually produces less greenhouse gas emissions than an electric oven. However, the differences between these two are not so clear cut, because some gas ovens use more energy than their electrical equivalents — especially if the gas oven isn't *fan forced*, using an inbuilt fan to circulate the heat.

If you already have gas appliances in the kitchen, get into the habit of using the cooktop — even if your gas oven is a fan-forced model. Steaming, boiling or stir-frying dishes on a gas cooktop is more energy efficient than cooking food in an oven or even a microwave. For more information about how to be sustainable in the kitchen, check out Chapter 5.

Lighting Up Your life

Any architect or interior decorator can tell you that lighting is a critical component in designing a home. For example, the right kind of lighting can transform your kitchen and save you lots of money, too.

The light that pours out of cities and towns at night is visible from space, and is the reason the night sky is invisible to most city dwellers. But if you visit the country on a clear night, the number of stars in the sky will simply boggle your senses. Most lighting is public, or commercial; domestic lighting 'only' accounts for 5 per cent of energy consumption in homes. That's still more than one tonne of carbon dioxide each year for the average Australian home, though.

The best way to cut back on your lighting bill is to turn lights off when they're not being used. For more tips on managing lighting in the home, see Chapter 5.

Appropriate lighting

Good design and good energy use are in agreement on this one: If you put the lighting where you need it, you'll need less lighting and end up with a warmer, cosier environment to live in. Smaller, individual lights dotted around rooms provide a much better atmosphere and more alternatives for lighting a room than one single, strong light.

You need good lights in doorways and entrance areas, as well as over work areas in the kitchen, bathroom, laundry and in study areas. Living and sleeping areas want subdued lighting at certain times. This can be achieved in a variety of ways: You can use low-voltage uplights in corners for subdued lighting, and strong ceiling lights for those times that require good vision.

Some energy-saving lights don't work well with dimmer switches. If you use dimmers to subdue the lighting in your home, look for globes designed for the purpose.

Seeking the low-energy glow

Alternative forms of lighting can help you reduce the amount of energy you spend on lighting your home. Each of the following types of lighting has its own characteristics, which make it suitable for some areas but not others.

Incandescent tungsten

The traditional light globe with a little coiled wire inside is called an *incandescent tungsten*. These lights consume between 60 and 100 watts of energy. Unfortunately, six of these lights used for four hours a day produce a tonne of carbon dioxide every three months (that is, if your electricity comes from a traditional coal-fired power station).

Incandescent tungsten lights provide a bright yellow and red light that creates a sharper edge to objects, which gives objects better definition.

Halogen

Similar to tungsten, except the colour characteristics are more constant over the colour spectrum. Halogens create a brighter light for the same power use and are often used to highlight ceilings and walls to reduce glare.

Halogen lights have a number of ecological drawbacks, mainly because of the way they're installed. Electricians scatter them widely, adding to their power consumption. They're usually installed in the ceiling by cutting a hole in the insulation to release the heat they produce. This reduces the effectiveness of your insulation considerably. As well, they're mostly installed with a transformer attached to each light globe, wasting power and producing more heat in the ceiling cavity.

Fluorescent

Compact fluorescents have become the darling of energy savers because they consume around one-sixth of the electricity that an incandescent globe of similar brightness would.

A fluorescent light produces a softer light that blends objects into the background, making them harder to see. It gives off blue and green colours, which are harder on the eye. A full-spectrum fluorescent allows the eyes to see items in a natural state, but it's still a soft light.

Because fluorescents don't generally work with dimmers, many people are reluctant to use them in their general living areas.

LED down lights

An emerging replacement for halogen lamps, these low-powered, solid-state lights are true energy savers, but also require transformers to convert your mains power into low-voltage direct current.

LED down lights tend to throw a blue-white light, with some of the same characteristics as halogen lamps.

Plasma lighting

Not commercially available at the time of going to press, this revolutionary new form of lighting comes in sheets. Rather than globes, you can place artificial skylights and windows onto ceilings and walls, even incorporating works of art into the light itself. Some companies are working on transparent plasma lights that will operate as windows during the day and lights at night.

Developers of plasma lighting say that the light that plasma lighting throws will be similar to that produced by plasma televisions and computer screens. This has similar qualities to fluorescent and LED lights: It diffuses the light, so does not define edges well.

Becoming an Alternative Energy Convert

Electricity is easy to generate. Unfortunately, the majority of electricity in this country is produced by burning coal, a huge polluter and one of the main sources of greenhouse gases that cause global warming. However, a number of alternatives to coal exist; the rest of this chapter describes some of them.

Most power plants burn fossil fuels, like coal, to make electricity. Mechanical energy is changed into electrical energy by burning the fuel in a boiler to produce steam. The pressure that builds up powers a generator that creates a magnetic field, which in turn causes the electrons in masses of copper wire to move from atom to atom, creating electricity.

This means that a lot of coal is mined (or oil is drilled) to meet your electrical energy demands. Reducing your reliance on this type of electrical power and converting to more sustainable, alternative energy sources is one way to become more energy efficient.

By the way, are you wondering whether nuclear energy is a green power source — or safe? To find out more, see the sidebar 'Is nuclear energy sustainable?'

Is nuclear energy sustainable?

You probably already know that Australia's Prime Minister, John Howard, supports nuclear energy and is considering building nuclear power plants around the country. Like Mr Howard, those in favour of nuclear energy proclaim that it's cleaner, greener and the only alternative to coal that's able to produce a large amount of energy from a relatively small amount of fuel.

Confused? Perhaps you're like me and have always considered that nuclear energy is bad for the environment — that it's dangerous, toxic and the waste generated by a nuclear power plant is a major global issue. Well, as this book went to press, I discovered that there's more to this issue than meets the eye. Here's what I have gleaned about the role that nuclear energy can play as an effective alternative-energy fuel:

⌐ A nuclear power plant generates power basically the same way a coal power plant does. The uranium undergoes a process called fission (a nuclear reaction that releases energy), which heats the surrounding water to generate enough steam that's fed into a turbine generator. The big difference between coal and nuclear energy is that greenhouse gas emissions aren't produced during the fission process.

⌐ Those in favour of nuclear energy state that a nuclear power plant generates a reliable source of power that's not reliant on the vagaries of weather (as wind and solar power is). And as long as the waste is contained, no-one's health is in danger.

⌐ Opponents of nuclear energy state that the extremely toxic and long-living radioactive waste that's generated from fission is enough of a disadvantage to rule it out as an energy alternative — it's just too dangerous to human health to even contemplate. For example, how can countries and organisations guarantee that the waste can be contained and disposed of safely? If released, plutonium (the main element of nuclear waste) is so toxic that the most minute amount can cause cancer in anyone exposed to it.

⌐ People opposed to nuclear energy also believe that the potential to use the uranium to create nuclear weapons is too great a risk.

One of the reasons why Australia is so keen to promote nuclear energy as an alternative power source is that Australia has large amounts of uranium ore (the Uranium Information Centre states that 28 per cent of the world's uranium supply is found in Australia).

So, from a sustainability perspective, you won't find me recommending nuclear energy as an alternative energy source in this book. Although some countries have started to increase their reliance on nuclear-generated electrical energy because it offers economic and environmental advantages, the waste and health issues realistically rule it out as being wholly sustainable.

Understanding green power

The following three sources are collectively known as *green power*, or renewable power, and are the main alternatives to powering your home with fossil-fuel-generated electricity:

✔ **Solar power.** Energy from the sun converted through solar panels (technically called *photovoltaic panels*) into electrical energy is the most popular alternative energy in Australia.

Solar hot water systems work differently. They simply trap heat from the sun. For more information about solar hot water systems, see the section, 'Using the sun to heat your water', later in this chapter.

✔ **Wind power.** Energy from the wind propels the blades on a wind turbine to create energy within a generator to produce electricity. Domestic turbines use different designs. For example, the Hush Turbine developed by Melbourne inventor Arthur O'Connor (shown in Figure 4-3) uses small blades that can turn at high speeds to generate electricity efficiently.

✔ **Hydro power.** Water flow creates enough force within a generator to create electrical output. For more information about how big hydro-electricity plants work, see the sidebar 'Where do energy suppliers get green power from?', later in this chapter. Small domestic hydro-power units suit properties that have their own source of continually flowing water.

Figure 4-3:
A quiet domestic wind turbine resembles a jet engine rather than a propellor.

You have two ways in which you can make the conversion to green power. One is to buy renewable energy instead of coal-fired power. The other way is to produce your own green power at home using one of the technologies I outline in this section. I cover these options in more detail in the rest of this chapter.

The Australian federal government offers rebates to households that install their own renewable power sources or solar hot water systems. The rebate can offset the cost of installation.

Signing up for green power

Many electricity suppliers across the country now allow households to sign up for green power. Although this option is slightly more expensive, the extra money you pay is invested in renewable energy sources. If everyone signed up for green power, renewable energy would become the dominant source of electricity in Australia.

In Australia, companies such as Neco and One Stop Green Shop, do a similar thing independent of the power companies. These energy traders allow you to invest directly in renewable energy. You get two bills: You still pay an electricity company to deliver your power, but you also pay the energy trader to generate the same amount of power from all renewable sources. The advantage here is that you know your money is being invested in building new power plants using renewable energy.

Some people think it's absurd that you have to pay more for green energy than you do for coal-fired power. But until demand increases for cleaner alternative energy sources, and initiatives like *carbon trading* are implemented as a way of penalising companies that own and operate coal power stations for the greenhouse gas emissions they produce, renewable energy will remain more expensive.

Using the sun to heat your water

A solar water heater can provide between 50 per cent and 90 per cent of your total hot water requirements, depending on the climate in your area and the model of heater you buy.

The basic principle is simple: Cold water is spread out over the roof in pipes or glass tubes and is heated by the sun. It is then pumped, or moved by its own heat, into a holding tank while more cold water is heated up. On a sunny day the water quickly reaches boiling point, so all systems are fitted with safety devices to stop the water from getting so hot that it burns people.

Just love that piping hot water

According to the Australian Greenhouse Office (AGO), in most households hot water is the largest energy cost and cause of greenhouse gas emissions. In fact, heating water accounts for about 27 per cent of an average household's total greenhouse gas emissions and energy use. This is an incredible luxury, especially when you consider the low cost of getting the sun to do it for you. If you can't afford to install a solar hot-water service, you can save energy by installing water-efficient fittings and appliances in the home. See Chapter 5 for more details.

Several types of solar heaters are on the market, all with different characteristics and varying degree of energy efficiency. Here is a run-down of the different solar heating models you may encounter:

✔ **Passive water collection heaters.** Cold water is collected in a tank in the roof, which is heated during the day by solar panel plates. Passive systems are the most energy-efficient solar heater because they don't use electricity to pump the water. You can choose between two types:

  • Open circuit system, where water flows directly from one tank to another.

  • Closed circuit system, where a heating fluid is warmed in the tank and then the heat from it is transferred to the water already sitting in the collection tank. The closed circuit system is commonly used in areas that experience frosts or freezing conditions in the winter. The fluid used to generate heat for the water in a closed-circuit system has anti-freeze properties.

Passive systems use either gravity fed or closed-coupled flow. The gravity-fed model has the water collector situated above the storage tank in the roof, and normal gravity moves the water through pipes from collection to storage and through to your taps. The closed-coupled system has the collector below the storage tank and uses normal water pressure to get the water to storage and through to your taps.

✔ **Active water collection heaters.** If you have limited space in the roof or a traditional hot water system, you may go for an active rather than a passive system. The storage tank on an active system can be located on the ground or under the house, with the heated water pumped from the collector tank to the storage tank.

Active pump systems, like the one shown in Figure 4-4, are good for converting your existing tank to a solar powered system, but you need to power the pump somehow, and the obvious way, unfortunately, is with electricity.

Figure 4-4:
An active
solar hot
water
system.

No matter which type of solar power system you choose, be sure to position the solar panel in the roof at an angle that takes advantage of the sun's rays. Also, think about what size tank you need to cater for your family; try not to buy something larger than you really need.

Whether you choose a passive or active solar water-heating system, if the sun's not shining, your solar power system can't heat the collected water. To overcome this, you can buy a *booster* to heat the water when the temperature falls below a certain point. The boosters can be powered by electricity, gas, petroleum or diesel.

However, boosters can waste energy if they're used too often. In fact, some boosters require more energy than normal off-peak electrical hot water systems. You're best bet is to install timers if you find your booster system is being used too much.

To find out more about solar water heating systems, including buying a unit that's suitable for your home, check out the AGO's Technical Manual for Environmentally Sustainable Homes at www.greenhouse.gov.au/yourhome/technical/fs43.htm.

Going the whole hog: Getting into the power business

Instead of spending your money on paying someone else to produce green power, you can create your own. Domestic solar panels, wind turbines and hydro power are reasonably affordable and make you virtually independent of the big power companies. If you produce all your own power needs, you never have to pay a power bill again or suffer from a power shortage (providing your own generators keep on ticking, of course).

You don't need a freestanding house or, more to the point, a large roof to run a solar power system. The truth is that many modern apartment buildings are also being designed to have much of their water heating and electrical needs centrally powered by solar energy. However, if you want to install a new solar power system, it helps if you have your own detached house, because you need *body corporate approval* (approval from the apartment complex) to install something new.

Where do energy suppliers get green power from?

Power companies draw on a combination of solar, wind and hydro power to provide renewable sources of energy.

Solar energy is one of the most popular sources of renewable energy. It uses no fossil fuels and emits no harmful greenhouse gases — nothing, naught, zero, zilch.

Solar panels. Large-scale solar power plants using photovoltaic cells use lenses or dish-shaped reflectors to concentrate the sunlight on the panel, making them more efficient. Another system uses mirrors that look like satellite dishes to track the sun and concentrate heat at one point. The incredible heat focused at that point can be used to drive an engine to create electricity.

Wind power. Energy from the wind propels the blades on a wind turbine to create energy within a generator to create electricity. Traditional wind turbines usually feature three large propeller blades that face the wind. The current big turbines are about 65 metres in diameter. Because of their size, this style of turbine can only operate at moderate wind speed. New, vertical axis models overcome this problem and can operate at high speeds.

Hydro-electricity. This well-established technology uses water cascading through large pipes to spin turbines that produce electricity. Although this method doesn't emit nasty greenhouse gases, hydro-electricity still impacts on the environment to a certain extent because the method interferes with the natural flow of rivers, and the dams often drown large areas of arable land.

Worldwide, the renewable energy sector is one of the fastest-growing parts of the economy. For example, Denmark recently committed to generating 100 per cent of its power from renewable sources. As a result the country has already created 16,000 new jobs and is exporting technology.

Besides space, you may also need approval from your local council to install domestic solar panels, wind turbines and hydro power.

Most people already connected to mains electricity remain connected, even after installing solar panels, wind turbines and hydro power. Staying connected to mains electricity protects them in case their gear fails, or it produces less energy than they expected. Staying connected also gives them the opportunity to earn income from their green power by selling it back to the electricity supplier. To do this they also need to install a reverse meter to measure the amount of electricity fed back into the electricity grid.

Chapter 5

Living Sustainably at Home

Tired of keeping up with the Joneses? Are you more interested in making your home a more non-toxic, energy and water-efficient environment?

In this chapter I get to the heart of lifestyle matters — the way you live at home. I take you from room to room and show you how each space provides you with some unique opportunities to use less energy, save water and reduce the number of toxins in the home. Along the way, I offer a range of money-saving and eco-friendly ways to run your home, most of which are simple ideas that you can start using today.

I even show you how easy it is to clean your home without using nasty chemicals. In fact, with some basic 'green' ingredients at hand, you can mix up a batch and clean just about anything!

Living the Sustainable High Life

You may be tempted to spend your hard-earned cash on extravagant appliances and justify your purchase by telling yourself: 'Well, why not — life is for living'. The implication here is that you damn the consequences and just do it.

Sales of the widest screen TVs, the loudest stereos, the coolest air-conditioners and the quietest dishwashers indicate that the *life is for living* rationale is very much alive. So much so that the word *affluenza* has been coined to describe excessive human consumption as a disease afflicting Western culture. (Refer to Chapter 2 for more on the effects of affluenza.)

When you consider the impact of over-consumption on the planet, you may start thinking about how to base your lifestyle decisions on ways that make your home a more comfortable, non-toxic and energy-efficient place. Here's a thought — if you turn around the phrase *life is for living*, you get *living is for life!* If you adopt this philosophy at home, you can refocus your lifestyle choices on what's best for you, your family and the environment for the rest of your life.

In fact, rejecting affluenza and living in a sustainable home is trendy. But you don't have to make a sea-change or a tree-change to live the sustainable high life. You can do it in the home you're living in now, wherever that is, and make your friends pea-green with envy.

Making Your Living Room a Comfort Zone

Your living room typically reflects the values you live by. The living room is usually the showpiece of the home. The most expensive furniture and appliances are located here, along with the family photos, framed paintings and prized collections. This section shows you many ways to bring your concern for the environment into the same room with these other things you value.

Most living rooms are also high-traffic areas and are set up to be the most comfortable area in the home — who doesn't like making a beeline for the sofa after dinner? Air-conditioning and heating are concentrated here, and lighting and entertainment systems grace the space.

In Chapter 4, I explain why good insulation helps maintain a comfortable temperature and reduces your consumption of electrical energy. Here I provide some initiatives to help you reduce your electrical energy consumption even further.

Entertainment systems — get real!

Some people's living rooms resemble a retailer's home entertainment showroom. I can't believe the size of the TVs — or are they movie screens? — in some of the homes I visit.

Do you really need a movie-sized TV screen or has the affluenza virus driven you to keep up with the Joneses? It might be more satisfying to show off a hand-woven rug by a local artist, a tropical fish tank, or your child's art projects (an ongoing gallery that changes often) than to have the same big screen as all the neighbours. The hand-woven rug will be worth more in ten years, too — and who knows about your child's artistic career if encouraged? The point is to think consciously about what fulfills you, and your family's actual wish list for fun and relaxation rather than simply assuming the latest gadget will bring joy.

The first question to ask yourself is — do you really need it? In other words, to what extent do you suffer from the affluenza virus? Do you really need to have a movie screen-sized TV when exactly the same message can be obtained from a smaller 51-centimetre TV?

After you've decided on the appliances and entertainment devices that are an important part of your lifestyle, use the advice in Chapter 12 to buy the longest-lasting and most energy-efficient ones. Whatever appliances you have, the way that you use them has the greatest impact on the energy you use.

For example, try to get into the habit of not turning things on just to create some background sound or vision. Only turn on the device if you really want it on; likewise, turn it off if you're not watching it or listening to it — especially if you actually leave the room. Reminding children to get into these habits often helps parents to remember them as well.

Furnishings and fittings

Furnishing your house with environmentally friendly and healthy materials has never been easier. In Chapter 3, I provide you with a list of sustainable flooring materials — such as bamboo, cork, naturally made linoleum and recycled carpets — that can be used in the home.

In fact, many of the tips provided in Chapter 3 for choosing sustainable materials to renovate your home apply to furnishing your home. Most household furniture is still made from timber, so seek out those items that are made from recycled timber materials or timber grown from renewable plantations. And more tables, chairs, lounges and beds are being made from timber alternatives, such as bamboo, cork, recycled rubber and plastics, and even hardened recycled paper.

If you have fabric-covered furniture that you like and it's in pretty good shape but you want a new look, why not simply reupholster it rather than replacing it? Natural fabrics such as linen, wool, cotton and hemp are resilient, contain little embodied energy and do not give off fumes when new, or if they are inadvertently burned. (For more information about embodied energy, refer to Chapter 3.)

New plant-based plastics, such as Zelfo, promise a range of furniture made from renewable sources using very small amounts of energy.

Chapter 12 provides you with a list of retailers that sell naturally made furnishings and fittings.

Lighting your lifestyle

How you use lights has an impact on your energy bill. The key to using lights efficiently — especially in large living areas — is to use them sparingly.

Here are some more pointers to help you save energy:

- ✔ Turn off the lights when you leave the room. Basic, I know, but you may be surprised how often people overlook this.

- ✔ For subdued lighting, use a lamp instead of dimmers. Lamps provide clear direct lighting where you need it (say, for reading). You can also select a globe that uses minimum energy.

✔ For romantic lighting, turn off the lights and light a few candles instead. (And definitely don't forget to blow them out when you leave the room, though you're actually more likely to be mindful of blowing candles out than switching lights off.)

✔ When everyone sits down to dinner each night, take a quick tour of the house and count the number of lights on. Turn them off and announce the count to the family — eventually, you'll irritate them to the point that they'll switch off, too (the lights that is, not their ears).

For best results, design the lighting in your home to be as energy efficient as possible. For details about the different types of lighting you can use in the home and their suitability for different areas, refer to Chapter 4.

Getting Eco-Friendly in the Kitchen

Your kitchen is where you can have a major impact on your ability to live sustainably at home. The food that you buy, the way that you store it, the methods you use to prepare and cook meals, and how you decide to clean up afterwards, can all be sustainable activities if you work in your kitchen thoughtfully.

Good morning, appliances

Like most people, when you walk into your kitchen you probably rely heavily on electrical appliances — so much so that you may find it hard to imagine living without them. After all, the late-night infomercial promised your cooking would become gourmet overnight with the new electric slicer-dicer-blender-whirrer-espresso machine! But the more you use these appliances, the more your electrical energy consumption goes up. The appliances in your kitchen may include:

✔ **Fridge (or combo fridge/freezer).** Okay, you need this appliance. Who can realistically get by without a greenhouse gas-producing, electrical energy-sapping refrigerator, especially when a lot of the food sold in supermarkets states on the label that you must *refrigerate after opening*? However, some fridges are better than others. For details, see the sidebar, 'How nasty is your fridge?' later in this chapter.

- **Stand-alone freezer.** Usually a staple in larger households and in rural areas, the freezer works just like fridge, only it's colder (and hopefully not opened as often).

- **Dishwasher (not the human variety).** Once a luxury, the automatic dishwasher is now a standard kitchen appliance in many homes. Dishwashers use a lot of water and electrical energy to heat the water, then more electrical energy to dry the dishes.

- **Electric oven.** Thanks to the cult of worshipping TV chefs, the electric oven has become more popular than the gas oven in Australian homes, even though electric ovens are less energy efficient (refer to Chapter 4 for more details).

- **Microwave.** *Brrrrrr — ping!* The microwave is now considered an essential cooking and heating device, but some people also use the microwave for defrosting. (For shame!)

- **Lots of other appliances, large and small.** On your bench sits an electric kettle, electric toaster and maybe an electric coffee maker. Take a look in your cupboards and drawers and count up all the electrical appliances and gadgets you own: Perhaps you're hiding an electric food processor, electric frypan, electric sandwich maker, electric juicer, electric blender, electric coffee bean grinder, electric carving knife and an electric can opener? Don't forget the electric ice-cream maker you use once every summer.

I know, I know, you're probably thinking that I'm now going to tell you to sell your freezer, microwave and other electrical stuff on eBay. Don't worry, I won't. (Anyway, if you're like lots of other people I know, you probably rarely use many of the smaller kitchen appliances.) But the right appliance for the job can actually save energy. A toaster, for example, uses less energy than an electric griller.

Take into consideration the energy efficiency of appliances you intend to buy. Purchase only appliances with the highest number of energy efficiency stars — refer to Chapter 4 for more details about energy-efficiency ratings.

Of course, doing some simple kitchen tasks — such as squeezing oranges — by hand not only saves your electricity usage, but saves the energy and resources that would have been spent manufacturing an electric juicer. And you may be surprised at how many non-electric tools you can find for specialised tasks at antique shops; previous generations made some highly efficient juicers that are still perfectly usable today.

Here are some more tips you can follow to reduce your energy consumption in your kitchen:

- **Refrigeration:** Keeping the temperature constant and being organised about how you store things in the fridge/freezer is the key to making this appliance work at its best.

  - Minimise how often you open the door — yes, the light magically turns off when you shut the door, but the fan and coolant that sprang to life when you opened the door don't.

  - Find the thermostats in both the fridge and the freezer compartments and set them to energy-efficient temperatures: 3 to 5 degrees Celsius for the fridge and –15 to –18 degrees for the freezer. Any higher or lower and you're unnecessarily consuming energy.

- **Defrosting:** Plan what you're going to eat the day before so you can defrost the food without needing to thaw it in the microwave. Take your frozen food out of the freezer in the morning and put it in the fridge. When you get home in the evening, your food has been defrosted quite a bit and doesn't require much more thawing, if any.

- **Cooking:** Develop a cooking method that increases your reliance on a gas-powered cooktop (if you've got one) and decreases your reliance on electrically powered ovens (for more details about using gas appliances, refer to Chapter 4). Even a microwave oven is a more energy-efficient cooking appliance than an electric oven.

If you have favourite family meals that cook best in the oven, try to cook more than one thing at once. For example, if you bake a casserole for an hour at a moderately high temperature, you can simultaneously bake a dessert. If the dessert requires a different temperature, at least use the preheated oven and bake the second item right after the first item comes out.

- **Washing up:** Reduce your use of the dishwasher by washing up some of the smaller plates, knives and forks in the sink. When you do use the dishwasher, always wipe or scrape off food scraps before stacking them (to stop clogging the drains and to reduce the need to use hot water washes) and only turn the dishwasher on when it's full. As soon as a cycle is done, turn it off and open the door so that the dishes dry naturally, rather than via the dishwasher's heater. Finally, when buying your highly-rated energy-star dishwasher, look for a model that provides an economy cycle and includes cold water along with hot water connections.

TECHNICAL STUFF

How nasty is your fridge?

The fridge is one of the most important appliances in the home. Your fridge and freezer use refrigerant gases to keep temperatures low enough to help preserve your food.

In the past, chlorofluorocarbons (CFCs) were commonly used as cooling agents. By 1986 a quarter of all global CFC production was for refrigeration, but when the hole in the ozone layer was discovered, CFCs were blamed because not only do they produce damaging greenhouse-forming gases, they also release a high proportion of chlorine atoms — the main culprit for ozone depletion. Fridge makers (and air-conditioning makers as well) were ultimately forced to find new cooling agents.

Refrigerator makers then turned to hydrochlorofluorocarbons (HCFCs) and hydrofluorocarbons (HFCs) as cooling alternatives because, in HCFCs' case, they release a lower proportion of chlorine atoms and have fewer long-term effects. HFCs actually release no chlorine atoms. This may have been okay if the ozone layer had been intact but, unfortunately, HCFCs still release enough chlorine atoms to damage the remaining ozone that is left. HFCs also produce enough greenhouse-effect-forming gases to exacerbate the problem.

So, once seen as a solution to phasing out CFCs, HCFCs and HFCs now also need to be phased out globally. One alternative is greenfreeze, a 'green' coolant promoted by Greenpeace, which uses hydrocarbon gases such as propane, butane and ethane for refrigeration. Hydrocarbons have no effect on the ozone layer, less impact on global warming than CFCs and HCFCs, are cheaper and are non-toxic. The energy efficiency of these hydrocarbon fridges has also proved to be as good as, or better than, those cooled with CFCs or HFCs — they can use up to 70 per cent less energy. The most energy-efficient fridge currently produced is completely CFC- and HFC-free, with an energy consumption equivalent to a 15-watt light bulb. Alternatives are also being developed that use helium gas as the coolant.

Greenfreeze-type refrigerators are becoming increasingly available to the market — except if you live in the United States, where they have been banned because manufacturers there deem hydrocarbon gases unsafe. Thankfully, everywhere else, including Australia, considers these fridges as safe as any alternative given that the amount of gas used in greenfreeze fridges is the equivalent of three cigarette lighters.

An increasing number of companies are developing ozone-friendly low-greenhouse-gas-emission appliances, although most are made overseas. These companies include Electrolux, Liebherr, Miele and Vestfrost. Unfortunately, most of the fridges in Australian stores use CFCs and HCFCs as coolants, so you'll need to shop around to track down ozone-friendly, energy-efficient fridge models.

If you're not ready to ready to replace your old fridge, check out HyChill, an Australian company that manufactures hydrocarbon refrigerants (but not the refrigerator itself). The company states that it can 'drop-in' refrigerants into domestic appliances that currently use the outdated and ozone-unfriendly gas systems. Check www.hychill.com.au for further information.

The ability to swap your refrigerants with environmentally friendly ones may become a great recycling solution, rather than throwing away your old fridge. If you are disposing of an old fridge, contact your local council so that someone can collect it and dispose of it properly. This is much safer than taking it to the dump yourself, where it'll slowly rot and release all those bad ozone-depleting gases.

Storing and preparing food more efficiently

Storing food in the fridge, the freezer or the pantry each have different sustainable impacts.

Foods requiring refrigeration use up much more electrical energy than foods that can sit in a pantry until they reach their use-by date. Of course, some staples such as milk, butter, margarine and juices obviously require refrigeration, but with some planning and sorting you can reduce the amount of foods you put in your fridge and freezer.

Consider the following tips for reducing your refrigeration and freezer needs:

- **Buy fresh.** Buying your food as you need it means less work for your freezer; so much so that you might find you don't need one. The ability to do this depends on how close you are to the shops.

- **Downsize.** Does all the food in your fridge really need to be there? Foods commonly found in the fridge such as bread, peanut butter, condiments, cordial, some fruit and vegetables and even water can realistically be stored at room temperature. You may find that you can get away with operating a smaller, more energy-efficient fridge.

- **Increase your pantry space.** Putting as many foods in the cupboard or pantry as you can fit saves you many dollars on electricity used to refrigerate your food. Pantry foods include the many (recyclable) tin products on the market, cereals, sugar, spices, condiments and all your back-up supplies of long-life milk, soft drinks and alcohol. When you start canning your own home-grown veggies, they go on the shelves here as well!

Disposing of kitchen waste — sort it out

Most household waste is dumped in landfill sites, but finding new sites and safer ways to dispose of waste has become a huge environmental headache for local authorities. Kitchen waste, whether food scraps or packaging, is the major contributor to the overall waste generated by households. Controlling what you put in your kitchen bin can help reduce the load sent to landfill sites (or maybe even burnt in large incinerators — a method still used in some regions). Both disposal methods are environmentally unsound.

Here are some basic guidelines to follow to help reduce the amount of rubbish you generate in the kitchen:

- ✔ **Reduce.** Every time you go shopping, consider how much of what you're buying is packaging, hitching a ride from the manufacturer via the shop to you (and then from your place in a truck to some distant landfill site). Fresh food sold straight over the counter — say at the butcher's or a delicatessen — is usually wrapped in a biodegradable bag and in paper, rather than pre-packed in plastic (as well as cardboard and other materials).

- ✔ **Reuse.** Instead of throwing out food scraps, put in a compost bin (or a worm farm) in your backyard. If you generate more food scraps than your compost heap can handle, try to cook only what you need each time or repackage leftovers (storing them in the fridge or the freezer) to eat another day. For more information about composting, see Chapter 6.

- ✔ **Recycle.** Most local councils recycle paper, cardboard, plastics, tins and glass. Your job is to sort these in the kitchen and place them in the correct recycling bin — because your council's recycling contractor ain't going to do it for you.

If you must line your kitchen bin with plastic, use biodegradable bags. You can now buy these in most supermarkets (and some supermarkets are even using them at the checkouts).

For more recycling tips, and ways to reduce waste in other areas of your life, see Chapter 8.

Bathroom Blitz

In the bathroom, you can wash your worries away. You can spend some quiet time by yourself, relaxing in your bath or showering away a day's worth of sweat and tears. Everyone's daily bathroom routines can also help reduce the stress placed on the planet.

Keeping water usage to a minimum

Water, water everywhere, nor any drop to drink. Although Samuel Taylor Coleridge's Ancient Mariner was talking about being stranded in a sea of salty water, the phrase also applies to the water that gushes into the sewer and stormwater system.

The waterless toilet

Of course, not every household can have one, but the waterless composting toilet is becoming popular in sustainably designed homes.

Similar to the backyard septic-tank *dunny*, this modern day variation can be installed within the home in the bathroom, with the waste collected in a container or chamber below the house for treatment to create compost for fertilising your garden. Unlike the smelly old backyard *dunny*, the modern composting toilet smells no worse and looks very similar to the flushing variety you're already familiar with.

Two types of composting toilets are on the market: The continuous composting toilet, which decomposes as it moves slowly through a composting chamber; and the batch composting toilet, where the waste is collected in a container and moved away to compost separately. You usually need at least two containers for a batch system so that you can alternate when you move a batch of waste away to compost separately.

There is no doubt that waterless composting toilets require more attention, especially at the composting end of the process, but the water that you save will be significant.

Several companies in Australia sell off-the-shelf composting toilets. Check the following manufacturers for more details:

- Rota-Loo: www.rotaloo.com
- Nature Loo: www.nature-loo.com.au
- Clivus Multrum: www.clivusmultrum.com.au
- Biolytix: www.biolytix.com

I deal with saving the water that runs off your roof and recycling water from your kitchen and bathroom in Chapter 7. By comparison, reducing you *consumption* of water greatly reduces the demands you place on the urban supply and helps you cut your water bill.

Most unnecessary home water waste occurs in the bathroom. Here are some guidelines to help you reduce the amount of water that may be pouring down your bathroom's drains:

- **Don't let taps run.** Some commentators say that if you allow the water to run for three minutes while you clean your teeth, wash your face or scrub your hands, approximately 15 litres of water goes down the gurgler. Another point: You're wasting a lot of good water if you allow water to run down the drain while you're waiting for it to heat up. If your plumber can't fix this 'hot water delivery problem', put the plug in the sink or catch some of the water in a bucket and use this to water your plants.

✔ **Reduce your showering time.** Sure, I know it can be difficult to take short showers, but if you set a daily time limit on your showering time, to maybe five minutes, you develop a routine that's easier to stick to.

Perhaps some things that you do in the shower, like shaving, can be done before or after you finish your shower. If you keep shower time for showering only, you can relax and enjoy it.

An average-sized bath holds approximately 150 litres of water, which translates into the same amount of water you would use in 7 minutes using a conventional shower head. So, if you take much longer than 7 minutes, think of having a bath. Or, install a water-saving shower . . .

✔ **Get water-saving shower heads and taps.** Many new homes are already installed with water-efficient AAA shower heads and taps. But if you live in an older home (that hasn't been renovated recently), call in a plumber and ask him to check your shower heads and taps and replace them if they're not up to sustainable standards. A new water-saving shower head can save up to half the amount of water that you'd normally use showering under an older shower head. You also need to heat less water.

✔ **Press the correct button on the toilet.** These days, most toilets have half-flush and full-flush options (called *dual-flush* toilets in most homeware stores). Use the half-flush when you can. Also, ensure that your toilet doesn't overflow and leak — a major source of water waste in the bathroom. Toilet leaks are usually a result of an incorrect setting in the cistern, which a plumber can fix in a couple of minutes.

✔ **Toilet paper.** Buy the unbleached, earth-friendly brands made from recycled paper. If you haven't tried it lately, try it again; it's softer than it used to be!

The Water Efficiency Labelling and Standards (WELS) scheme, shown in Figure 5-1, rates the water efficiency of taps and shower heads. Unlike other labelling schemes mentioned throughout this book, it's not yet compulsory for manufacturers to submit their products for water conservation rating and to display this label on their wares. However, due to water restrictions and the like, most companies interested in making sales are doing so. For more information, visit the WELS Web site at www.waterrating.gov.au.

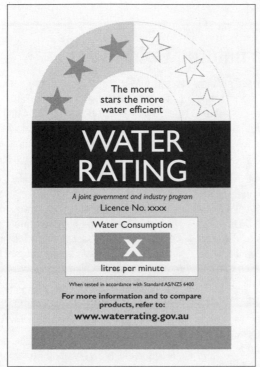

Figure 5-1:
Water rating labels on new products indicate how water-efficient they are. The more stars highlighted, the better.

Lathering up without poisoning yourself and polluting the planet

You probably use a range of personal hygiene products in your bathroom — shampoos, conditioners, soaps, cleansers, moisturisers and deodorants, to name just a few. The trouble is, bodycare products are notorious for containing long lists of bewildering ingredients, making it difficult for anyone other than an industrial chemist to figure out which ingredients are plant-based and which ones are petroleum-based (see the sidebar 'Not so natural, Goldilocks' for more information).

Not so natural, Goldilocks

During the writing of this book, one of the editors suggested I add an extra *Real-Life Story* in this chapter, so I said to her, 'Give me the list of ingredients printed on the back of your shampoo bottle, and I'll tell you if they're harmful or not.' Here's the list, to the letter:

Water (Aqua), Ammonium Lauryl Sulfate, Disodium Cocoamphodiacetate, Polyquaternium-39, Cocamine MEA, Stearic Acid, Dimethicone, Laureth-8, Succinoglycan, Glycol Distearate, Persea Gratissima (Avocado) Leaf Extract, Hydroxypropyl Guar, EDTA, Dimethlypabamido-propyl Lauryldimonium Tosylate, Propylene Glycol Stearate, Citric Acid, Fragrance (Parfum), DMDM Hydantoin. Not tested on animals.

Not tested on animals? That's a relief. I asked a chemist to tell me more about this cocktail of chemicals that my editor is putting on her head every second day. The following is what he said:

Shampoo is basically detergent that strips out grease and dirt combined with a series of compounds that deposit a film onto the hair to add shine and body.

The detergents are the active component and raise the most health concerns. Detergent breaks up the bonds in water molecules so they dissolve the grease and dirt in your hair. Chemists describe such compounds as surfactants, because they reduce the surface tension of water. Add a drop of any detergent or shampoo to a drop of water and it will collapse. If mosquitoes try to land on water containing detergent they will fall through the surface of the water that they would normally walk on. Detergents have been used in the fight against malaria.

Detergents allow other chemicals to penetrate the skin more easily. Concerns have been expressed that because surfactants break down skin cells they can accelerate the ageing process. Some classes of surfactants — the nonylphenols — have been reported to interfere with the sexual development of wildlife.

The surfactants in this shampoo include Ammonium Lauryl sulfate, Laureth-8, Disodium Cocoamphodiacetate, Cocamine MEA

Cocoamphodiacetate is a surfactant derived from coconut oil with a very good toxilogical profile.

MEA (monoethylamine) is considered responsible for creating carcinogenic compounds that are absorbed through the skin. It is considered less dangerous than DEA (diethylamine) which has been banned in the US but is prevalent in Australia.

Other active chemicals that are not involved directly in the cleaning process include EDTA (ethylenediaminetetraacetic acid). It is used to soften the water by depositing mineral salts and locking them up in the shampoo foam. It also preserves the shampoo.

DMDM Hydantoin is a preservative that works by releasing formaldehyde into the shampoo to prevent mould, fungus and bacteria growing in it. Formaldehyde is a known carcinogen.

The second group of compounds are those left behind on the hair to replace the natural oils. These compounds are relatively inert, though their manufacture may cause industrial pollution.

Stearic Acid is made from blasting animal fat or saturated vegetable oils with water at high temperature and pressure and is used to give body to the shampoo. Propylene Glycol Stearate and Glycol Distearate are related compounds.

The addition of avocado oil Persea Gratissima (Avocado) Leaf Extract into the mix does little to interfere with the underlying chemistry of the shampoo.

This shampoo also contains Polyquaternium-39 (cellulose derived from cotton), the silicone-based Dimethicone, as well as Succinoglycan and Hydroxypropyl Guar. Dimethlypabamido-propyl Lauryldimonium Tosylate is included to protect it from ultraviolet radiation.

The third main group of compounds are used to add fragrance. This shampoo label simply calls this group 'Fragrance'. Over 4,000 chemicals are used to manufacture fragrances, 95 per cent of them derived from petroleum and 84 per cent which have never been tested for safety. Fragrances are considered trade secrets so do not have to be declared on product labels. This is just one shampoo product. Conditioners contain a similarly strange mix of chemicals, and hair-colouring products that use synthetic dyes are probably even worse. For example, they may contain coal tar colours, listed on labels as FD&C and D&C, and made from bituminous coal. Or, they may contain phenylenediamine, another cancer-causing agent. Some even contain lead. This is not only bad for you, but also for the environment.

The only way you can ensure that you're using sustainable products — those that are non-polluting to the environment and won't harm you — is to always choose products that don't have *any* synthetic chemicals in them at all. This means selecting products that don't contain manufactured fragrances, preservatives, colourants, detergents and other petroleum-based nasties. Usually, the least ingredients the better.

The best bodycare products are made from all organic ingredients, or at least contain only natural plant or herb extracts, minerals and oils. Healthfood stores and outlets such as the Body Shop specialise in selling these kinds of products (see the sidebar 'The Body Shop phenomenon' for more details). Some of the online sources I list in Chapter 12 also sells them.

The Body Shop phenomenon

The Body Shop was one of the first companies to put sustainability principles into practice and use only natural ingredients in its bodycare and beauty products, use recycled materials for packaging, adopt a no-animal testing philosophy and run campaigns to help local communities. This approach has earned the company a nice tidy profit over the years and a reputation as being one of the most trusted companies in the world. Although many other companies large and small now make bodycare and beauty products using natural and organic ingredients,

The Body Shop phenomenon continues to grow: The business that began as one store in Brighton in the UK in 1976 (founded by Anita Roddick) has now become 1,900 stores worldwide — 72 in Australia alone. The company also has a strong online presence and sells its range of wares at www.thebodyshop.com.au.

The Body Shop uses a range of natural ingredients in its products, such as like olive oil, coconut oil, seaweed, tea-tree oil and grapeseed oil.

Bedroom Nirvana

Unless you're living a precarious or nomadic existence, you spend a third of every day in your bedroom, just sleeping. The bedrooms in most homes also take up a large percentage of household space, so they're also used as retreats or study rooms, and may include TVs or computer equipment.

I know that what you do in your bedroom is your own business, but you'll live far more sustainably if you make this room, where you spend most of your time, naturally comfortable and energy efficient.

- **Minimise electrical equipment.** All electrical equipment gives off EMFs and ELFs — electromagnetic frequencies that may cause disturbance to the cells of your body. At the very least, turn off computer equipment at the switch before you go to sleep.

- **Organise the living space.** Work out the main activities that the bedrooms in your home are used for, then organise the rooms accordingly. For example, place desks or play areas near windows so that you or family members can make the most of natural light during the day.

- ✔ **Outfit the room with furniture sourced from renewable and sustainable materials.** Choose wardrobes, drawers, side tables and desks made from recycled timber or timber from sustainable plantations. (For more information about timber products, refer to Chapter 3.)

- ✔ **Sleep on eco-friendly mattresses.** Many mattress manufacturers add highly toxic fire-retardant chemicals to mattress covers. However, environmentally aware companies have managed to minimise the health impact of this by adding a very thick cotton cover or a layer of pure new wool, which are both naturally fire-retardant materials. Pure new wool is the more environmentally friendly of the two.

- ✔ **Use natural bedding.** Choose materials that can keep you naturally warm or cool. For example, buy sheets and comforters made from hemp or organic cotton. Use woollen blankets to stay warm. Check out Chapter 12 to find out where to buy sustainable bed linen and blankets.

The best thing about adopting these tips is that you create a more serene, eco friendly sleeping space.

While you're sleeping

Because you spend a lot of time in your bedroom doing nothing except sleeping, you shouldn't be consuming energy during this time, right?

Here's how to ensure that you use as little electricity as possible while you're asleep:

- ✔ **Add layers to stay warm.** Doonas or comforters are just as effective as heaters and electric blankets in keeping you warm. Layers of woollen blankets work well, too.

- ✔ **Use thermostats and timers.** Most heaters have automatic thermostats and timers that you can set so that they'll turn on only when air temperature drops to a certain low temperature, or at a set time — usually the early hours of the morning, just before you need to get up. If your heater doesn't have such a control, buy a timer to control when it turns on.

- ✔ **Let in the night air to stay cool.** Open windows during warm weather (but make sure you windows are fitted with screens to keep the mozzies out). Night time is always cooler than day time; opening the windows allows the cool air to enter. If the night is hot and still, use a ceiling fan or freestanding fan to help create ventilation.

Okay, sometimes you may need to resort to using artificial ways to cool down or warm up a bedroom. If you follow these tips and insulate your home as I describe in Chapters 3 and 4, you'll greatly reduce your need to use air-conditioners, heaters and electric blankets while you're asleep.

You're not living sustainably if you leave the air-conditioning on all night to keep cool. And some heaters (like electric radiators) are big fire risks — these cause most of those house fires you see on the news during the winter months.

Before you go to bed, go around the house and turn off all the electrical appliances (except the fridge and freezer, of course). Turn them off at the power switch, because energy is still being used when appliances are left in standby or sleep mode. (I talk more about how to save energy and using electrical appliances in Chapter 4.)

Kids' rooms can be sustainable, too

These days, kids' bedrooms are multifunctional — bedrooms are play rooms and study rooms, as well as places to crash out for the night. An increasing number of kids (and adults for that matter) are spending more time in their bedrooms than previous generations did. This is particularly true of bedrooms in apartments, which inevitably serve a variety of functions.

As well as equipping kids' rooms with natural furniture and furnishings to ensure they get a good night's sleep, you can encourage them to be more sustainable in their own space. For example:

- If an electrical appliance, such as a computer, a monitor, a TV or electronic game is the room, place a small sign nearby as a reminder to turn the appliance off at the switch. Or, place some subtle environmental and energy-efficiency messages, posters or books in different parts of the room. Don't overdo it, though — it's their room!

- Provide a low-wattage night light and show them how this provides enough light to help them find their way to the bathroom during the night. Older kids can turn on a low-wattage lamp. Even better, teach them to get used to the dark — after all, humans have slept in the dark for hundreds of centuries.

- Encourage a tidy and clean room so you don't have to use the electric vacuum cleaner more than necessary. Explaining why you require a tidy room — to save our earth — may get a more positive response than telling them to do it, 'because I told you to'.

To efficiently heat and cool kids' bedrooms, follow the same rules you apply to heating and cooling other areas in the home. Refer to Chapter 4 for more details.

Consider sharing a family computer or television rather than giving in to the current trend to put one in every bedroom. Working out a schedule of who gets to use the Internet when makes your family more mindful of how much time you're spending on it and whether you're Web surfing as efficiently as you could be. If you do allow your child to have a television or computer in his or her bedroom, lay down some ground rules about how long it can be on at a time and what time it definitely needs to be turned off. Teach your children that they can still play Solitaire without using energy — the old-fashioned way, with cards.

Laundry Time!

The laundry is often the least-liked room in the home — it usually reeks of chores and hard work. All those detergents, bleaches, polishes and other chemical nasties can give a laundry a distinctly unsustainable smell, making it a no-go zone for children and an unfriendly place for you to visit, too.

Doing an eco-wash

Thanks to good engineering, washing machines are easy to use — you can simply load 'em, then set and forget. A washing machine can use a lot of water and electrical energy, though, especially if it's the workhorse in an above-average sized family.

Calculate how many times a week you put your washing machine through its paces, then use the following tips to eco-wash your clothes:

- **Wash in cold water.** If you set your washing machine to the cold water cycle, instead of the warm or hot cycle, you're not using electricity to heat water. Usually, a cold wash is more than adequate for most loads; you can individually soak or hand-wash more troublesome items in hot water using a bucket.

- **Wash less often.** A small load of laundry may use less water, but it usually uses the same amount of electricity as a full load. (Make sure you don't overload your washing machine, though.)

- **Use eco-friendly washing detergents.** Unlike regular commercial brands, eco-friendly washing detergents don't contain phosphates or petrochemicals, so they won't harm the environment when they enter the water system. Look for earth-friendly products in your supermarket.

✔ **Get a front-loading washing machine.** Front loaders use less water than top-loading washing machines, and require less detergent. Some states in Australia even offer government rebates if you buy one of these water-saving washing machines. I cover buying whitegoods in more detail in Chapter 12.

✔ **Reuse the waste water.** The *greywater* waste generated by your washing machine (and also your shower, bath and sinks) can be used to water your garden. For more details about how to capture your grey water and pump it out to the garden to keep your plants alive, see Chapter 7.

Drying your gear

Perhaps the weather's too wet or cold for drying clothes outside, you work long hours or you've got kids . . . a clothes dryer sure does come in handy! On the other hand, clothes dryers shrink and crease clothes and cost a fortune to run.

If you can't hang your washing on the clothesline outside, get yourself a drying rack or two: These are inexpensive to buy and can be set up anywhere in the home. In fact, a drying rack may be your only alternative to using a dryer if you live in an apartment, but keep in mind that strata restrictions may not allow you to put the drying rack on the balcony.

Yes, yes, I know — a full load of washing won't fit on a regular drying rack. I get around this by doing smaller washes so that everything fits on the drying rack. Using the washing machine this way may not be ideal, but this method is still more energy-efficient than washing a full load in the machine and then stuffing some items in the clothes dryer.

If you really must use a dryer regularly, consider buying a model that runs on natural gas. The new range of gas clothes dryers are more energy efficient and cheaper to run than standard electric clothes dryers; the only prerequisite is that your home can access mains natural gas.

Green Cleaning Around the Home

Supermarkets devote long aisles of shelf space to nasty household chemical cleaners, but you don't need to buy them. Alternative, eco-friendly products are now on the market, and those old-fashioned concoctions your grandparents swore by can work just as well — the trick is knowing what solutions work, and when and how to use them.

No stains, less strain

Yes, it's true that most of the highly toxic cleaning products can remove really stubborn stains. But if you clean your kitchen appliances, ovens, benches and floors with eco-friendly solutions regularly, you're unlikely to reach a stage that stains become so stubborn that to need those heavy corrosive products.

Sorting out what's toxic and what's not

Most commercial cleaning products that are designed to get everything spick and span contain chemical ingredients that are dangerous to living things. Even if you heed the warnings on their labels and use them carefully, when you rinse them down the drain, the chemicals enter the ecosystem.

Some of the less environmentally responsible products that you may be using in your home include:

✔ **Regular detergents.** Most mild household detergents contain phosphates, which work as water-softening agents and behave like fertilisers when they reach the environment. Phosphates encourage the build-up of algae in waterways, which depletes oxygen from the water and destroys aquatic life.

✔ **Oven, drain and other corrosive cleaners.** The acids or alkaline salts in these products are extremely toxic to skin, eyes, throats and stomachs, and are responsible for the majority of household-related emergency calls made to medical centres each day of the week. (I don't have enough room in this chapter to explain what happens when these products reach ecosystems!)

Note that most dishwasher detergents contain corrosive, burning alkaline salts, too.

✔ **Cleaning products sold in flammable spray cans.** These types of sprays emit damaging greenhouse gases into the atmosphere (as well as a cocktail of chemicals into the air).

✔ **General purpose cleaners that contain bleach and ammonia.** Products with these toxic chemicals in them can irritate eyes, lungs, skin, and if accidentally ingested can cause even more harmful effects. Detergents based on enzymes and oxygen bleach also have these effects.

Even mild chemicals can be readily absorbed through the skin (refer to the sidebar 'Not so natural, Goldilocks' earlier in this chapter for more details). Alternative cleaning products made from natural, non-threatening ingredients at the very least are better for your health and can tackle everyday cleaning jobs.

So what should you be looking for when buying alternative cleaning products? Read the labels. Seek out products labelled 'non-toxic', 'biodegradable' and 'phosphate free', then scrutinise the list of ingredients. Look for natural oils, citrus extracts, herbal blends and other plant-based ingredients. For online resources that you can visit to find out what's in green cleaning products, see Table 5-1.

Table 5-1	Researching green cleaning products	
Site Name	**Web Address**	**Features**
The Eco Shop	www.ecoshop.com.au	An online shopping Web site for environmentally friendly products that lists eco-friendly cleaning products and their ingredients.
Safer Solutions	www.safersolutions.org.au	Information and product resources.
Eco Shout	www.ecoshout.org	A Melbourne-based eco Web site that features an online database.
Green Pages Australia	www.greenpagesaustralia.com.au	A fast-growing online shopping directory. Click on the Home category for cleaning products.
One Stop Green Shop	www.onestopgreenshop.com.au	An online shopping directory based in northern New South Wales.

Cleaning with all-purpose baking soda

One of the most popular multipurpose cleaning alternatives is baking soda (also called bicarb soda or, if you know some chemistry, sodium bicarbonate). Baking soda occurs naturally in living things, but is produced in large quantities for commercial use by combining soda ash with carbon dioxide. You can pick up a box of baking soda at your local supermarket.

Cleaning the kitchen

The following techniques using baking soda work quite well (experiment with small proportions to get the mix right):

- ✔ **Drains:** Pour half a cup of baking soda down the drain, then add a half-cup vinegar chaser, followed by some boiling water. This breaks down fatty acids, which usually cause drainage blocks.

- ✔ **The oven:** First, ensure that the oven never gets too dirty: Place some foil on the bottom of the oven to catch oil and fat spills. When you need to clean the oven, moisten the inside of the oven with a damp cloth and then sprinkle baking soda over the surfaces. Wait for an hour before wiping clean with a cloth.

  If the stains in your oven are far too stubborn for baking soda, a specialist green oven cleaning product should do the trick (refer to Table 5-1 for resources).

- ✔ **The refrigerator (interior and exterior):** Dissolve three tablespoons of baking soda in half a cup of warm water, then wipe down with a damp cloth. To keep your fridge smelling fresh, put some baking soda in a small open container and place it in a shelf in the door (the baking soda will absorb smells for up to a week).

- ✔ **Pots and pans:** Fill a sink with hot water, then add two or three tablespoons of baking soda. Let the pots soak in the sink for about an hour and then scrub them clean with an abrasive scrubber.

- ✔ **Benchtops and appliances:** Apply small amounts of baking soda to a damp cloth and then simply wipe them down.

Cleaning the bathroom

Some people are very serious about how clean their bathrooms are. So much so that a quick inspection shows that the bathroom is by far the cleanest room in the house. This can be both good and bad: Good because a super-clean bathroom probably has fewer bacteria in it, but potentially bad when you consider that a cocktail of chemicals may have been used to get it sparkling clean.

Good old baking soda can work wonders in the bathroom. Here's how:

- ✔ **Toilets:** Sprinkle the bowl with baking soda then pour some vinegar (a good deodoriser) on top of it. When the frothing subsides, use a toilet brush to scour the bowl clean.

- ✔ **Tubs and showers:** Sprinkle baking soda everywhere just as you would with cleaning powder, rub with a damp cloth to clean all over, before rinsing off.

- ✔ **Taps and other chrome fittings:** Mix three or four tablespoons of baking soda into half a litre of water, wipe all over before rinsing.

- ✔ **Lime deposits and mildew in the shower:** Dip your cloth into some vinegar and use elbow grease to get it off.

For general-purpose cleaning — for example, cleaning sinks and kitchen and bathroom surfaces — mix baking soda with warm water, or try combining vinegar and salt.

Housekeeping with other natural products

You can replace all those heavy-duty, general-purpose cleaners that you store in the laundry with do-it-yourself, sustainable alternatives. Try these ideas for specific cleaning jobs around the house:

- ✔ **To kill germs:** A product called borax, which can also be used as a cleaning alternative to baking soda, is good at killing bacteria. Borax (sodium borate), a mineral found in the earth, is a little toxic, so containers should be well labelled to warn children or visitors. Fortunately, like most things found naturally, borax has very little adverse impact on ecosystems.

- ✔ **To remove stains:** On carpets, try blotting some soda water on the stain and dabbing it away. To lift red wine or coffee stains, good ol' trusty baking soda can be poured on the stain, rubbed in, then brushed or vacuumed away. Some people recommend using corn starch (also called cornflour) on more stubborn stains instead of baking soda.

- ✔ **To polish furniture:** For furniture polish, try a mixture of lemon and olive oil (mix one-part lemon juice with two-parts olive oil). Apply like you would any other polish and smooth off with a dry cloth.

- ✔ **To clean windows:** How about spraying some vinegar or an equal mix of vinegar and water and wiping down with a dry cloth?

- ✔ **To scent your bathroom (or any other room in the house):** Use essential oils. Get yourself an oil burner, some small candles and your favourite naturally scented oils. Essential oils also smell more natural than commercial air fresheners, especially fresheners that come in aerosol spray cans.

Give these alternatives a go. Spend one weekend making up all your mixtures, place them in clearly labelled containers and store them in a space out of reach of children.

For more green-cleaning tips and information on how to prepare your home-made cleaners, check out the Australian Environmental Labelling Association's General Purpose Cleaner's Web page (www.aela.org.au/gec/ General_Purpose_Cleansers.html). Click on the Clean and Green link at the bottom of the page to reach the recipes page.

Goodbye bugs (and other indoor pests)

Nearly every insect spray on the market claims to be safe to use in the home, and the impression I get when I see fly spray ads is that you can just about breathe in the fumes as if it were oxygen. Well, maybe that's my warped take on things, but I hope you get the point. Along with oven cleaners, household pest sprays contain some of the most toxic chemicals you can find around the home. Chemicals like Tetramethrin, Bioallethrin, Bioresmethrin and anything else with 'methrin' in its name don't sound too inviting, do they? You only have to read the warning panel on most cans to understand why: Do not spray directly on humans and pets; do not inhale spray mist; do not spray near eyes or near face.

Again, you can catch those pesky insects by using some clever and more natural solutions.

Old-timers can tell you that boric acid (borax mixed with mineral acids) mixed with flour to form little dough balls is a great way of enticing and knocking out cockroaches and other creepy crawlies. Just make sure your own little human crawlers don't try out the concoction first. Commercial names include Boracic Acid.

For intruders that fly in and out of your life, natural essences and potpourris generally do the trick. Mosquitoes usually shy away from citronella scented candles, and flies and bugs tend to stay away from a potpourri mix of rosemary, lavender, spearmint, cedarwood and other pleasantly scented dried plant extracts.

To ensure flying insects, spiders and other bugs don't get inside in the first place, install screens on your windows and doors.

Chapter 6

Greening Up Your Garden

*Y*ou'd think it would be easy being green in the garden. All that lawn, and all those flowers, tree and shrubs . . . they make many homes look like shrines to the natural environment.

Appearances can be misleading, though. A well-manicured garden can drain resources from the environment. Take a moment to think about it. A constant supply of water is required to keep poorly designed gardens alive and green. The usual tools employed to keep a garden neat and tidy are motorised lawnmowers and other power tools. And toxic chemicals promise to keep pests at bay and feed the soil and roots.

With some direction and guidance, you can turn this around and create a garden that makes a resoundingly positive impact on the environment. In a sustainable garden, you grow and eat your own organic produce; you recycle your food scraps to feed and replenish your plants; you create your own compost; and you add value to the local ecosystem by growing native and indigenous plants.

Even if you live in an apartment block, you can use pots to bring nature into your life and enjoy the benefits of cool green leaves, colourful flowers and growing your own fresh food or herbs.

In this chapter, I help you create your own sustainable garden. I show you how to design and plant your own fruit trees and vegetable patch, and set up a composting system. I also introduce you to the types of plants and shrubs that complement this approach. In particular, I encourage you to plant native Australian species, because they need less watering, encourage indigenous birds and animals, and require less effort to maintain.

Finally, I deal with the lawn. You probably already know that large tracts of grass require extensive watering, weeding and mowing to look immaculate and evergreen. Nevertheless, a lawn provides a great space for playing or to hold a party. I show you how to keep your lawn at its best without poisoning the planet.

By the way, the advice in this chapter only scratches the surface, so to speak, of gardening. For more good gardening techniques, check out *Gardening For Dummies,* Australian Edition (published by Wiley Publishing Australia Pty Ltd).

Designing Your Garden

Everyone can have a garden. Some people keep a small potted garden on an apartment balcony, or have a plot in a community garden that belongs to the whole neighbourhood. Others have more space to work with and maintain a traditional suburban backyard garden, or run a large market garden that feeds the local community.

Whatever the type of space you have, the objectives of creating a sustainable garden are the same:

- Minimise the amount of water and chemicals you use.
- Grow plants and veggies to reduce your impact on the environment.
- Create your own plant food through recycling your waste. (Compost is a critical component of any sustainable garden. I explain how to get compost started in the section 'Composting Your Waste' later in this chapter.)

Begin by landscaping

Before you go out the back and start digging soil and planting seeds, step back and think about what you want. You need to work out what's achievable in the space that you have and its geographic and climatic limitations. Most importantly, you need to design a garden that you'll enjoy maintaining and using.

To begin, map out a rough design or landscape plan. Sit down, take a deep breath, and on paper sketch out how you'd like to fill the space. Here are some suggestions to help you get started:

- ✔ Identify the things you want to keep in your current space — for example, the clothesline, the barbecue and seating area — and what you'd like to move or downsize. Do this even for a balcony garden. Your design needs to take into account all the activities that take place in the area.

- ✔ Plan where you want to put pavers, pergolas, and other functional landscaping features, such as a bird bath.

- ✔ Break the space into different functional areas — some for growing food, some as a home for local fauna, and some to simply look good or provide flowers to decorate your home.

- ✔ Identify on your plan the shady and sunny areas, and the areas that will be easy to water or get plenty of rainfall. (For more details about how to do this, see the following section 'Working with the lay of the land'.)

If you're limited in space, don't be afraid to put plants close together. Many gardeners promote vertical growing — placing plants in containers on racks one above the other — in spaces that are tight. Less space also equals less soil and less watering.

If you're stuck for ideas on how to landscape your sustainable garden, check out magazines and a good gardening book, or chat to your local nursery.

Planning what to plant

After you've mapped out the space, consider what plants you want to grow and how often you'll use them. For example, the kitchen garden, with herbs, leaf vegetables and other regularly used plants, is better off close to the house.

- ✔ The compost heap and the worm farm (and any animals) are better off some distance from the back door, but need to be easily accessible for the once or twice-a-day trip you need to make to reach them.

- ✔ Fruit trees and bushy herbs such as rosemary, bush basil and lavender need less attention, as do larger food crops such as corn, potatoes, eggplants and sunflowers.

- ✔ Soft fruit crops like strawberries and tomatoes warrant regular attention, so they're better placed closer to the house — or, at least, visible from the kitchen window.

✔ Fruit trees and veggies usually require more sun and rain than other plants, so make sure they're out in the open — away from fences and shady areas — without being exposed to howling winds or other damaging weather that may be prevalent in your area.

Don't forget to place vegetable gardens and fruit trees where you can get plenty of water to them. Rainwater from the roof and waste water from the kitchen, bathroom and laundry can all be delivered by a dripwater system to keep your plants vibrant and healthy (but if your house is low on the block, you may need a pump; see Chapter 7 for more details).

As you juggle these components around on your sketch, you'll probably discover that some things find the 'right' spot straight away. You can start organising the rest of the garden around these items. Obviously, any building or major earthworks needs to be done before you can plant anything that will be disturbed by construction.

Working with the lay of the land

To create a sustainable garden, you need to work with nature and minimise the amount of effort and water you'll use. Here are some questions to consider before you begin planting:

✔ **What is your local climate like?** For example, do you experience frosts, very little average rainfall, or a relatively humid climate with a good level of moisture? Plants requiring sun, and those that can cope with heat — like many fruit varieties and veggies — can be placed in more exposed areas. More sensitive varieties can be planted in shady zones or areas not exposed to prevailing winds.

✔ **How much area do you have to work with?** A large area provides more scope for fruit trees, whereas a small area requires you to be selective about what you can grow. A large area also needs more maintenance, so create some areas that can look after themselves.

✔ **What is the slope like on your property?** Does the property drain well? Or is it basically flat and retains water? Plants requiring more shade and moisture are best placed near fences or near the side of the house, as well as on any downslopes and low-lying land where water drains to.

✔ **How does the shade fall across the garden?** Keep the sunny aspect — the northern side in Australia, the southern side in the northern hemisphere — for plants that enjoy full sun, and put low trees on the other side, which won't create too much shade in winter. Identify the areas that get shade for most of the day and some of the day, so you can plan and plant appropriately.

✔ **What's the soil like?** If the soil is sandy it can drain well. If the soil is thick with clay it can't. The best growing soil has an equal mix of sand, organic matter and clay. Check the requirements of the plants you want to grow with your local garden centre. It may be that you need to buy some organic soil to grow the plants you want.

✔ **How often does it rain?** Yes, I've left the best question for last: How are you going to water your sustainable garden? Hardy plants, like Australian natives, can look after themselves, but tomatoes require lots of water. (For more information about watering a garden, see the section 'Mind your water usage' later in this chapter.)

No, that mango tree can't grow in a temperate climate, but an apple tree can. When you get a feel for what grows in your local conditions, you can plant accordingly.

Growing Your Own Fruit and Veggies

You can grow your own food wherever you are — mushrooms can grow in a cupboard and bean sprouts can sprout on a window sill. Fruit trees can fill a backyard with delicious food for a minimum of effort. Of course, each situation requires a different approach . . . and investment of time. I take you through some of these so that you can apply whatever works best for you.

Getting food from your backyard

Suburban sprawl may be responsible for environmental problems, such as the overuse of cars and the reduction in agricultural land, but one advantage of living in the suburbs is that you have the opportunity to grow your own food on your own land.

Eventually, the soil in your backyard will nourish your different fruits and veggies. Unfortunately, when your first dig it up, most backyard soils don't contain the quality nutrients required to grow nice healthy food. All you have to do to correct this imbalance is to add homegrown compost to the soil.

Compost heaps and worm farms are great ways to recycle your waste and turn it back into food. Combined with capturing and recycling your own water, they can significantly reduce your dependence on external resources. (I explain how to get your compost going in the section 'Composting Your Waste' later in this chapter.)

Creating the kitchen garden is a great place to start when you're ready to head outside and get your hands in the dirt. First, plant the herbs you use regularly and any fast-growing plants that are due for planting now — consult a regional seasonal planting guide if you're not sure. When you start picking food from the garden, you'll be inspired to keep going.

If you have determined the permanent location of any trees you wish to plant, they can also go in the ground straight away. Start early, so your garden takes shape around you. Most fruit trees are best planted in spring, but some species are suitable for planting at other times. Obviously, the full heat of summer and the depths of winter are not optimum times.

You may have to buy manure or compost for these first plantings — that is, until your own compost heap starts to produce. Dig your garden beds and the holes for your tree much deeper than the plants require — say an extra 20 centimetres — and fill the hole with compost and water. Let the water drain into the soil and plant in the moist soil. To keep the weeds down, the moisture in and the soil warm, cover with a good layer of mulch.

Juggling your annuals and perennials

Most vegetable crops are *annual*: The plant lasts for one season and is then composted. The cycle of planting, cultivating, harvesting and composting is as old as agriculture itself. It puts many people off gardening, however, because there always seems to be another chore to do.

If a vegetable garden sounds like too much hard work to you, you can still turn your suburban block into a sustainable paradise by planting trees and other *perennial* plants that do not need to be dug up and replaced every year. Food plants that are native to your area require the least maintenance of all.

Planting perennials that produce food

Fruit trees are perennial and keep producing for 20 years or more. They require some fertilising and pruning to remain fully productive, but that's a small price to pay for the abundance of food they provide.

Many seed and nut trees that are common in other cultures are also perennial, but because these have fallen out of use in European gardening, you'll have to track down specialist nurseries that supply them. Varieties that come to mind are the Neem tree, the Moringa Oliefolia and the Carob tree. All three produce staple foods in many countries.

Some perennial varieties of common annual herbs exist, as well: Bush basil is a woody plant that just needs to be pruned back every couple of years; and prickly coriander is useful in hot climates where traditional coriander goes to seed quickly.

Native fruits are not only perennial, they're pest resistant and well adapted to the local climate. They may not be as productive as standard fruit trees, and often have strong or unusual flavours, but you can have fun exploring your local varieties. You can plant them as interesting decorative plants in the garden and then treat the fruit as an experimental bonus.

Getting more from annuals

If you grow varieties of annuals that produce viable seed, let one or two plants go to seed and allow the next year's crop to spring up in the same bed. This approach works well for annual and biannual herbs such as basil and coriander, and for some root vegetables, like carrots and beetroot.

If you use *heritage seeds* (seeds that cannot reproduce), rather than commercial hybrid seeds, you can collect your own seeds at the end of its season to keep your vegetable patch going. These maintain plant diversity as well as ensuring that you maintain a sustainable food supply. Heritage seeds, or traditional vegetables, are available from many hardware stores and nurseries these days. (By the way, in the United States, heritage seeds are called heirloom seeds.)

You will need to keep the compost coming to ensure the garden beds continue to produce good crops, though. Also, consider *crop rotation*: Changing the type of plant you grow each season in a plot of ground ensures the soil isn't depleted of nutrients.

Even many annuals will continue to produce for much longer than one season if they're healthy and you're careful as you pick them. Some plants — like tall lettuces, celery, silver beet and broccoli — can last the full year or more, depending on the climate, by careful picking and pruning.

Dealing with a confined space

If you live in a city, without a yard, you're probably thinking that all this talk about sustainable gardening is all very interesting, but not very relevant to you.

Well, you may be surprised how much you can grow in pots on a balcony. You're basically looking for foods that you can pick without digging up the plant. This includes most of your greens — from beans through to lettuce and herbs. Fruit bearing plants such as strawberries, tomatoes and peppers are also suitable for growing in containers.

After you've decided what you want to grow, use these tips to get started:

- **Pots:** Select your containers carefully. Make sure the pots are deep enough to allow adequate root growth (about 20 to 25 centimetres) and that they have some holes in the bottom to allow water to drain right through the soil. Use trays to catch the water so you don't flood your balcony and the downstairs neighbours! Also, try to find recycled containers or clay or terracotta pots, which are the most naturally made of the pots on the market. Even better, look for locally made pots.

- **Soil:** Use pre-packaged or home-made organic potting mix, which contains natural ingredients such as soil, plant mulch, compost, manure and sand. Compost created from an indoor worm farm would be an excellent additive. Soil straight from a garden generally has too much clay and doesn't allow moisture to get through the soil to the roots.

- **Position:** Try to position plants that prefer the sun in the open to capture a good amount of sun and rainwater. Build a frame for tall plants to grow on, and try to position the containers so the rain runs into them without the sun drying out the soil. Put plants that like shade, such as mints and ferns, in the shade of other plants.

- **Composting:** Consider an indoor worm farm or a composting system that enables you to recycle food scraps without mess or smells. Even in a small apartment you can use a small closed system, such as the BioFermenter shown in Figure 6-1. With the help of an organic fermenting agent, the BioFermenter creates a nutritious liquid that you use as plant food.

Don't forget to check your pot garden regularly. The key to nurturing living things is to pay them attention. Notice when they need water, when caterpillars or adult insects are eating them and when it's time to pick off dead flowers and leaves. To deal with bugs and nurture your balcony garden, see the tips about using natural pesticides and fertilisers in the section 'Maintaining a Sustainable Garden' later in this chapter.

You can also find out more about container gardening by visiting the Container Gardens Web site (www.container-gardens.com). In fact, this site has so many pages of information about growing plants and veggies in containers, you'll be raring to go.

Figure 6-1:
A small compost bin suitable for apartments (or houses) that uses microbes to quickly turn kitchen waste into plant food.

Community living and eating

Another option for growing food in cities, or other situations where you don't have your own space, is to participate in a community garden. Community gardens have been a common part of the urbanised world for centuries, and are now becoming popular in many Australian cities. As well as offering a solution for densely settled areas, they enable you to share skills with other people, and to enjoy the benefits of working with a group.

When you join a community garden, you get your own plot to work in and can take home the produce you grow, in exchange for assisting in the running of the garden. Usually, members of the garden community vote for a committee that ensures the smooth running of the garden.

The land provided for many community gardens is generally donated through a local council, a community group such as a church, a school, health care facility or, in some cases, the state government.

To find out more about getting involved in a community garden project in Australia, visit the Community Garden Web site at www.communitygarden.org.au. The site provides good information about gardening, as well as how to establish a new community project.

Maintaining a Sustainable Garden

Your research should have identified plants that do well in your climate, and the soil, moisture and sunlight conditions that those plants prefer. This information determines where in the garden the various plants need to go, and what you need to do to keep them hale and hearty.

Mind your water usage

Some people living in drier regions have no qualms about turning on the sprinkler and watering to their heart's content. This approach is short-lived and gets more difficult as water restrictions become a permanent feature of Australian life.

The simplest method to reduce your usage of mains water is to install water tanks to capture and store rainwater from the roof of your house and sheds. Water tanks are becoming so popular again that they are now the norm in many new housing developments. Some state governments in Australia even offer a cash rebate on rainwater tanks to encourage their use.

Waste water from the sink, shower or washing machine is known as *greywater*, named because the soap it contains sometimes turns it that colour. Greywater needs some treatment to prevent it clogging up the pores of the soil and making it hard and water resistant. It should also be used quickly to prevent bacteria building up in tanks and, ideally, soaked into the ground using an agricultural pipe or drip-filler system, rather than poured on the surface. For more information about greywater systems, see Chapter 7.

A healthy garden makes light work

The key to maintaining a sustainable garden is healthy soil. Good soil reduces your need to use unnatural additives to maintain the health of your plants. Also, by designing your garden to take advantage of the natural conditions of your local ecosystem, you give yourself the best chance of success.

Here are some tips to improve your garden's health so that it's easier to maintain:

- **Discourage pests.** Rotate your crops from season to season, prune in winter, harvest your crop just as your food becomes ripe and make sure you don't leave anything behind that might rot away.

- **Reduce weeds in your garden.** Weeds can attract unwanted pests which can ruin your seedlings and plants and compete with your veggies for sunlight, water and nutrients. Nipping weeds in the bud, so to speak, before they get a hold is the best way to reduce their influence. However, don't be tempted to use toxic chemicals to kill them off quickly.

You can also reduce the influence of weeds by adding mulch to your garden beds. Organic mulch keeps the weeds at bay and also insulates roots on hot days and retains soil moisture. Consider mulch as insulation batts for the backyard.

✔ **Use organic fertiliser to feed your plants.** Organic fertiliser contains rock minerals and animal manure that has been produced from sustainable farming methods. Your own composted material, or the liquid from the bottom of a worm farm, can also be used to fertilise your plants. For more details, see the section 'Composting Your Waste' later in this chapter.

✔ **Use organic insecticides.** Try mixing this: Garlic, chillies and dried pyrethium. This natural insecticide won't poison the environment. In fact, garlic has been used as the main base for naturally made insecticides for thousands of years. The chillies and dried pyrethium add more punch (to deal with today's mutant grasshoppers — just kidding).

The chemistry of healthy soil

The key to healthy soil is making sure you keep up the nutrients. You can do this quite nicely by feeding your soil with the following natural materials:

✔ For phosphorus upkeep, which stimulates seed and root growth, use rock phosphate or any other minerals containing phosphate.

✔ For nitrogen and protein upkeep, which stimulates green growth, feed compost piles with alfalfa or cottonseed meal. Grow peas or pea bushes such as pigeon pea.

✔ For potassium upkeep, which helps plants resist disease, use glauconite, sulfate of potash or even wood ashes.

✔ For calcium upkeep, which helps with root and leaf growth, use gypsum.

✔ For magnesium upkeep, which helps plants stay green and healthy by promoting the production of chlorophyll (the good stuff that plants use to process carbon dioxide), use dolomite lime.

✔ For sulfur upkeep, which helps feed the life that works away underneath the soil, use gypsum.

✔ For oxygen upkeep, it's not necessarily what you add but how you garden. Ensure that the compost, manure or any of the minerals you add are turned over and through the soil regularly to maintain air pockets and encourage good root growth.

After you've added some of these nutrients to help your soil to be healthy, you simply need to regularly add compost to maintain its health. For more information about creating and maintaining a sustainable garden, check out the online resources listed in Table 6-1.

Table 6-1	Online Gardening Resources
Resource	**Web Address**
Introduction to sustainable garden techniques	www.gardensimply.com/technique.shtml
Developing a sustainable produce garden	www.sgaonline.org.au/ info_producegardening.html
Produce gardening	www.sgaonline.org.au/ info_producegardening.html
Growing fruit and veggies in containers	www.container-gardens.com
Sustainable pest control	www.greenharvest.com.au/pestcontrol/ general_purpose_spray_prod.html
Getting involved in a community gardening project	www.communitygarden.org.au
Sustainable composting techniques	permaculture.org.au/?page_id=22
Setting up a worm farm	www.epa.nsw.gov.au/envirom/ wormfarm.htm
Water-wise gardening	www.sgaonline.org.au/ info_waterwise_gardening.html

Specialist approaches

When you research sustainable gardens, you come across a variety of techniques designed to achieve a healthy garden with a minimum of resources. These techniques each take a particular approach to growing food naturally. They include:

✔ **Organic gardening.** This approach encourages the use of feeding and maintaining soil by using natural methods. Essentially this is gardening without the use of petroleum-based products and artificial chemicals.

✔ **Permaculture.** Developed in Australia, this technique promotes the development of your own ecosystem so that the garden maintains itself. For example, kitchen waste can feed chickens and the compost heap to fertilise your garden soil, which creates the food you eat. The waste-water from your house can be treated in ponds that support fish and plants and then used to water your plants. Perennial plants form an important part of a permaculture garden.

✔ **Biodynamic gardening.** A study of life in soil and water has led to this philosophy of gardening and farming. Special compost and food preparation improves the quality of the food and plants grown. See Chapter 10 for more details about biodynamic farming.

✔ **Fukuoka farming.** When is a technique not a technique? When you farm the Fukuoka way! Plant your seeds and then just leave everything to the elements, with no assistance whatsoever.

✔ **Bio-intensive farming.** This technique involves growing food and plants in a very small area. You can do this by planting seeds and plants in raised boxes on top of each other. This is a bit like promoting living in apartments as being more sustainable than living in low-density areas because it involves less consumption of resources. Bio-intensive farming results in you using less water and less energy (human and natural) to keep the garden healthy.

Composting Your Waste

Composting is nothing to turn up your nose at. When you realise all the benefits, you may actually be eager. Composting is a magic formula for maintaining a healthy and sustainable garden. In fact, composting creates your own household mini-ecosystem where the waste that becomes the food, becomes the waste, becomes the food . . . in a never-ending cycle. It doesn't get any more sustainable than that!

Not only is compost essential in producing and maintaining many of the nutrients that give your garden vigour, it also helps the soil perform at its peak when your plants start growing. Here's how:

✔ A rich, health soil retains much of the moisture that it receives, which means that you don't have to overdo it when using your captured rainwater.

✔ Compost is full of living things that hold the nutrients, so the roots of your plants get the chance to absorb them before they leach from the soil.

✔ The organisms in compost keep the soil healthy by reducing soil-borne disease and the need for chemicals that try to do the same job.

Composting also gives you an opportunity to get rid of your kitchen waste sustainably. Composting is all good news.

Beginning an outdoor compost

You can go to your local garden supply to buy compost — but you probably don't need to. It's very likely that you produce enough varied waste in your kitchen, which can be mixed together to form your own compost. Here's what to do:

1. **Get a sustainably made compost bin (or make one of your own).**

   You can buy a nice, sustainably made outdoor compost bin at most plant centres or hardware stores. (For information about indoor compost bins, refer to the section 'Dealing with a confined space' earlier in this chapter.)

2. **Get your ingredients together.**

   The key to a good compost is balance — the organisms that break down your food scraps work best when mixed with water, air and a good balance of leaves. Don't overdo it with any one ingredient, though, or you may end up with a stinking pile of rotten food.

   You don't have to go too far to find the two key ingredients of compost: Carbon and nitrogen. Take a walk to your household paper recycling bin to find some carbon (paper, bark and sawdust, for example), then go to your kitchen bin to find nitrogen (fruit peels and vegetables wastes). Add some grass clippings, manure (trot down to your local stables for some) and weeds to the mix and you'll have some great compost on your hands.

   Equal proportions of each in the mix typically do the trick, as long as everything is mixed, watered and aerated well.

3. **To maintain your compost, keep the mix moist, but not wet.**

   As you're adding material to your compost, make sure you keep the heap of festering compost moist. Water and air allow the thousands of bacteria and fungi to do their work. Too much moisture and you'll create some of the most pungent smells your neighbours have had the pleasure of whiffing. Too dry, on the other hand, and nothing will happen.

   The key to keeping air available for these micro-organisms is to turn the compost over regularly (for example, once a week) with a garden fork and allow as much oxygen to enter the process as you can.

4. **Harvest the compost.**

   A good compost brew looks like dark soil and contains no recognisable food scraps. (This can take anywhere between two and ten weeks, depending on local conditions and the mixture of ingredients.) You can then scoop out what you need and dig it into your garden.

The composting that I've just helped you set up can be defined as *warm composting* — anyone who has lifted the lid on a composting bin can appreciate this. In fact, the organisms that break down the food can produce so much heat that grass clippings can turn to ash — that's why it's important to make sure your compost stays moist.

Keeping chooks

The humble hen has been an integral part of human settlement since the dawn of agriculture. Whether you call them chickens, chooks, pullets or poultry, *Gallus domesticus* — to give them their scientific name — can produce a bounty of free-range eggs and speed up the process of recycling your kitchen waste. They're usually kept by people living in rural residential areas, on small acreages or with larger backyards.

A small hen-house, chook-shed or chicken coop in one corner of the backyard with three or four hens can keep most families in organically grown, free-range eggs. You may never need to buy an egg again. Your hens also produce an ongoing supply of nitrogen-rich fertiliser.

Let the chooks out into the garden — keeping them away from seedlings and delicious low-growing fruit — and they can keep down snails, caterpillars and grasshoppers and turn over the top layer of soil with their powerful fork-like feet.

Follow these tips to make sure that you and your chooks live happily together as a harmonious sustainable whole:

✔ Make sure the shed has plenty of air, but the birds are not sleeping in a draught.

✔ Keep the floor of the shed dry and clean out the manure every couple of months.

✔ Design the shed to keep out cats and other predators common to your region (like pythons, if you live in the north of Australia).

✔ Design the water supply to last a couple of days so you can go away for the weekend.

✔ Remove uneaten food scraps and put them into the compost.

✔ Complement your hens' diet with commercial pellets, but don't be surprised if they turn up their beaks and wait for more table scraps.

✔ The more often you let them out into the garden, the happier they will be.

✔ Think carefully before introducing a rooster. They're noisy and aggressive — so noisy they may breach council regulations.

Rodents see chook sheds, and compost heaps, as a free supply of food. By building strong enclosures and feed containers that keep the food tidy, and by removing waste on a regular basis, you can minimise the rodent problem.

One word of warning: Some councils have rules about keeping chooks, such as a limit of four birds in some metropolitan areas or a 'no noisy roosters' regulation. Check with your local authority before you proceed.

Setting up a worm farm

Worm farming is *cold composting*. A worm farm makes a great composting alternative if you don't have a backyard (or use an inside composting system like the one I describe in 'Dealing with a confined space' earlier in this chapter).

Worm poo! Hard to imagine, but a *worm farm* is one of the most effective composts you can create. It can all take place within a confined cool space, like a laundry or a well-shaded balcony. Or your worm farm can sit quietly on a back porch or on an inside bench and produce nutrient-rich juices and humus, without many of the smells associated with regular compost bins.

Becoming a worm farmer is easy. The following information can help you get started:

✔ You can buy a worm farm or box from your local council office (check the council Web site to find out whether it stocks them), or make your own worm farm from scratch.

To make your own, get hold of some storage boxes or crates that aren't being used for anything else — you'll need four for maximum effect. The bottom container needs to be waterproof and large enough to take the weight of the other boxes when full of soil.

✔ Many of the worm farms you can buy have all the necessary startup material contained in the box, from the right types of worms down to the soil. Most experts recommend two types of worms: Red worms or tiger worms. Don't bother with your average garden worm — they don't do the job, so to speak.

✔ For a worm farm to work, you need to have a good supply of vegetable scrap waste. Also, make sure that there are enough holes, or perforations, in the bottom of each box (except for the one that sits at the base) for the worms to move from box to box. Start with three boxes plus a waterproof container at the bottom to collect the worm juice.

Armed with the preceding information, follow these steps to get your worm farm underway:

1. **Set up box one.**

   Line the bottom of the first box with soil and newspaper, add some fruit and veggie scraps, then add the worms and block as much light to the box as you can by placing a hessian cloth or some more newspaper over the top. Place this box on top of the waterproof container.

2. Feed and nurture your worms in box one.

Worms don't like acidic food, so don't put orange and lemon skins in the worm farm. Raw onion, tomatoes and pineapples are no good for them, either. Remove the newspaper or hessian each time you add food scraps and replace it afterwards. Add leaves, paper or other bulk with every second or third batch of food scraps. Spray the contents with water every now and then to keep it moist.

After a couple of weeks of monitoring, the worms in box one will grow larger and multiply and the box will be full.

3. When box one is full, set up box two, then later, box three.

Set up box two the same way you set up box one (in Step 1). Then remove the hessian or newspaper from the top of box one, and place box two on top. Keep adding scraps to box two, the same way you did for box one. When box two is full, do the same with box three.

4. Harvest your worm compost material in box one.

By the time box three is full of food scraps, the worms will have finished eating all the food in box one and moved on. Lo and behold, all that will be left in box one is an accumulation of compost material that you can spread over your garden or through your pot plants.

5. Harvest your worm juice.

Now that your worm farm is well established, the waterproof container at the bottom of the stack will regularly fill with liquid fertiliser (don't worry, it won't stink). Dilute this worm juice — two-parts water to one-part juice — then pour this mix onto the plants you want to fertilise.

Planting Native Shrubs and Plants

Growing Australian native plants is good for the environment. They're also easy on you: Native plants and shrubs don't need much looking after.

Natives don't require as much watering as imported species because they're adapted to the generally arid Australian conditions. They also provide food for bird and insect species, ensuring your garden is the hub of an active community.

Another environmental advantage is that you're helping preserve the local plant stock. Humanity's spread across the planet has been responsible for replacing rich, diverse plant communities with a small number of favourite flowers and fruits. You can reverse the trend, and buy a local plant from a local nursery.

Not only should plants be native to your country, it's best if they're also indigenous to the local area you live in. Indigenous plants are adapted to local conditions and interact with the local ecosystem more effectively than other species. For example, the plants indigenous to the Snowy Mountains area in New South Wales are different to plants indigenous to Queensland's tropical north. Indigenous plants in both of these regions differ from one another because they've evolved to work best with the average rainfall and heat in their own regions, as well as the local birdlife, insects and soil conditions.

Choosing indigenous plants

It's impossible to list all the different regional conditions that exist around Australia, and the types of shrubs and plants that should be planted in each area. Instead, here's a list of the main types of indigenous plants that you can use as a guide:

- **Wattles (acacias):** Most acacia plants can be grown in many regions of Australia, especially coastal, mountain and arid inland areas.

- **Banksias:** Most of the banksia species originated in the southern region of Western Australia but are diverse enough to be grown in most regions of Australia.

- **Boronias:** A variety of boronia species can be found throughout Australia, although they rarely flourish in humid or arid areas.

- **Bottlebrushes (or callistemon):** Bottlebrushes work well in heavy rainfall areas and along waterways in forested areas.

- **Dyandras:** One of the many species that occur naturally in south-western Western Australia. They seem to work best in areas of dry summers and wet winters and in sandy soils.

- **Eucalypts:** The species that forms much of the Australian bush and is commonly called a gum tree. Eucalypts grow just about anywhere except in rainforests.

- **Grevilleas:** Another native that grows just about anywhere. The flowering capabilities of the grevillea make it one of the more popular garden plants.

- **Melaleuca (or paperbarks and honey myrtles):** These are generally found along watercourses in woodlands and shrublands all over Australia. They're popular landscaping plants that require moist conditions to flourish.

For some online resources that cover more indigenous plant species, check out Table 6-2.

Table 6-2	Sources of Native Plants in Australia
Type	*Web address*
How to choose the best plants	www.sgaonline.org.au/ info_choosing_local_plants.html
List of native species nurseries	www.greeningaustralia.org.au/GA/ NAT/TipsAndTools/Nurseries.htm
List of indigenous plants for different regions	www.floraforfauna.com.au
List of native species	http://farrer.riv.csu.edu.au/ ASGAP/acacia.html

Living With a Lawn

Millions of suburban gardens are little more than a lawn surrounded by a few shrubs. Keeping the lawn lean and green takes up all the time many people set aside for backyard chores.

Getting more from your lawn

Much of the time you spend on manicuring your lawn is probably unsustainable. Here are the main reasons why:

✔ Using petrol-powered lawnmowers and other cutting devices to keep things trim is an unsustainable practice. That Sunday sound of suburban lawnmowers keeping the grass at a tidy height and the edges nice and clean means a large amount of fuel is being used, adding to greenhouse gases.

✔ The amount of water you need to keep the lawn green and healthy is wasteful. Mown grass is a water hog because it does not produce shade and has relatively shallow roots.

✔ Chemicals used to rid the lawn of weeds and pests and to keep the lawn green are pretty toxic.

One key consideration in sustainable garden design is to reduce the amount of lawn and to use that space as part of a mini-ecosystem that has its own fruit and veggie garden, water collection system and compost area.

To get more out of your lawn, try these hints:

- ✔ Use the grass clippings for your composting system.
- ✔ Reduce the size of your lawn by placing pavers along the areas where you walk most.
- ✔ Plant some trees and shrubs in the middle of the lawn.

If you don't have a clothesline for drying your washed clothes, the lawn is a great place to put one.

Tool shed tips

How does your tool shed or garage rate from an environmental perspective? If you take a good look you're likely to stumble across some of the most toxic products on the market: Garden chemicals, pest control, old fridges and freezers. Then there is the range of fuel-guzzling tools and machinery.

It doesn't have to be like this. Downsizing your lawn and developing your own sustainable garden ecosystem also enables you to rid yourself of garden and pest chemicals. You can even replace your engine mower and other petrol-powered landscaping machines with hand-held versions.

Powering your tools by hand

In the old days, all tools were powered by hand, from lawnmowers through to drills. Hand tools require a little more of your energy, but are often as fast and effective as the powered alternative. Working this way can also be better for you. No-one ever heard a Zen monk saying, 'When you switch on the leaf blower, do it with all your energy and attention and find stillness within'.

If you do give away, resell or safely dispose of all the unsustainable products from your tool shed and garage, all you should have left are some manual tools that enable you to be a do-it-yourself handyman without expending any energy other than your own. Table 6-3 lists some of the gardening alternatives.

Table 6-3	Manual Alternatives to Power Tools
Powered	*Alternative*
Electric or petrol lawn mower	Push reel mower
Electric lawn edger	Foot-powered lawn edger
Electric whipper-snipper	Long-neck grass shears
Electric or petrol chainsaw	Manual pocket chainsaw or hand saw
Electric or petrol leaf blower	Garden rake or yard broom
Electric drill	Rechargeable battery drill or hand drills

Part III
Use It Again, Sam

Glenn Lumsden

'Are you sure only the two of us live here?'

In this part . . .

Sorting out your rubbish so that paper, glass, plastics and metal can be recycled is now an everyday activity that most people take for granted. But there's plenty more you can do.

Water is one of the most important resources that people can make better use of. I explain why water is a declining resource and suggest ways you can conserve, reuse and recycle what goes down your drain.

You can also recycle perfectly good clothes, furniture, books and everything else that you don't need any more. Giving your possessions a new life by passing them on to someone else has become popular again in the age of the Internet, especially through online trading sites like eBay.

Chapter 7

Water: A Precious Resource

● ●

In This Chapter

▶ Understanding how water is supplied to your home

▶ Using water wisely

▶ Drinking tap water versus bottled water

▶ Living with drought

▶ Coping with reduced rainfall in rural areas

● ●

*H*ave you ever woken up and gone to the bathroom, turned on the tap, and discovered that nothing comes out? In your initial panic, you probably wondered how you were going to get through the next few hours — you can't take a shower, make breakfast or clean your teeth.

Your no-water crisis may have been caused by something like a broken pipe, which can be quickly fixed. Yet over one billion people in the world today have no guarantee of water from one day to the next. And if current trends continue, in less than 20 years, two-thirds of the world's population will suffer regular water shortages. Even the industrialised world is running out of water.

The bare facts are that there's simply not enough water to supply increasing demands. Since 1900, the world's population has grown two-fold, but global water use has increased six-fold. Reduced rainfall caused by climate change is now exacerbating the problem (refer to Chapter 2 for more details about global warming).

In this chapter I explain how water supplies work and why the way water is delivered will change radically over the next ten years. I show you how these changes may affect you, and what you can do to make sure you're not left high and dry.

Understanding Why Water Is a Precious Commodity

Some facts about water can help you appreciate how dramatic the shortage situation is.

Up to 41 per cent of the world's population lives in regions that are under *water stress* — in these areas, water supply is much less than the global average. These parts of the world include northern and central Africa and the Middle East. By comparison, in urban areas of Australia, the United States and Europe, water supply is much higher than the global average. Despite this, the developed world also faces water shortages.

Where your water comes from

The most common way water is delivered to homes and businesses in large urban areas follows these steps:

1. **Water from rivers and streams is collected in strategically placed dams and reservoirs, or drawn from natural underground sources.**

   Most big cities rely on many dams. Places such as Perth and Alice Springs get their water from underground sources.

2. **The water is delivered to filtration plants.**

   At the filtration plant, much of the sediment and minerals is removed, chlorine is added to kill any living things and fluoride is added to prevent tooth decay.

3. **The water is delivered to homes and businesses via a network of pumping stations and pipes.**

   These networks are extensive. For example, Sydney's network of underground water pipes is approximately 21,000 kilometres long — the same distance as flying from Sydney to New York via London.

For agricultural and farming purposes, the method is more direct: Irrigation water is pumped straight from a nearby watercourse or groundwater supply. Also, many rural towns pump their water supply straight from natural waterways and channels, and rely on residential rainwater tanks for back-up (for more details about rainwater tanks, see 'Tanking it' later in this chapter).

REAL-LIFE STORY

Who's drinking the dam dry?

According to research conducted by the CSIRO (Commonwealth Scientific and Industrial Research Organisation), Australia receives up to 3.3 million gigalitres of rainfall each year, but Australian homes and businesses consume only 20,000 gigalitres. This ratio suggests that there's plenty more water available for everyone, right? Well, not really.

Of the 3.3 million gigalitres that Australia receives in rainfall each year, 88 per cent evaporates into the atmosphere.

Of the remaining 380,000 gigalitres, agriculture uses 80 per cent.

That leaves 72,000 gigalitres, but the majority of this disappears through leaky pipes. (In fact, in some urban areas, an incredible 80 per cent of the water supply is lost to leaks.)

The 20,000 gigalitres consumed in homes and industry is a large proportion of all the currently available water. Melbourne, Sydney, Brisbane, Perth and Adelaide all face serious water shortages in the next five years.

Many of the methods used to deliver water are unsustainable. Here's why:

✔ Damming natural waterways and concreting streams and rivers interferes with and, in some cases, destroys the natural ecosystem.

✔ Drawing too much water from rivers and streams reduces water flow; the removal of vegetation near rivers and streams intensifies sunlight; and agricultural runoff and sewage fouls waterways with the wrong kind of nutrients. Algae blooms which kill aquatic life, flourish under these conditions.

✔ Water drawn from rivers and underground water supplies for irrigation contains mineral salts. When this water evaporates, the salts are left in the top layers of the soil. This increased *salinity* makes the soil useless for farming.

✔ Unless it rains, dams simply dry up. This drying up is accelerated by evaporation and by rates of rising consumption.

✔ Ageing pipes and infrastructures used to deliver water in urban areas are susceptible to leakages and contamination.

Where your wastewater goes

It's one thing to get water to your home, your business or your farm. But it's another thing to get rid of the wastewater after you've used it.

The term *wastewater* is used to describe all the water that has been used and then poured down the drain. Here are some of the more common components of wastewater:

- ✔ Water that runs down the kitchen sink
- ✔ Water that's flushed down the toilet
- ✔ Water from showers and baths
- ✔ Water from washing machines
- ✔ Water used in industrial processes

This *wastewater* is also known as *sewage* and is distributed through *sewerage* pipes to plants near urban areas. These plants separate the gunk and sludge from the water. After treatment, the water is then returned back into the environment via a nearby watercourse or the ocean. The separated sludge is usually disposed of in landfill or piped out into the ocean. Both processes have a negative impact on the environment.

Stormwater is the water that runs off roofs, streets and roads. Stormwater is managed separately to wastewater and usually runs straight into watercourses, along with the debris collected along the way, separated by grates and litter traps. The oil, grease and chemicals in stormwater cause up to half of the pollution in watercourses.

All this water can be recycled. Here's how:

- ✔ **Greywater:** You can safely reuse the wastewater from your washing machines, sinks and showers in your garden. This *greywater* contains relatively small amounts of pollutants and bacteria. (For information about reusing your greywater, see 'How grey is your water?' later in this chapter.)

- ✔ **Sewage:** Advances in sewage treatment systems allow the water separated at the sewage treatment plant to be put straight back into waterways or used in industry. (For more information about sewage recycling, see 'Recycling urban wastewater' later in this chapter.)

- ✔ **Stormwater runoff:** Although most stormwater currently runs straight into waterways or the sea, this source of water could potentially be stored and reused, with the gunk collected along the way separated from the water. At home, you can capture some of your own stormwater runoff from your roof by installing a rainwater tank. (For more details, see 'Tanking it' later in this chapter.)

Adopting a Drier Lifestyle

Governments around the world face dwindling water supplies and growing populations demanding more water. To resolve this, they're acting on two fronts:

- **Technological innovations.** Governments apply new technology to better manage the water supply. These developments enable water to be either recycled or drawn from new sources.

- **Behavioural measures.** Education and financial incentives encourage people to use water more conservatively to take the pressure off the water supply. In urban areas, 70 per cent of water consumption occurs in and around homes, so any changes in domestic consumption can have a significant impact.

Government actions aimed at changing your behaviour involve a combination of the 'carrot and the stick'. The *carrot* approach uses mainly financial incentives, designed to encourage you to conserve water. These include rebates for purchasing water-efficient washing machines and rainwater tanks. The *stick* approach forces you to do something, usually by introducing regulations that carry the threat of a fine. For example, water restrictions limit your use of water when supply levels get seriously low, and carry severe penalties. Watering gardens and washing cars are usually the first targets — these restrictions are permanent in some cities and towns. Another approach is raising the cost of water to discourage those who guzzle more than their fair share.

So how do you reduce your water consumption when temperatures rise? Actions you can take include the following:

- **Don't waste a drop.** Yes, that's right — this is all about being frugal with water. See the following section for more details.

- **Collect your rainwater.** Check out 'Tanking it' later in this chapter.

- **Recycle your own greywater.** For more details, see the section 'How grey is your water?' later in this chapter.

Don't pour water down the drain

Consuming less water is not so difficult. By eliminating wastage and using water more efficiently you can significantly cut your water consumption — and coincidentally your water bill.

 Check for leaks regularly. If your toilet continues to run after flushing, or you have a dripping tap (inside or outside), call in the plumber. Just one leaking tap can waste up to 500 litres of water per week!

Place aerators on the faucets of all the taps in your home. This can reduce water flow by up to 50 per cent without reducing water pressure.

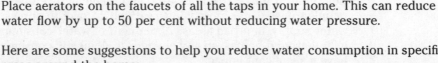 Here are some suggestions to help you reduce water consumption in specific areas around the home:

- ✔ **Bathroom:** You know the drill — install water-efficient devices and turn off those taps! For extra tips about how to be wise with water in the bathroom, refer to Chapter 5.

- ✔ **Kitchen:** Focus on how you use water at the kitchen sink. You can waste up to 7 litres of water per minute by rinsing things under the tap. Put the plug in the sink before washing fruit and veggies and rinsing dishes. I include more washing-up tips in Chapter 5.

- ✔ **Laundry:** A front-loading washing machine uses 60 per cent less water than a top-loading washing machine. You can also conserve water by washing full loads less often, rather than washing smaller loads more often. For more information about saving water in the laundry, check out Chapter 5.

- ✔ **Garden:** Put away your hose. Watering your lawn, hosing your pathways and raising exotic flowers consume lots of water. In arid climates like Australia, grass lawns are water hogs. Historically, lawns have accounted for up to 90 per cent of water used in Australian gardens, according to Sydney Water Corporation. For more information about maintaining your garden, refer to Chapter 6.

If you have a swimming pool in your backyard, you can reduce water evaporation and avoid constant topping up by covering the pool when it's not in use — hey, this is more practical than banning the kids from doing water bombs in the pool or splashing water over the sides, don't you think? Many companies supply custom-made pool covers, but more popular are solar pool covers, or blankets, that can raise the temperature of the water in the pool by 8 degrees Celsius so that you can swim in it more often.

For guidelines about restrictions, and conserving water inside and outside the home in the area you live in, check with your local water supply agency. Table 7-1 lists key online resources across Australia. You can also get more water-saving tips at the Savewater Alliance Web site (www.savewater.com.au).

Table 7-1	Australian Water Supply Resources
Water Supply Agency	*Web Address*
ACTEW Corporation, ACT	www.actew.com.au
Barwon Water, Victoria	www.barwonwater.vic.gov.au
Brisbane Water, Qld	www.brisbane.qld.gov.au
Central Highlands Water, Victoria	www.chw.net.au
Coliban Water, Victoria	www.coliban.vic.gov.au
Esk Water, Tasmania	www.eskwater.com.au
Gippsland Water, Victoria	www.gippswater.com.au
Gold Coast Water, Queensland	www.goldcoast.qld.gov.au/gcwater
Goulburn Valley Water, Victoria	www.gvwater.vic.gov.au
Grampians Wimmera Mallee Water, Victoria	www.gwmwater.org.au
Hunter Water Corporation, NSW	www.hunterwater.com.au
Lower Murray Water, Victoria	www.lmrwa.vic.gov.au
Melbourne Water Corporation, Victoria	www.melbournewater.com.au
North Queensland Water, Queensland	www.nqwater.com.au
PowerWater, NT	www.powerwater.com.au
South Australian Water Corporation, SA	www.sawater.com.au
South East Qld Water Corporation, Queensland	www.seqwater.com.au
South East Water, Victoria	www.southeastwater.com.au
Sydney Water Corporation, NSW	www.sydneywater.com.au
United Water, SA and Victoria	www.uwi.com.au
Water Corporation, WA	www.watercorporation.com.au
Yarra Valley Water, Victoria	www.yvw.com.au

Tanking it

Almost as effective than curbing how much water you use is collecting your own water for free, from the sky. A *rainwater tank*, which you hook up to your guttering to collect water runoff from the roof, can pay for itself within a few years (if it rains). Most state governments in Australia offer rebates on rainwater tank purchase and installation. In fact, with a rebate, a small tank can effectively cost you next to nothing to set up.

Today's rainwater tanks are more sophisticated than the round corrugated icon tanks of yesteryear. These days, water tank systems include a range of options, such as first flush filters to wash away leaves and debris that would otherwise enter the tank; and valves that enable you to switch between using either mains water and tank water to supply the toilet or to supply the hot-water system. Rainwater tanks come in a range of shapes and sizes, which means there's almost certain to be a shape and size that meets your particular requirements for installation. For example, they can be:

- ✔ Integrated into the walls of the house.
- ✔ Stashed away under the floor (which also helps cool and heat your home).
- ✔ Installed in the garden, as shown in Figure 7-1.

Figure 7-1: Rainwater harvesting: This rainwater tank is designed to fit under the eaves in a confined outdoor space in the garden.

In rural areas, tank water is the preferred source of drinking water — an extra tap is fitted in the kitchen. The water pumped from rivers and dams and supplied as tap water is often too muddy and loaded with nutrients and other contaminants to be safe for drinking (although it's usually safe enough for washing dishes, and to use in the bathroom and laundry).

If you intend to use a rainwater tank for drinking water only, you need a tank that's somewhere between 400 and 1,000 litres in capacity (depending on the size of your family), which range in cost from $500 to $800. Double the size if you want to use the tank to also supply water for your garden. You also need to install a filter to make sure you're drinking clean water.

To minimise electricity, installation and repair costs, install the tank in a position higher than your kitchen sink. That way, gravity delivers the water from the tank to your drinking glass with no need for a pump.

How grey is your water?

Why not reuse and recycle water that is otherwise washed down the drain to water your garden? Governments do it and, thanks to improvements in technology and regulations, you can do it too, at home.

Water agencies define *greywater* as the wastewater from showers, baths, sinks, laundry tubs, washing machines, dishwashers and kitchen sinks (but not toilets — this is called *black water*). The average 3.5-person Sydney household produces approximately 400 litres of greywater each day, which you can easily divert to the garden. This saves you from drawing on water stored in a rainwater tank, or turning on a tap and using fresh drinking water from the mains water supply.

To capture the greywater, you can install either a greywater diversion system or a greywater treatment system. Some of the more sophisticated systems treat the water so well, you can reuse the water again in your toilet or even the washing machine.

Greywater diversion systems

In a greywater diversion system, water runs directly from the house through pipes and into the garden.

A basic *direct diversion system* uses gravity: The greywater simply runs down the pipes into the garden. The water flow is controlled by a greywater tap or a valve, and the flow is directed below the soil to an irrigation system within your garden. You can purchase a simple greywater diversion system at a local hardware store and install it yourself. Usually, installing one of these systems doesn't require council approval.

You can also get a *pumped diversion system*, which includes a tank that holds the water to control the flow and avoid possible flooding. Obviously, gravity flow is easier, cheaper and more sustainable, because the pump uses energy at the same time and costs money to install and run. Plus, you need a plumber and electrician to help install a pumped diversion system to ensure you meet local regulations.

Greywater diversion systems should only connect to your least polluted greywater sources, such as the laundry tub or your bath. (Other greywater sources may not be so good for the health of your garden.)

Domestic greywater treatment systems

Greywater treatment systems remove much of the soap and other sediment that exists in greywater, avoiding problems that can occur with bacteria and the build-up of waterproof sediments in the soil. You also need to employ a plumber and electrician and get council approval before installing a greywater treatment system.

These systems are popular in sustainably designed apartment complexes, because the large setup cost can be shared between all apartment owners. Pipes connect all greywater sources to the collection and treatment tanks, as shown in Figure 7-2. Different systems use different filters though, such as sand and soil filters, and different methods of treatment; for example, some use aeration and some use disinfectants.

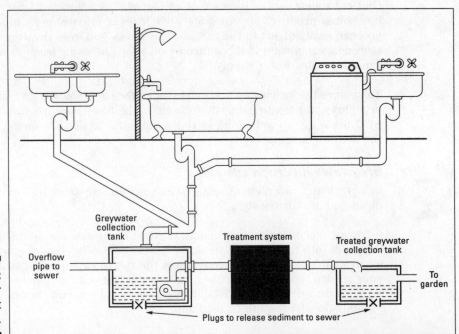

Figure 7-2:
A greywater treatment system.

Greywater collection tank

Overflow pipe to sewer

Treatment system

Treated greywater collection tank

To garden

Plugs to release sediment to sewer

Drinking the Stuff

A chapter about water would be incomplete without a comparison of the two main types of water that people drink: Tap water and bottled water. Yes, I thought you might be wondering . . .

How safe is tap water?

Despite treatment processes that remove harmful pathogens (bacteria, viruses and protozoas) from tap water, outbreaks in New South Wales of cryptosporidium and giardia in 1998 led to some serious gastroenteritis cases in the community and raised concerns among many people about the quality of the water supply.

All government agencies and water supply agencies say that there's nothing wrong with drinking tap water. In fact, they recommend it because fluoride is added to most water supplies, which helps protects teeth, especially in children. On the other hand, the same agencies don't advise drinking the water from a rainwater tank in city areas, mainly because of potential pollution and contamination problems. Country folks can, though (for more information, refer to 'Tanking it' earlier in this chapter).

Can you reduce your water bill by not drinking tap water? Not really. The water you drink is a minor component of the water you use. Finding alternative sources for drinking water is not going to make much difference to the amount of water you take from the mains supply.

If you're worried about the quality of tap water, yet baulk at the cost of buying bottled water, you can invest in a water filter that sits under the sink. These devices filter out the minerals contained in water, making the finished product a cleaner, clearer and more natural-tasting product.

In Australia, tap water does vary in taste, look and quality from area to area, but as long as your regular water supply meets the Australian Drinking Water Guidelines, then it's fine to drink.

Bottled water is 90 per cent energy

Why do so many people buy bottled water? With tap water selling for a fraction of a cent per litre, why are people worldwide drinking more than 150 billion litres of bottled water each year?

Here's why:

- **Health reasons.** Drink manufacturers market bottled water to the health conscious as a more pure source of water (fewer chemicals and minerals).

- **Water quality and safety.** Some people harbour fears that waterborne diseases could enter the water system, so they prefer the bottled stuff.

- **Taste.** Some people prefer the tasteless and consistent purity of bottled water.

The extent of the environmental impact of having tap water delivered to your home pales in comparison to the impact of the processes involved in producing bottled water. Bottled water is the more unsustainable of the two because

- Bottled water requires plastic bottle production. Many of these bottles can't be recycled in some areas.

- Some popular bottled water brands are imported from overseas, increasing the transport costs required to get these products to you.

- Manufacturers use between three and five litres of water to make a one-litre bottle of water. Some estimates are many times higher.

All of these factors make the cost of bottled water around 1,000 times more expensive than a similar amount of tap water. Also, bottled water offers no relative health benefits. In fact, some commentators argue that the lack of fluoride in bottled water is responsible for declining dental hygiene standards.

Australia, You're Baking In It — Adapting to a Drier Climate

In Australia, governments at all levels are scrambling to come up with solutions to address water shortages. Population growth is outstripping available resources, while factors such as drought and climate change are reducing those same resources. Building more dams is no solution when not enough rain falls to fill them.

As a voter, you have a say in how government plans to supply your water or treat your waste. Understanding the issues, and participating in these debates, empowers you politically and makes you a part of the sustainable solution.

Recycling urban wastewater

Governments and water supply agencies recycle wastewater in sewage treatment plants. This wastewater is now of such high quality it's considered to be an additional water source, rather than a disposal problem.

Major cities in Australia, Europe and the United States already drink recycled water mixed with fresh water drawn from rivers. Sewage is treated and returned to the river at one town, and then the mix of river water and treated effluent is re-treated and supplied as drinking water in the next town downstream. Adelaide uses this approach to treat water from the Murray River.

Large projects that pump recycled water from an urban area for use by industry are also in the works. Smaller scale solutions are possible within urban areas as well. In these solutions, recycled water is used in the bathroom, laundry and garden and is supplied separately from fresh tap water. This requires placing a third pipe alongside the water supply and the sewerage system pipes, and is only practical in new residential estates (or in large industrial and recreation areas).

The United Nations Environment Program estimates that in the next decade, one-quarter of the world's major cities will incorporate recycled waste water into their drinking supply. A handful of cities in Japan, the Middle East and Europe already recycle effluent in their water supply. However, in 2006, Toowoomba residents, in Queensland, voted not to use recycled water to supplement their diminishing water supplies. Residents of Toowoomba now face the prospect of paying trucks to deliver water to their town.

Removing the salt

Desalination plants treat sea water and turn it into drinking water. Although the sea may seem to offer a potentially unlimited supply of water, the technology used in desalination plants still needs to overcome these hurdles:

✔ The process of desalinating water is energy-intensive (and emits greenhouse gases). Powering the process with solar energy may be one way to address this problem.

✔ The cost of desalinating water is currently prohibitive for many governments, although as technologies improve these costs will become lower.

✔ The disposal of the salty brine byproduct has its own environmental impact. Where and how to dispose of brine without harming the environment remains an unsolved problem as yet. The best solution for disposal will depend on where the desalination plant is located. If located on the coast, the salty brine can be disposed of in the ocean. If inland, dedicated brine ponds would be required, which has major environment and cost implications.

These problems are very real and alarm ordinary people. Western Australia gets a significant proportion of its water supply from desalination plants, but that's because that region has no alternative. In late 2006, the New South Wales government decided to go ahead with its plan to build a desalination plant in Sydney — in response to a worsening water supply problem — even though residents had previously protested, citing costs and the potential greenhouse gas emissions the plant would produce.

Coping with Agricultural Water Shortages

Farmers face serious difficulties coping with a decreasing water supply. Rural areas are affected by reduced rainfall, changing river systems due to the construction of new dams and reservoirs and, the big one — the siltation of rivers and streams.

Impact on agriculture

Because 80 per cent of Australia's water is used by agriculture, any reduction in the water available for irrigation purposes affects Australia's economy. Whether or not this water can be used more effectively is a hotly debated topic, but there's no doubt that rural Australia faces a serious water crisis.

Programs underway to make more efficient use of the water available include

  ✔ Concreting and covering existing irrigation channels, or replacing them with pipes to reduce losses due to evaporation and leakage.

  ✔ Understanding how much water each crop actually requires, to help farmers use only the water they need.

  ✔ Introducing drought-tolerant species, especially wheat, in dry areas, and more intensive farming practices in high rainfall areas.

Some of these efficiency innovations, however, create new problems.

  ✔ New species created by genetic modification lead to major concerns about the health impacts of eating genetically modified food (see Chapter 10).

  ✔ Intense land use in high rainfall areas may increase silt and pollution in nearby waterways, creating new areas of non-productive land.

Impact on remote communities

Communities not connected to mains water supply usually get their water from nearby groundwater, rainwater tanks or a combination of both.

Groundwater is the most reliable source of water in central and southern inland Australia. Some of these infrastructures are poor, though, which compromise water quality. The good news is that upgrades are in the works in many regional areas of Australia.

Many rural properties also sink their own bores to reach groundwater. This involves boring down to reach the underground water table underground, then pumping the water to the surface and storing it in a tank.

When remote communities really run short on water, short-term remedies include transporting water from reservoirs.

Chapter 8

Waste Not, Want Not: Minimising Your Rubbish

*Y*ou may think you're living in the computer age or the information age, but wouldn't the *disposable age* be more to the point? Unfortunately, disposable products dominate society: Takeaway food containers, tissues and napkins, microwave dinners, plastic cutlery, appliances that can't be repaired . . . the list goes on. I'm sure you can think of many more things that you throw into a bin every day.

Every bit of waste consumes natural resources. It takes resources to make, to deliver and to get rid of stuff once you've used it. Consumption and waste go hand in hand: Increased consumption equals increased waste.

Most of your waste ends up in landfill, hidden away from view on the edge of your city or town. Yes, that's right — most of your rubbish is just dumped in the ground. Resource prices, a shortage of landfill sites and concerns about pollution all add up to make waste a really big problem. This chapter shows you how to do your bit to help solve the problem.

The Road to Zero Waste

One of the more popular waste-disposal concepts is called *zero waste*. Sounds good, doesn't it? If you don't generate any waste, the problem goes away.

The key to achieving zero waste is adopting the *three r's* (reducing, reusing and recycling). Each 'r' is an important part of the zero waste concept, but the third — recycling — gets the most attention in communities. When you look at the materials sent to the average rubbish dump, however, recycling is the least effective of the three. (I discuss the relationship between reducing, reusing and recycling in more detail in the section 'Why Less Is Best' later in this chapter.)

Domestic or household waste comprises about 33 per cent of the stuff that gets sent to a landfill site, and includes the following:

- Food waste (40 per cent)
- Garden waste (15 per cent)
- Recyclable metals, plastics, glass and paper (20 per cent)
- Non-recyclables (25 per cent)

The other two-thirds of the rubbish that gets buried is a mixture of commercial, industrial, construction and demolition waste.

If you recycle your food and garden waste at home or in the community, you halve the amount of rubbish you send to landfill sites. The other way you can make a big difference is to simply buy less stuff that ends up being thrown out: Avoid packaging, throwaway items, and cheap toys, tools and clothes that can't be repaired.

How governments are helping

Around the world, governments and community groups are adopting zero waste policies to save money and stop damaging the environment — you have to be very careful about what resources you use, if you plan to throw nothing away!

In Australia, South Australia and Western Australia lead the way with formal zero waste intitiatives (check out the following Web sites for more details: www.zerowaste.sa.gov.au and http://zerowaste.com.au).

Government initiatives include

- Grants to establish recycling and collection depots.
- Free hazardous household waste collections, along with information about using sustainable cleaning products instead of dangerous chemicals.

✔ Regulations to ban non-degradable plastic bags from retail stores. In some places, funding has been provided to promote the region as plastic bag free.

✔ Grants for research into recycling and waste-free alternatives.

✔ Funding for zero-waste events.

These initiatives are a great start, but no accreditation yet exists for zero waste products. It's up to you, the consumer, to play your role in forcing the market to provide you with zero waste goods.

The power of your dollar

You can turn around the disposable culture you live in by shopping carefully. Why wait for governments to pass new regulations — you could be waiting a very long time. Tell the manufacturer what you want, every time you shop.

Manufacturers respond quickly to consumer demands. If you insist on products that don't harm the environment, manufacturers *will* make them. They're in business to supply what consumers will pay for. To get your message across, it's important to understand exactly what to demand in the products you buy. Here are some key factors:

✔ **Minimum waste in production.** The resources used to manufacture a product are critical, from the raw and recycled materials sourced, to the energy sources used to produce the product. Buy (or demand) products made from renewable resources with the lowest possible *embedded energy*. To find out more about embedded (or embodied) energy, refer to Chapter 3.

✔ **Repairable appliances.** Companies encourage you to buy new things instead of fixing old ones. Insist on products with replaceable components and products that can be repaired.

✔ **Products made from recycled materials.** If you buy products made from recycled materials, companies will provide collection depots and recycling facilities to acquire the necessary raw (well, half-cooked, perhaps) materials.

✔ **No wasteful packaging.** Refuse extra packaging or bags and only buy products packaged in a minimum of recycled material.

Packaging is a major source of waste and deserves special attention. I provide practical tips in the section 'Packaging is a problem' later in this chapter.

Making a buck out of waste

More and more companies are recognising the value in reusing, reducing and recycling products. They are proof that if more people demand products that support the zero waste philosophy, the market will react. These businesses stand out:

✔ Visy Industries, at `www.visy.com.au`: This leading paper-recycling company has eight paper-recycling mills, six of which are located in Australia.

✔ Y, at `www.ywebsite.com.au`: Y is a Brazilian company that manufactures and sells products using recycled raw materials. Its most recent innovation is making shoes, bags and accessories out of used truck and car tyres. Y sells its products through `www.brazil2you.com.au` in Australia.

✔ Mobile Muster, at `www.mobilemuster.com.au`: This company was set up by the mobile phone industry of Australia to recycle and reuse mobile phone handsets.

✔ The Body Shop, at `www.thebodyshop.com.au`: The Body Shop is proud of its recycling program. The company will take off your hands those empty plastic containers numbered 4, 5 and 6 and recycle them for you. (To find out more about the numbers on plastic bottles and what they mean, check out 'Recycling household products' later in this chapter.)

Why Less Is Best

To achieve zero waste, you need to do the following:

✔ *Reduce* the waste that you generate.

✔ When goods reach the end of their useful life, *reuse* them as much as possible.

✔ If you end up with something that can't be reused, send it off for *recycling*.

Reducing waste is not hard to do

The order in which you tackle reducing, reusing and recycling is important. Reducing waste has to be the first step, because it leaves less to reuse and recycle.

The simplest way to reduce waste is to buy less stuff in the first place. This conserves resources and reduces your overall impact on the planet along the way. It's basic, really: If you buy less, you have less to throw away. Makes sense, doesn't it?

The easiest way to avoid throwing things away is to buy better-quality products that last longer. For example:

- ✔ Buy your kids a small number of toys that don't break easily, instead of giving them cheap plastic things that fall apart after a week.
- ✔ Use cloth napkins instead of paper ones.
- ✔ For outings, invest in a picnic set that you take home and wash (instead of throwing away a bin full of plastic plates, cups and cutlery).
- ✔ Buy tools and appliances that can be fixed. Metal items held together with screws are easier to fix than plastic goods that have been joined by melting the seams together.
- ✔ Buy well-made clothes woven from natural fibres. (For more information about buying clothing, see Chapter 11.)

After you get the hang of shopping for keeps, you'll stumble across other examples every time you scan the shelves. Pretty soon, you'll find yourself surrounded by quality instead of clutter. You'll shop less often, saving money to buy more good-quality products.

Good-quality products usually cost less in the long term, even though they're nearly always more expensive to buy upfront.

Packaging is a problem

To reduce the amount of waste you generate, be conscious of the packaging that comes with your purchase. Packaging not only generates waste, but also consumes energy when it's manufactured.

Most products are overpackaged. Packaging helps sell products, so manufacturers go to town, presenting their products in fancy dress. Some packaging is useful, though, because it protects food from spoiling or makes it easier to handle. For example, it would be pretty icky carrying home food like peanut butter if it weren't in a container. In a zero waste society, such packaging would be reusable or at least recyclable.

Unfortunately, a lot of common purchases are grossly overpackaged. Take-away food, for example, generates a huge amount of waste. In fact, all processed food involves a large amount of packaging. Another culprit is bottled water: The cost of the packaging in this case is many times the cost of the contents (refer to Chapter 7 to find out more about bottled water).

Here are some tips to help you minimise packaging when you go shopping:

- Use your own reusable shopping bags rather than accept the plastic shopping bags you're offered at the cash register.

- When you buy fresh food, pop it directly into your bag — or just carry it. If the food needs to be wrapped, ask for a (recycled) paper bag.

- Shop at a fresh food market instead of at a shop that prepackages fruit and veggies. (For more information about buying food, turn to Chapter 10.)

Buying unwrapped food may be an easy strategy to adopt, but what can you do about all the boxes and plastic foam that comes with a new TV or stereo? And what about all the nasties used to package kids' toys — these days, you often need a screwdriver to get toys out of their packs. Even some clothes, like mens' business shirts, come in fancy packages. How do you buy these products without 'investing' in the packaging?

When you're buying household utensils, appliances and other products, look for natural or recycled packaging that has been produced using low levels of embodied energy (refer to Chapter 3 for more details about the energy used in production processes).

I know some people who ask shop assistants to unwrap larger goods before they leave the stores they shop at, so they don't have to take all the wrapping home. Imagine hundreds of *For Dummies* readers making the same kind of request whenever they go shopping — this might encourage retailers to discuss wrapping habits with manufacturers. (Well, here's hoping, anyway.)

Campaigns to eliminate toxic plastic carry bags in everyday shops like supermarkets have begun to impact on the two billion 'singlet bags' sold in Australia each year. (Retailers still need to carry these bags for shoppers who don't bring along their own shopping bags — *tut tut* — or get caught at the store without one.) The best type are *biodegradable* bags that disintegrate easily after use without leaving behind harmful residues. For more information about biodegradable plastic bags, visit the EPI Environmental Products Web site at www.epi-global.com.

Reusing your refuse

If you shop carefully, your rubbish bin will be lighter, but it won't be empty. You'll still generate some waste, such as food scraps, containers and things you just don't need any more.

Reusing things that have served their original purpose means they're no longer waste; they turn into useful things that you got for nothing. Free, no-cost, zippo. Reusing a product is also more environmentally friendly than recycling the materials from the product, because no energy or new resources are consumed in giving the product a new lease of life.

I show you how to reuse waste generated by specific activities in several chapters in this book. For example:

- ✔ Cooking in the kitchen generates vegetable scraps that are great for making compost to feed your garden (Chapter 6).
- ✔ The water you send down the drain can be collected and reused in the garden or diverted back into the house (Chapter 7).
- ✔ Reusing and recycling your clothes, furniture and other domestic goods reduces overall consumption, as well as your own waste (Chapters 9 and 11).
- ✔ Taking home scrap paper from the office to be reused at home saves water as well as trees (Chapter 14).

Here are some everyday strategies you can adopt to reuse stuff around the home:

- ✔ Repair things that break instead of buying a new product.
- ✔ Save your bottles, glasses, plastic containers and so on for storing food and other bits and pieces, rather than buying new containers.
- ✔ Buy used goods, such as 'retread' tyres, used furniture and secondhand clothes.
- ✔ Keep unwanted paper in a pile to use as notepads, craft material or wrapping paper.
- ✔ Keep boxes and containers and use them to wrap gifts in.

Your imagination is your only limit when it comes to reusing things — many artists have made their name by creatively reusing old products.

Take the product's afterlife into account when you're shopping. For example:

- ✔ Buy food in containers that can easily be washed.
- ✔ Choose packaging suitable for other purposes.
- ✔ Buy clothes made from good fabric that can be turned into something new again.

Your waste mountain is now shrinking. After you've reduced and reused to the limit, you're left with a smaller pile of rubbish that, hopefully, can be recycled. Ideally, to live the green life as an individual, you reduce your waste to zero. Realistically, though, this is difficult to achieve.

Recycling — Déjà Vu

Recycling turns old products into another type of material to make new products. Glass bottles are melted down and made into new ones, for example, or rags are reduced to fibres to make high-quality paper.

The recycling bin is now part of everyday life. Today, it's second nature for most people to look for the right receptacle when they want to throw something away. It's rare to walk into someone's house these days and find that there's no recycling bin standing beside the standard rubbish bin. And at most public outdoor events you see colour-coded bins to help people pre-sort their garbage.

Some products, such as glass, can be recycled any number of times. Other products, such as paper, deteriorate with each use. High-quality papers have long fibres, which break during recycling; ultimately, the short-fibred pulp ends up as egg cartons or other soft packaging.

Recycling is not all good news

I want to make one thing clear before espousing the advantages of recycling: On its own, recycling is not the answer to reducing waste. It takes energy to melt glass, chemicals and water to turn rags into paper, and highly toxic solvents to dissolve plastics so they can be reformed into new products.

The best way to reduce your waste is to buy goods that contain no wasteful packaging or properties. The next most effective step is to reuse old goods in a new way. Recycling is the final step in the process. Recycling reduces the amount of material that ends up in landfill. It also reduces the pressure on using natural resources in the production process.

However, recycling requires an energy-intensive manufacturing process, similar to manufacturing natural resources. Reducing the amount you buy and reusing materials does not entail the use of energy.

One form of recycling that doesn't fit this general rule is composting. Recycling your food scraps in your own backyard is all good news. The only energy that gets used is yours (or the energy provided by the worms in your worm farm). The byproducts of compost are good rich humus and nutrient-rich worm juice, which both help keep your garden healthy. For more details about composting, refer to Chapter 6.

Recycling pros

Here are some facts that highlight the bright side of recycling:

- ✔ The recycling process is more energy-efficient than producing primary materials. Recycling steel, aluminium, copper, lead, paper and plastics saves between 65 to 95 per cent of the energy used to extract the raw materials from the ground.

- ✔ The global recycling industry is a major employer, adding positively to local economies around the world.

- ✔ Recycling technology has influenced the development and design of products so they're more easily recycled when they reach their use-by date.

One organisation that advocates recycling is the Bureau of International Recycling. To reach this organisation on the Internet and get more juicy facts about recycling, go to www.bir.org.

Recycling cons

Ultimately, recycling is not fully sustainable. The reasons why are because

- ✔ Recycling materials requires energy and resources. The energy consumed can create greenhouse gases if it's not supplied by renewable energy sources. The resources involved may also include solvents and chemicals that are toxic or not renewable.

    Just because a material is recyclable, this doesn't mean the material itself is environmentally friendly. For example, plastics contain high levels of toxic chemicals and embodied energy.

- ✔ Collecting and sending materials to a recycling plant costs local governments up to five times more than simply sending them to a landfill site. This cost reduces the amount your council can set aside for other local community services.

- ✔ In some cases, the total energy requirements of recycling — transporting, sorting, reprocessing — are greater than those needed to extract new raw materials.

Recycling household products

Recycling helps you reduce your contribution to the global waste pile. It pays to understand what you can recycle and what happens to stuff after it leaves your home.

Most urban councils in Australia offer to pick up and transport your stuff for recycling. Some council areas recycle a greater range of materials than others. For more information on what your council area offers, and who you can contact to find out more, check out the Planet Ark Web site at www.recyclingnearyou.com.au.

Paper

Paper is the most popular recycled product, partly because it's so easy for households to organise. Most paper can be recycled, including newspapers, cardboard, packaging, magazines and wrapping paper.

Some people aren't sure whether they can or can't recycle square milk and juice cartons, which is understandable given that recycling technology is continually evolving. Milk and juice cartons are made from cardboard sandwiched between very thin layers of plastic, creating a product that contains some materials that can be recycled, and some that can't. Long-life cartons are even more complex because they contain a foil layer to enhance the life of the product they protect.

Some recycling plants separate the plastic and even the foil in these products, then they recycle the cardboard. Place these products in your recycle bin, anyway — they'll be recycled if one of these type of plants operates in your region.

Plastics

Most plastics are recyclable, but different types require a different recycling process. The Plastics Identification Code, as shown in Figure 8-1, is a voluntary system that identifies the plastic resin that each type of plastic is manufactured from. In Australia, this code is managed by the Plastics and Chemicals Industries Association (PACIA), online at www.pacia.org.au.

Plastic containers that display codes 1, 2 and 3 (usually underneath) can be recycled for use in similar consumer products. These include

- PET (polyethylene terephthalate) bottles, used mainly for soft drinks.
- HDPE (high-density polyethylene) bottles, used mainly for milk, juice and bodycare products.
- V (polyvinyl chloride, PVC) containers and products, used for cordial bottles, plumbing pipes and blood bags.

Other plastics, marked 4, 5, 6 and 7, can be recycled, but the high cost of implementing recycling systems can be a deterrent. These *polymers* (or plastics) can be mixed to create other plastic products: For example, outdoor furniture, signage, bollards and traffic management systems.

These plastics include:

- Low-density polyethylene (plastic 4 — ice-cream lids and black plastic garbage bags).
- Polypropylene (plastic 5 — takeaway food containers and straws).
- Polystyrene (plastic 6 — yoghurt containers, plastic cutlery, whitegoods and electronic equipment).
- Other plastics (plastic 7 — all other plastics including acrylic and nylon).

Keep in mind that just because a plastic product displays a symbol, this is no guarantee that the plastic can be recycled in your community. Check with your local council for more details.

At the very least, buy products displaying the 1, 2 or 3 symbols, because these plastics are more likely recycled.

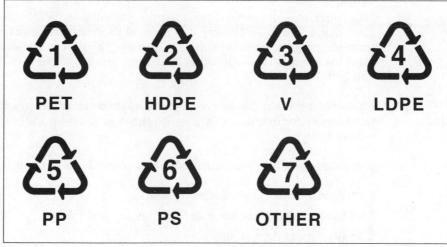

Figure 8-1:
Look for these recycling numbers on the bottom of plastic containers.

Used with permission from PACIA

The reincarnation of the car tyre

Perhaps you've seen pictures of tyre mountains in the middle of nowhere. Old car tyres are a major waste problem. Car tyres do not break down quickly, and they leach toxins into the earth where they're stored.

Several innovative uses for shredded car tyres can offer them a more useful retirement:

✔ Tyres can be broken down into rubber granules and used to provide a springy surface for playgrounds and sports pitches. (Some of the world's largest stadiums are now laying artificial surfaces that include recycled tyre granules in the mix.)

✔ The shredded rubber from tyres can be used to manufacture mats and tiles. Several carpet companies use recycled tyres in their products.

✔ Some tyres are broken down into a fine powder that's added to concrete and asphalt to provide elasticity and reduce noise. The approach has been tried successfully in Europe.

✔ Tyre scraps have approximately the same calorific value (energy) as coal and can be used as an alternative fuel. (But I worry about the pollution aspects of this approach.)

Of course, old car tyres are also recycled into new car tyres, as retreads. To find out if a tyre recycling facility is set up in your area, check out the Planet Ark Web site at www.recycling nearyou.com.au.

Glass

Like paper, most household glass has the potential to be recycled. In fact, glass manufacturer ACI claims that some of its glass containers are made from 100 per cent recycled glass. On average, the percentage of recycled glass used across the entire glass industry is around 45 per cent, which is not half bad.

Glass products that can be recycled are all those clear, green and amber bottles used for drinks and jars — like the ones used for sauces, jams and peanut butter.

Some glass products are currently not recycled. These include

✔ Window and car windscreen glass.

✔ Heat-treated glass, such as Corningware and Pyrex.

✔ Glass from light globes.

Metals

Many steel cans and containers can go into the household recycling bin. These include steel cans that hold perishable foods and the lids of bottles and jars. Aerosol cans and old toxic paint tins need to be disposed of separately; some councils offer a pickup service for these materials, and some don't. Contact your local authority to find out what you can do with this type of waste.

These days, many cans are made of aluminium, especially soft drink cans. These are recyclable, along with the aluminium foil you use in the kitchen.

Of course, you're unlikely to generate many sheet metal or iron bar scraps around the house, but if you do, they're also recyclable. The difference with these large iron-based items is that it's your responsibility to get them to a local recycling plant — they won't be picked up by council or the recycling contractor.

One of the largest metal recyclers in Australia is Sims Metal. Visit the company's Web site at www.simsmetal.com.au for the location of the factories.

Chapter 9

One Person's Trash Is Another Person's Treasure

Not so long ago, buying and selling secondhand goods seemed a quaint hobby to me. You wouldn't see me in op shops and at the local markets, or visiting garage sales in the suburbs.

Well, not any more. The Internet has opened my eyes to the advantages of buying and selling used goods. You can even make some money by selling the things you don't need anymore. More importantly, from a sustainability perspective, every secondhand item you sell is one less new item that needs to be manufactured, as well as one less item to be disposed of.

On the Internet, you can buy and sell used products anywhere in the world, if it's worth the cost of transporting them. In this chapter, I show you which Internet sites help you trade your used goods online. I also give you the heads up on why eBay attracts so much attention and why it works so well.

Trading used items online has also introduced me to the vibrant world of street markets, garage sales and the secondhand trading community. Armed with this new-found enthusiasm, I show how to get your pre-loved goods out the door, to make a profit or help a worthy cause.

Valuing Your Stuff, Instead of Throwing It Away

You're not only kicking the consumer habit of throwing things away when you fix or find a new home for your secondhand goods. You also go a long way towards reducing the amount of waste you create.

Spending a little time and effort making your unwanted possessions more attractive and usable also enables you to get the best price for them. Who knows, you may fall in love with them a second time, and save money by not having to buy a new replacement product.

Who wants that old toaster, anyway?

Many retailers and community organisations specialise in bringing old or disused goods back to life. This saves you the trouble of learning how to fix antique clocks or reupholster old furniture.

Here are some examples:

- **Cooperative reuse and repair centres.** One of the best-known cooperatives in Sydney, the Bower Centre (www.bower.org.au) collects, repairs and resells reusable items bound for the waste dump. The organisation also runs workshops to show you how to repair seemingly unusable goods and how to make things from scrap metals, wood and other throw-away materials. Other cooperatives in Australia include Reverse Garbage (www.reversegarbage.com.au), which is located in Sydney and Brisbane; Resource Tipshop, a Tasmanian business online at http://resourcetipshop.com; and the Bowerbird Tipshop in the Northern Territory (www.alicesprings.nt.gov.au/council/services/tipshop.asp).

- **Antique repair shops.** To find someone in your local area who repairs and brings back to life old antique goods, such as furniture, jewellery, clocks and even books, check out the Australian Antique Dealers Association Web site, at www.aada.org.au.

- **Furniture repair shops and upholsterers.** Check your local yellow pages directory to track down local stores and specialists near you.

- **Clothing repair shops.** Your local tailor and boot repair shops can give your clothing new life, or a fresh look.

- **Toy and doll repair shops/hospitals.** Lifted straight from the pages of Enid Blyton, these services restore old teddy bears, dolls and prams so they can be passed on from child to child. Check the Internet or the yellow pages to find doll and pram repair shops in your area.

Finding a trader

How much old stuff do you have lying around your home that could be used by other people? Think twice before automatically throwing these things away — they could be a nice little earner if you do decide to move them on.

Here are some of the most popular items competing for attention at car boot sales, garage sales, street markets and your local charity store:

- **Books, magazines and CDs.** How often do you throw unwanted books and magazines in the recycling or garbage bin? Why not put them in a storage box or crate when you don't need them anymore? When the box is full, sort them into some sort of order and take them down to your local secondhand shop.

- **Clothes.** Used and vintage clothes have been the mainstay of many a street market, and now they're just as popular on the Internet. It's worth getting into the routine of going through your wardrobes and drawers before each new season arrives and seeing what you might want to either mend, give away, swap, sell or even turn into useful rags.

- **Computers and printers.** Companies now collect computers or anything electronic, fix them up, install up-to-date software and sell them cheaply or even give them away to schools and charities. (See the following section for one source that offers this service.)

- **Furniture and household items.** I don't need to tell you how expensive it is to outfit a home. I know some people who do the rounds of the local garage sales and markets with the sole purpose of finding that quirky, but much less expensive, lounge suite or coffee table.

The idea is not to become a hoarder, with boxes and crates of old books, clothes and other once-precious items stuffed into every nook and cranny in your home. Instead, get into a routine and figure out a system to keep your old things moving on.

Charity Begins at Home

You can donate just about anything of value to someone else or to a worthy cause. There's one proviso, though: Take care that you're not burdening anyone with your gift. For example, there's no point in dumping a three-legged chair at your closest charity shop just because you have no space for it at home.

Sending stuff in the right direction

Some of the most popular organisations accepting donations across Australia include:

- ✔ **Salvos Stores** (salvosstores.salvos.org.au): Run by the Salvation Army, these stores accept pre-loved clothing, accessories, furniture, homewares, electrical goods, books, toys and manchester. Go to the Web site to find your nearest outlet. You can also use an online form at the Web site to arrange for the Salvos to pick up your donation.

- ✔ **St Vincent de Paul Society** (www.vinnies.org.au): St Vinnies accepts furniture, books, clothing, bric-a-brac, toys and blankets, and even non-perishable food. You drop items in St Vincent de Paul Society collection bins or take them to your nearest Vinnies Centre.

- ✔ **Green PC** (www.greenpc.com.au): Green PC refurbishes and recycles old computers that offices and homes don't need anymore. The recycled PCs are then offered to low-income groups and community organisations.

The Giving Centre on the Our Community Web site, at www.ourcommunity.com.au/giving, can also tell you exactly where you can take your surplus clothes, furniture, blankets, computers, mobile phones and much more. When you select a category on the Giving Centre page — such as the Blankets category — the resource provides links to donation centres in your area, as well as specific community groups looking for blankets, such as animal shelters for abandoned pets and specialist homeless care groups.

Joining the freecycling world

Another way to give a new lease of life to your unwanted possessions is to offer them a new home on the Freecycle Network. More than 2.1 million freecycling members are located across the globe, participating in some 3,500 local freecycle communities. Who knows, you may actually be living next to a freecycler.

The Freecycle Network (http://freecycling.org) is a Yahoo! Groups online community. It enables people in community groups all over the world to give away or get something (for free). If you have something that you don't want anymore — say a mattress, chair or garden shed — you 'post' a message online to your local group's Web page. When you see something that you want that's listed on the Web site, you respond to the online message displayed there, and then the giver contacts you. The rules are simple: Everything posted online must be free, legal and appropriate for all ages. You need to be a member to participate, though. To sign up, follow the links on the Freecycle Network home page until you reach your local freecycle group, then click the Join This Group button.

As a sustainable project, freecycling is close to perfect. Not only are you giving your possessions an extended life, but giving within your community reduces the amount of transport required for people to obtain their new goods. This reduces fuel consumption and greenhouse gas emissions.

Secondhand Shopping — for Fun and Profit

Okay, you have a lot of pre-loved stuff accumulating at home and want to convert it into cold hard cash. In the rest of this chapter, I tell you about the outlets you can trade with, or how to sell them from home — by advertising, hosting a garage sale or selling them online at eBay.

Choosing the right outlet

If you prefer to sell your secondhand jewels in the real world rather than the e-world, you have plenty of choices. These include

- **Pawnbrokers and secondhand dealers.** No, I'm not talking about the shady world of laundering illicitly acquired goods — the police keep a close eye on these activities. Secondhand business is corporate these days, and franchises are everywhere. These include Cash Converters, Cash Convenience, Cashwise and Happy Hockers.

- **Secondhand books and music shops.** These places never go out of style, because they provide great alternatives to the more expensive commercial operations. When you've filled a box with old books or CDs, take them down to your closest secondhand book or CD shop and either trade them for some others in the shop or see how much cash you can get for them.

✔ **Antique shops.** If you like the finer things in life (or perhaps I should say, those fine old things), and love to browse older parts of cities and towns, you already know all about antique shops. If you're new to antique shops, you may be quite surprised how much you can get for that old painting that's been sitting in the garage for years.

✔ **Auction houses.** These places sell jewellery, fleets of used cars, unwanted office furniture, household furniture and entertainment units (among other things) at regular, well-publicised times. Bidders get to touch the goods, rub shoulders with other enthusiasts and boast about the great little purchase they made last week. Many people find a real-life auction much more exciting than the online alternative.

✔ **The classifieds.** Some people love to buy and sell their goods through the classifieds section in their local newspaper or favourite magazine. Classifieds are still going strong, although many now have an online presence as well.

Holding a garage sale

Garage sales are great for getting rid of a whole heap of household items in one big hit. They're especially good if you're moving house or if you have hoarded too many things over the years. They can be a great social occasion, too.

As with any business activity, you need to do some preparation and planning to ensure that your garage sale works. For example:

✔ **If required, get a permit.** Contact your local council or check its Web site to find out if you need a permit to hold a garage sale.

✔ **Ask for help.** If your garage sale successfully attracts local bargain hunters, you're going to need someone to help you with sales and enquiries. You'll probably need a hand setting up, too. Ask some friends or family members to help out, and to entice them, suggest that they throw in some secondhand goods of their own to sell.

✔ **Set the scene.** Ensure that the space you select for the sale — whether it be your garage, the front lawn or the driveway — has enough space to cater for what you want to sell, is well shaded or protected from the elements.

Don't hold your garage sale inside your home. At the very least, you don't want perfect strangers trampling through your front door, eyeing off the stuff you don't want to sell and bugging you about it.

- ✔ **Categorise your items.** To make browsing easy for would-be buyers, sort the goods into different boxes based on designated categories or different price ranges.

  Things that sell well at garage sales include old furniture, baby items, toys, electrical appliances, books, CDs and tools.

- ✔ **Fix a date.** Obvious, I know, but hold your garage sale on a Saturday or Sunday when most people aren't at work. Start as early as possible and run your garage sale for at least four hours to maximise your chances of getting as many people as possible to visit.

- ✔ **Advertise.** Putting signs on power poles around your neighbourhood is only the icing on the cake when it comes to advertising your garage sale. Three relatively cheap ways to get the word out prior to your garage sale day are to place a classified ad in your local paper or neighbourhood newsletter, advertise on the Internet at sites such as Garage Sales Australia (www.egaragesales.com.au) and put up notices on community boards at local stores and community centres.

- ✔ **Be realistic about pricing.** I suggest that you price each item at less than half the retail price you paid for it. Older or worn items should be cheaper. Spend a little time at garage sales for a couple of weeks before you hold yours, to see what your potential customers expect. At the end of the day, be prepared to haggle with customers who seek a lower price.

To ensure that your garage sale goes as smoothly as possible, and everyone (including you) has an enjoyable time, make sure that you have plenty of cash and small change on hand, refreshments for yourself and your potential customers, and lots of smiles to give away for free.

Online buying and selling

Why sell your secondhand items the old-fashioned way when you can use the Internet to reach more potential buyers? By extending your market reach online, you're more likely to get a better price for your possessions than you would from a local, secondhand shop or through a garage sale. And when you're shopping, you're more likely to find more secondhand goods online than on the street.

Internet shopping is good for the environment because shoppers don't have to drive in cars to find the bargains they're looking for. However, the goods still need to be delivered, so transport is still a factor. I discuss the sustainability pros and cons of online shopping in more detail in Chapter 15.

The most popular Internet sites for buying and selling used goods are:

✔ **eBay** (www.ebay.com.au): eBay sells just about everything and anything. See the following section for more information.

✔ **OZtion** (www.oztion.com.au): Australia's second-largest online auction site. The best thing about OZtion is that all the products, and the shoppers, are located in Australia.

✔ **Trading Post** (www.tradingpost.com.au): The online version of the paper classifieds that's dominated secondhand trading in Australia for a century.

Joining the eBay bandwagon

Whether you like it or not, eBay is now recognised as *the* leading online auction Web site. Although a few other Web sites have tried to duplicate eBay's success, eBay is far and away the leader of the pack — the McDonald's of the buying and selling world, so to speak.

The best thing about eBay is that it champions reusing secondhand goods. You can sell just about anything on eBay — the market will quickly tell you if your pre-loved wares are hot or not.

eBay itself doesn't sell a thing; eBay members do all the buying and selling. eBay provides the space for people to set up shop (auction pages) to sell their stuff. The unbeatable advantage of selling on eBay is that you can run as many auctions on eBay as you want. (To use eBay, go to www.ebay.com.au. To find out more about how eBay works, check out *eBay For Dummies*, Australian Edition, published by Wiley Publishing Australia.)

eBay is unique because:

✔ Members can participate in online auctions the world over. As a seller, this means you can make a nice little profit because your market reach is potentially huge. As a buyer, you have the best chance to land yourself a bargain.

✔ The Web site uses a rating system to give members credibility and security. The more you buy and sell on eBay, the better your reputation becomes in the community. It works like this: Everyone who buys on eBay checks the selling history of the person they're buying from before they proceed. This helps allay fears of being sold a dud, not getting your money for shipped goods and so on.

How to use eBay

Becoming a seller of secondhand goods on eBay is easy. This rough guide maps out the basic process:

1. **Get started.**

   You need to register as a member to become a seller on eBay seller, then create a seller's account. After you've registered (it's free) you receive an email confirming your user account and password information, which you use to logon every time you want to access the site. You also get your own My eBay pages, where you're encouraged to set up an account with eBay's preferred payment system PayPal (www.paypal.com.au). Buyers can use PayPal for free, but sellers are required to pay a small fee every time a transaction occurs.

2. **Prepare to sell your item.**

   Before you can list an item for sale, you need to inspect the item for any flaws, write a description about the product, and if you want, take a digital picture of the item to include on the item's auction page. At this stage you also need to set the auction start price and weigh the item so that you can calculate your approximate shipping costs.

3. **Run the auction.**

   eBay charges a small fee to list your auction page. When you submit your item auction page, it appears as a new entry in eBay's category listings so people can find out about it, and the auction automatically starts. To increase your changes of getting higher bids and a better price for your item, you communicate with potential buyers in the eBay community. This ensures that you become a highly rated and trusted eBay seller.

4. **Complete the sale.**

   At the end of a successful auction, you receive an email that includes your buyer's shipping address and payment method. After you receive an online payment confirmation from PayPal or a cheque or money order from the buyer, you then carefully package and ship the item to them.

If you're interested in using eBay and would like more details about how the whole auction process works, check out the eBay Help pages http://pages.ebay.com.au/help/index.html.

So what makes eBay more sustainable than other secondhand selling methods? By bringing a global community of buyers and sellers together, eBay encourages people to reuse items on the largest scale imaginable.

Don't forget that buying things locally is more sustainable because you reduce the need to ship and transport the goods long distances. This reduces the greenhouse gases and pollution associated with long-distance shipping.

In the United States, eBay is a member of the Rethink Initiative, which encourages the reduction of e-waste by putting people in contact with companies or individuals that accept old or disused computers, mobile phones and other electronic equipment. To find out more, visit `http://rethink.ebay.com`.

Part IV
Sustainable Shopping

Glenn Lumsden

'How do they expect us to shop here if they don't provide decent-sized parking bays?'

In this part . . .

Money doesn't grow on trees, nor do most of the things you buy. However, if you want to maintain a sustainable lifestyle, you need to think 'green' when you go shopping.

This means choosing organically raised produce over the mass-produced variety when you're food shopping, selecting energy-efficient appliances and homewares made from natural or recycled materials when you're renovating your home, and dressing yourself in clothes that don't only make a fashion statement but are 'politically correct' as well.

These types of eco-friendly products are not only kind on the environment, but better for your health, too.

Chapter 10

From Farm Gate to Dinner Plate

In This Chapter

▶ Finding out what's really in food

▶ Defining 'organic'

▶ Shopping for organic food

▶ Understanding genetically modified food

▶ Adopting a sustainable diet — for vegetarians and meat-eaters

*H*ere's one way to make an omelette and salad: Use the tomatoes you bought from your neighbour who grows things organically, select that locally handmade cheese you bought at the wholefood deli, dig out the free-range eggs and lettuce you purchased at your local farmers' market last Saturday, then pick some fresh herbs from your own garden.

Wouldn't shopping and eating well be so much easier if you knew that every one of your foods was produced in the same sustainable way? You'd have no reason to worry about eating food that was genetically modified or whether it contained strange chemicals and drugs. You could live a much healthier lifestyle and cause less damage to the environment. And when your food is produced locally, you keep your country cousins in work.

In this chapter I show you how to choose food that's produced sustainably, and discuss the sustainability issues as your food travels from the farm gate to you. I look at some of the nasties lurking in non-organic food, along with how organic food helps you avoid these. Plus I show you where to shop for the best organic food in Australia.

I also tell you about the important role that food labels play in guiding you towards sustainable food choices, and explore one of the more interesting scientific topics of this era — genetically engineered or modified food. I even show you some of sustainable food choices you can make if you're a vegetarian and — surprise, surprise! — how if you're a meat-eater, you can make sustainable eating choices, too.

You Are What You Eat

Do you know exactly what went into your body at dinner time? Lots of unnatural chemicals and other additives enter the regular food-production process and many of these may be compromising your health.

Some of the things that you may not know about food production include

- **Additives:** Most packaged foods you see on supermarket shelves contain additives that help preserve, add flavour and alter the colour of food. Many additives are chemically generated and can be a source of food allergies.

    Also, watch out for those foods that are unpackaged, like processed deli meats or fish products that don't have any labelling requirements. They may contain additives as well.

- **Antibiotics:** Much of the mass-produced meat we eat contains drugs used to quicken the growth of animals and increase production, and to stop them from getting sick. Well over 50 per cent of antibiotics imported into Australia is used in stockfeed — approximately 20 per cent more than what's used for human medicine.

- **Genetic engineering:** The process of transferring genes from one plant or animal to another in order to improve the quality and production of food is extremely controversial. The technology has not been properly tested and no-one seems to really know whether food produced this way is safe to eat.

- **Farming methods:** Factory and caged-style farming produce many more emissions, chemicals, pollutants and diseases than more organic and natural styles of farming. And the fruit and vegetables grown on many factory farms are not tested for pesticide residues.

- **Imported foods:** Your fruit, veggies and other favourite foods are increasingly imported from halfway around the world. This not only reduces the demand for locally produced food but increases the amount of fossil fuels burned (and pollution generated) to transport the goods. Imported fruit and veggies usually also escape the net when it comes to testing for pesticide residue.

These methods of food production are actually relatively new — your grandparents (or possibly great grandparents, depending on how old you are), and everyone before them didn't buy prepacked frozen meals or casserole bases, or fruits and greens sprayed with chemicals and grown in soils supported by fertilisers — let alone animal products pumped with antibiotics. Back then, farmers had no choice but to follow sustainable practices in order to get the most from their land. (See the following section for more details about modern farming practices, plus 'Getting the Gist of Genetically Modified Food' later in this chapter.)

One way of ensuring that you're eating foods that have been produced in a sustainable way is to buy locally produced organic food. Being organic implies that most of the unsustainable food production processes have been avoided. Being local, less transport is involved.

Understanding Why Organic Means Sustainable

Shop locally, and eat organically. Follow this philosophy and you're well on the way to adopting a sustainable diet.

The National Standard for Organic and Bio Dynamic Produce (Edition 3.2, October 2005) defines *organic* as

✔ The application of practices that emphasise the use of renewable resources.

✔ The conservation of energy, soil and water.

✔ An environmental maintenance and enhancement program that allows for the production of optimum quantities of produce without the use of artificial fertilisers or synthetic chemicals.

The Biological Farmers of Australia defines *certified organic products* as those grown and processed without the use of synthetic chemicals and fertilisers and which are not genetically altered.

For these reasons many people believe that organic fruit and vegetables contain more vitamins, nutrients and cancer-fighting antioxidants than non-organic mass-produced and chemically altered food. Organic farming is much friendlier for the earth and the local economy than mass-produced products. Here's why:

✔ Organic farming of fruits, vegetables and grains utilises traditional methods of ploughing and rotating the soil, which results in better fertility for long-term continual growth, rather than relying on chemical pesticides and fertilisers to get high yields. Farming in a more traditional manner also reduces the likelihood that chemicals run into nearby rivers, streams and the water table below. In turn, you're less likely to be ingesting any chemicals used to keep bugs at bay and to boost the soil.

✔ The same environmentally-friendly farming methods can be applied to the production of meats, eggs, milk and other animal products. Organic meat is produced from pasture-raised animals with no chemicals or drugs given to the animals while they graze and feed.

The life and times of a factory-farm chicken

You only have to look at how chickens are treated on a factory farm to understand how health problems in humans might arise, not to mention the welfare issues related to treating animals with little compassion. The Animal Welfare League (on the Web at www.animal liberation.org.au) provides an insightful overview of how chickens are raised and treated during their lifecycle. Here's a summary:

✔ Many hens born and raised on a factory farm can live their whole lives crammed inside cages next to other chickens — something like 20 or more birds per square metre, with most never seeing anything outside the cage in which they're housed.

✔ Most hens raised on a factory farm have never walked or stretched their wings.

Instead, they're forced to sit unnaturally for most of their short lives.

✔ Because of their desire to move around, the hens can become aggressive and peck at the other chickens around them. To get around this, they're raised in darkened sheds to keep them quiet.

✔ The chickens are fed on grains that promote rapid growth, which makes them predisposed to disease and physical abnormalities. Many of these birds die of heart attacks, dehydration or starvation because they can't even stand or walk to feeders.

✔ After six weeks of rapid growth, the chickens that have survived the factory farm process are rounded up and taken to the slaughterhouse.

Compare the organic approach of farming animals to the factory farm, which stuffs animals in cages and pens, and pumps them full of drugs (see the related sidebar 'The life and times of a factory-farm chicken' for more details). Factory farming concentrates too many animals in a limited space, which results in an overflow of animal waste on each farm. Most factory farms apply lots of water and chemicals to assist in removing the waste, which subsequently results in an oversupply of chemicals leaching into the soil and, ultimately, the water table. The organic approach may be a lot slower and less productive, but it leads to a much cleaner and healthier product — it doesn't take long for the land on which factory farming takes place to become contaminated and extremely unhealthy for the animals living on it.

A major problem with eating non-organic, mass-produced meats could be the effect it has on human health. Free-range meats and eggs are much more likely to have less total fat and fewer calories than their factory-farm cousins, because the animals haven't been artificially fattened. They're also much less likely to carry bacteria like E.coli.

Although organic food is generally more sustainable than factory-farm production, its popularity creates its own problems. Big businesses are interested in its money-making potential and will use their marketing clout to undercut or muscle out local businesses. This may increase factory and transport emissions.

When buying organic, read the labels (turn to the section 'Reading the Label' later in this chapter for more facts about labels) or check the manufacturer's Web site to see if its production processes cover all sustainability bases.

Some questions to ask about a product include

- **Is it locally produced?** Large corporations do produce organic food, but you also need to check whether a product is grown locally — many products labelled as organic actually use imported ingredients and even import the whole product from overseas. The amount of 'food miles' it takes from the farm to the dinner table varies from country to country. The Australian Conservation Foundation (ACF) states that no known study of food miles has been undertaken in Australia. However, the organisation states that in the United States the food eaten during a typical meal has travelled an average of 2,100 kilometres to get to the table. The pollution generated and energy required to transport imported organic food can easily outweigh the nutritional benefits of eating the produce.

- **Are animals contained or free-range?** A big difference exists between free-range in contained sheds or cages, and free-range on pasture. Organic farmers and producers can use the free-range label as long as the animals have access to outdoors — but they don't actually have to let them go out.

- **What packaging is used?** The food itself may be organically and locally produced, but if it arrives on the shelves in a non-recyclable container then it's compromising some of the benefits of buying organic in the first place.

If no labelling or produce information is displayed where you buy your food (especially in the fruit and veggie section), consider the following tips when deciding what to buy:

- Eat organic fruit and vegetables that are in season — they're more likely to have been grown locally. Those fruits and veggies that you know are not in season but are still sitting up on the shelf are likely to have been imported or trucked from the other end of the country.

- Avoid 'exotics'. Some foods and ingredients, such as coffee, grapes and mangoes, just can't be grown locally; they require specific growing conditions. Check your local or regional area specialties and develop a taste for these to support your local growers.

- Get a feel for those Australian companies that produce, package and transport your food staples (such as bread, rice, milk and so on) from local warehouses.

- Check with the Australian Organic Directory — this Web site can help you track down local shops and distributors near you. You can find the company on the Web at enviro.org.au/organics-directory australia.asp.

Now you know some of the key things to look out for when researching what to buy and eat. You're ready to go to shopping and buy a basketful of sustainable food.

Hunting and Gathering — Where to Find Organic Foods

Buying organic food is the answer to many of your sustainable eating issues. You may be thinking though, 'But how do I really know it's organic?' Good question.

A product can only claim to be *certified organic* if it really has been certified as organic by a governing agency. Standards are internationally recognised and organic producers are regularly audited as part of their certification process.

These days, labelling and other forms of product identification ensure you're aware whether something is organic or not. If your shop doesn't put organic foods in a separate organic foods section, look out for labels that prove that the food has been certified organic.

According to government data and independent reports, Australian Certified Organic (ACO) currently certifies about 55 per cent of the Australian organic industry. The organisation's *bud* logo, shown in Figure 10-1, appears on about 70 per cent of all certified organic produce in Australia.

Other certified logos to look out for include those endorsed by the National Association for Sustainable Agriculture Australia (NASAA), as shown in Figure 10-2, and the OGA Certified Organic logo, shown in Figure 10-3.

Figure 10-1:
The
Australian
Certified
Organic logo.

Figure 10-2:
The NASAA
Certified
Organic logo.

Figure 10-3:
The OGA
Certified
Organic logo.

For details of Australian organic label certifiers, check out Table 10-1:

Table 10-1	Australian Organic Label Certifiers
Organisation	*Web Address*
Australian Certified Organic	www.australianorganic.com.au
Organic Food Chain	www.organicfoodchain.com.au
Safe Food Production Queensland	www.safefood.qld.gov.au
Demeter (Bio-Dynamic Research Institute)	www.demeter.org.au
National Association for Sustainable Agriculture Australia	www.nasaa.com.au
OGA Certified	www.organicgrowers.org.au
Tasmanian Organic-Dynamic Producer	tas_organicdynamic@yahoo.com

Because not all food on the shelves is locally produced or processed, look out for labels associated with the following international certifying bodies:

- Bio-Gro (New Zealand)
- Ecocert (based in Germany)
- IBD (Instituto Biodinâmico: Brazil)
- ICEA (Istituto per la Certificazione Etica e Ambientale: Italy)
- OCIA (Organic Crop Improvement Association International: USA)
- Quality Assurance International (USA)
- The Soil Association (UK)

Also, look out for endorsements provided by the Australian National Standard for Organic and Bio-Dynamic Produce, which fruit and vegetable farmers use. Different levels apply, depending on how long a farm has been operating without the use of pesticides and fertilisers. See the sidebar, 'The farmer's road to organic certification' to find out more.

By the way, according to the Australian Bio-Dynamic Research Institute, *biodynamics* is the process of farming to 'culture' the soil. In biodynamics, every aspect of primary production is based on the dynamic interplay between soil life, plant and animal health, and how these all benefit each other.

Many urban and rural areas are dominated by one or two big supermarket chains that provide a wide variety of reasonably priced foods for us to eat. In Australia, Coles and Woolworths are the two main supermarket chains providing a surprisingly good range of organic food. The alternatives are small, specialty organic stores, which are supplied by businesses specialising in organic foods, and local organic farms, co-ops and producers.

Getting organic in the supermarket

Recent reports state that the number of certified organic operators in Australia has grown by nearly 200 per cent since 2000. One of the benefits of the increasing number of organic suppliers is that this has helped increase competition and enabled prices of organic food to become relatively affordable. Most shoppers realise that organic food is generally more expensive than conventional items, which has meant that people have been hesitant to buy organic. However, the entry of the big supermarket chains into the organic food market as a result of increasing demand for organic food is driving supplies and, through economies of scale, lowering prices.

The farmer's road to organic certification

It takes time to rid soils of chemicals like pesticides and fertilisers, and entrench good sustainable farming practices. When applying for organic status, farmers must meet and adhere to a set of nationally agreed standards listed under the National Standard for Organic and Bio-Dynamic Produce. Use of this standard provides transparency and credibility for the industry and is designed to protect you, the consumer, against deception and fraud. Here's how it works:

At the beginning of the first year, a grower is inspected by an approved certifying organisation to confirm that the farm's activities comply with the standard. The grower is then classified as Under Supervision.

At the beginning of the second year, another inspection is carried out and if the grower complies with the standard, he or she is classified as Organic In Conversion and receives an individual certification number that accompanies any produce the grower sells.

When the third year rolls around, another inspection occurs and if the farmer again complies and has carried out any corrective actions that may have been required, full certification is given.

Then at the beginning of the fourth year, after another inspection and compliance, the farmer receives full organic status and an 'A' number (rating).

You're now more likely to be able to find a greater variety of well-labelled, organically produced foods in large supermarkets than in some local fruit and veggie shops or your local corner store. Have a look in the fruit and vegetable, health food, breakfast cereal and tinned products sections; these sections tend to have the majority of the organic food on offer. Don't forget, though, that if a product is not certified by one of the major bodies listed earlier in this chapter, then it's unlikely to be truly organically grown as per the standards.

A friend of mine now buys organic milk, organic nuts, flour and coffee at her local supermarket. This wasn't possible a few years ago. Before then, she had to run around and visit a range of specialty foods stores, and each item cost significantly more.

Coles and Woolworths have also started developing their own brand of organic products to cater to the upswing in demand. The question then must be asked, 'If large-scale retailers move into the organic market, will this squeeze the little shops and markets out?' Probably not. Although the big supermarkets usually offer a cheaper and larger range of organic products, many lack the character and ethics of your local specialty organic food shop, co-op or local market.

Finding organic suppliers

A surprisingly large number of smaller specialty shops and co-ops sell organic, sustainable food products. Some of these shops only sell organically produced and labelled food, whereas others combine organic food with health food, vitamin and mineral supplies and other wellbeing and fitness-related products.

These suppliers are popping up everywhere in cities and towns around Australia and are increasingly moving into many large 'big box' shopping complexes, such is the demand for organic food lines.

In Table 10-2, I list some of the better-known and larger certified organic shops by state, plus some of the larger produce markets that exist in metropolitan areas throughout Australia.

TIP

If an Internet connection is handy, I also recommend that you do a Google search to find out whether co-ops exist in your area, because these businesses are more likely to source locally produced food.

Table 10-2	Organic Retailers and Markets in Australia	
State	*Shop*	*Location*
New South Wales	Macro Health Foods (www.macrohealthfoods.com.au)	Bondi Junction, Crows Nest
	Granny Smith Natural Food Market (www.grannysmith.biz)	Hampden Avenue, Wahroonga
	Annabel's Natural Food Store	Willoughby Road, Crows Nest
	O-Organic Produce	Mitchell Road, Alexandria
	Fresh and Wild Organic Food Market (www.freshandwild.com.au)	Manly West Public School, Balgowlah
	Flemington Markets	Flemington
	Paddy's Sydney Markets	Sydney
	Organic Food and Farmers Market — Leichhardt	Orange Grove Public School, Leichhardt
	Organic Food and Farmers Market — Chatswood	Chatswood Public School, Chatswood
	Organic Food and Farmers Market — Bondi Junction	Oxford Street Mall, Bondi Junction

State	Shop	Location
	Organic Food and Farmers Market — Frenchs Forest	Parkway Hotel, Frenchs Forest
	Organic Food and Farmers Market — St Ives	St Ives Showground, St Ives
	Organic Food and Farmers Market — Hornsby	Hornsby Mall, Hornsby
Victoria	Organic Wholefoods (www.wholefoods.com.au)	East Brunswick, Fitzroy and Daylesford
	Savi Organics	Station Street, Fairfield
	Queen Victoria Markets	Melbourne
	Prahran Markets	Chapel Street, Prahran
	Collingwood Children's Farm Farmers' Market	St Helliers Street, Abbotsford
Queensland	The Meat-ting Place	Flockton Street, McDowall
	Allsop & England Butchers	Old Cleveland Road, Coorparoo
	Green Harvest	Kilcoy Lane, Maleny
	Organic Essentials	Days Road, Grange
	Organic Growers Market	Northey Street, Windsor
	Organic Gold Coast Farmers Market	Miami State High School, Miami
South Australia	Fruit to Boot	Semaphore Road, Semaphore
	The Organik Store	The Broadway, Glenelg
	Wilsons Organics	Gouger Street, Adelaide
	Organic Pasta Shop	Gouger Street, Adelaide
Online	Organics4u (www.organics4u.com.au)	
	Gingers Organics (www.gingersorganics.com.au)	
	Farm Fresh Organics (www.freshorganics.com.au)	
	Totally Organic (www.totallyorganic.com)	
	Australian On-line Farmers Market (www.farmersonlinemarket.com)	
	Ecoproduce (www.ecoproduce.com)	

Source: Biological Farmers of Australia

Meeting the grower at your local farmers' market

Farmers' markets, the traditional way that food reached tables, have increased in popularity the last few years. Farmers and their employees go to towns and suburban locations perhaps one day a week to set up their stalls and sell their wares. They cater to locals interested in buying fresh, cheap, and often organic produce, and to tourists interested in learning a bit about what's grown and eaten in the region.

Not all of the farmer's selling produce will be certified organic, though. Some may be still be going through the certification process (refer to the sidebar earlier in this chapter) and others will be hobby farmers or backyard growers with green thumbs. But at the very least, you're able to sample and buy local fruit and vegetables that are in season, and chat with the growers about their produce — they're usually passionate about the things they grow.

Reading the Label

Buying food has become a little confusing. You're told you need to buy foods that are low in cholesterol, saturated fats, sugars and salt, but high in calcium and antioxidants, and that are produced in Australia. I'm now suggesting that you also check that they've been produced organically and haven't been genetically modified.

You know that you're pretty safe if you're eating organically grown fruit and vegetables, but what about the rest of the food groups — packaged breads, meats, fish and foods you buy in tins and from the freezer section? How do you know what's really in them?

When you consider how intricate and technological the food-making process is, it's no wonder that the health and safety of the foods has become such a critical issue. Luckily, Australia is among the more diligent countries when it comes to labelling food, which means you can find out what goes into your food.

Food Standards Australia and New Zealand states that labelling is important because it's the only source of information about the nutritional content of the food you buy. Labels show you, for example, the percentages of the different ingredients contained in the food and the presence of potential allergens in foods.

Comparing organic to non-organic

When you start looking at labels, you'll no doubt find it very interesting comparing the types of ingredients that are in an organically produced food to those in a normal, off-the-shelf product. Peanut butter, for example, is one of the most popular and simply produced foods on the market. Well, simple if it's organically produced.

Organically produced peanut butter

Ingredients — 100 per cent organically grown Australian peanuts.

Manufactured peanut butter

Ingredients — 95 per cent imported and local peanuts, 5 per cent canola oil, with Antioxidants E319 (tert-Butylhydroquinone), 320 (Butylated hydroxyanisole) and Antifoam E900 (Dimethyl-polysiloxane).

When buying a product, you can find out if it has arrived on the shelf from an organic or sustainable production process by checking out the following information on the label:

- **Ingredients list.** Understanding the ingredients and their nutrients gives you an excellent feel for the quality of your food. Heavily processed food is likely to have plenty of salt to assist in preservation and taste, and several chemicals for flavouring and colouring, whereas naturally prepared food will be low in salt, sugar and saturated fats, for example. You'll be amazed at how many chemicals are added to your food once you start looking — so much so that most of them are officially numbered so the manufacturer can fit the list on the label, tin or packet.

   You can take a look at this numerical list of food additives (and what they do) by visiting the Food Standards Australia and New Zealand Web site. Go to www.foodstandards.gov.au and use their Quick Links menu to find the Numerical List of food additives.

- **Genetically modified info.** The law requires manufacturers to label whether a food has been modified genetically. And the impact of genetic modification is still being worked out, as I explain in the section, 'Getting the Gist of Genetically Modified Food' later in this chapter.

- **Animals used.** Some animals and fish have become protected species due to their near-extinction from being over-farmed or culled. Check the label to ensure that your food does not use or harm animals that are protected, such as dolphins and whales.

Getting the Gist of Genetically Modified Food

Genetically modified (GM) foods have ingredients in them that have been modified by altering the biological characteristics of a food crop by using genetic material and proteins from another source.

Many scientists consider genetically modifying food (or *GMOs — genetically modified organisms* — as they're also called) a controversial process because it introduces new allergens, toxins, disruptive chemicals, soil-polluting ingredients, mutated species and unknown protein combinations into people's bodies and the wider environment. Basically, the fear is that by altering the genetic makeup of a species, the natural order of things will be lost, with abnormal animal and plant life evolving as a result.

Scientists who support GM food suggest that there has been no real proof that problems have been caused by GM food. They say that as long as the process is strictly controlled, any negative effects can be controlled by science.

The food and agricultural industries are interested in GM food because it promises to overcome some of the major difficulties facing large-scale farming. Food can be modified to withstand higher doses of herbicides and pesticides or to produce toxins in the plant or seed to kill insects, saving millions of dollars on wasted crops. The GM process also allows additional vitamins and extra taste to be added, and even makes foods last longer.

But do you want to take the risk? *Choice* magazine recently published a list of some of the foods that are now genetically modified, including

- **Soybeans:** Soya is currently one of the main sources of genetically modified ingredients in food, and can be found in everything from chocolate to crisps, margarine to mayonnaise, and biscuits to bread.
- **Canola:** GM canola may be used in animal feed and to produce potato chips.
- **Cotton:** Some snack foods are made using GM cotton seed oil.
- **Potato and sugarbeet:** Processed foods or those containing sugar may contain GM potato and sugarbeet.
- **Corn:** GM corn is mainly used as cattle feed but is also found in all sorts of packaged food, like breakfast cereal, bread, corn chips, confectionary and gravy mixes.
- **Milk:** Cows in the United States and some other countries (not Australia) are being injected with a genetically engineered growth hormones to increase milk production. Some imported products such as cheese may contain this hormone.

The good news is that so far, under Australian law, no fresh fruit and vegetables grown in this country, whether on organic farms or not, can sprout from GM seeds. Only varieties of cotton grown in this country are genetically modified. Still, plenty of products on supermarket shelves, whether imported from halfway across the globe or using ingredients shipped in from overseas, have genetically modified ingredients in them.

You know whether the food you're buying is a GM product because of labelling requirements. A GM food must be labelled using the words 'genetically modified' together with the name of the food, or by listing the specific ingredient modified. However, you may be unknowingly eating a GM food when you order a meal at a restaurant or fast food outlet.

Unlike organic food, no logo or icon has yet been officially endorsed to indicate that a food or ingredient has been genetically modified. You need to study the fine print on labels. Still, to cut to the chase, Greenpeace has produced a *True Food Guide* that shows you what and how much of the food you buy is genetically modified. You can check out this information, go to the Greenpeace Web site at www.greenpeace.org.au/truefood.

Vegetarianism Is Eco-Friendly — Myth or Reality?

Vegetarians (not the fish and free-range chicken-eating variety, but real non-meat-eating vegetarians) become vegetarians and even *vegans* (no dairy or other animal byproducts at all) for a purpose. Many become vegetarian for health reasons or philosophical reasons or even both. More vegetarians tend to align philosophically to sustainable lifestyle choices than not.

A major study reported in the *British Medical Journal* in 1994 found that of 5,000 meat-eaters and 6,000 non-meat eaters, the vegetarians had 40 per cent less risk of cancer and 30 per cent less risk of heart disease than the meat-eaters. The vegetarians were also less likely to die from these diseases (Oxford Vegetarian Study).

So, does simply being a vegetarian guarantee you're living a sustainable lifestyle? Possibly, especially if your fruit and vegetable choices are grown organically, but this is certainly not a guarantee. Even vegetarians can end up eating fruit or vegetables produced by an intensive and invasive farming production process, just like many meats are. And although a vegetarian's choices mainly revolve around food and more recently clothing and accessories, vegetarians still turn on the lights at night and produce garbage — they have other sustainable living issues to face just like everyone else.

One of the big issues vegetarians now have to deal with is the GM phenomenon. Many vegetarian products on the shelves, like tofu and textured vegetable protein (TVP), are based on soybean, which has become one of the most popular food types for modification, genetically speaking.

Knowing that many of their customers care about this issue, companies like Sanitarium are making it well known on their labelling when their foods are GM free. And Food Standards Australia, as the controlling body for what goes into processed food, has a mountain of information on GM food and the labelling associated with GM-free food (visit www.foodstandards.gov.au for more information).

When you ask people why they choose to be vegetarians, you often find they're protesting against the meat industry's barbaric way of producing meat. Others forsake meat in favour of vegetarianism because they're alarmed by health issues, such as:

✔ **Mad cow disease:** This killer disease reared its ugly head on a wide scale in the mid-1990s. Found in both humans and cows, it's not a virus or a bacteria, but a *prion*, which is an infectious protein that causes dementia and possible death in those infected. Safe to say that the sale of beef went down significantly when the disease became prevalent in certain parts of the world.

✔ **Toxicity:** Artificial hormones, steroids and other chemicals injected or fed to animals to make them grow faster and bigger are, not surprisingly, foreign to the human body and can make vital organs break down.

✔ **Bacteria:** The antibiotics pumped into animals actually result in them resisting strains of bacteria like E. coli. The overuse of antibiotics means you're in with a greater chance of buying meat with undetectable forms of bacteria in it.

✔ **Saturated fats:** In simple terms, many meats are high in fat and a major cause of obesity. As well, factory-farmed animals are grain fed (soybeans and corn) rather than pasture fed (grass). This results in high acidity levels in the animal's digestion system, which causes an increase in the diseases carried by the animal at the time they are slaughtered for consumption.

As if health issues weren't reason enough, consider also the resources that go into the production of meat. Grain feeding animals in a factory farm is resource intensive. Lots of power is used for lighting or other machinery and water to flush away effluent. Even though Australian farms run cattle and sheep out in the paddock, drought, overgrazing and other factors mean their diets are often supplemented with grains.

The Global Resource Action Center for the Environment states that a bull must consume about 7.5 kilograms of grain in order to yield a kilogram of meat. Such a typical grain-fed animal consumes approximately 1,200 kilograms of grain by the time it's ready for market.

Some countries that do not have a large meat-producing industry or that worry about local meat being infected (particularly countries in Asia and Europe), prefer to import their meat from 'safe' countries, such as Australia. The transport energy required to service the meat-eating demands of these countries is extremely large. Transport emissions also apply to shipping livestock across this country.

Fishy business

You probably already know that eating fish is good for you. Here's some of the good oil: The National Health and Medical Research Council states that fish is low in fat, high in protein and an excellent source of omega 3 fatty acids. In fact, if you eat fish regularly, you're probably reducing your risk of developing heart disease, diabetes and asthma — especially when compared to eating red meat.

But maybe it's not as well known that eating all the fish you can get your hands is a sustainability issue — depending on the fish you eat and where it was caught. It's not an exaggeration to state that the world's oceans continue to be plundered. The United Nation's Food and Agriculture Organisation provides the following statistics to back up the claim: 52 per cent of commercial fish species are fully exploited; 17 per cent are overexploited; and 8 per cent are depleted.

The Australian Marine Conservation Society (AMCS) at www.amcs.org.au monitors and supports sustainable fisheries. Some key points that you can further investigate on the Web site include the following:

- Due to intense fishing in Australian waters, there are few natural ocean refuges left in Australia where marine life can thrive. And the list of overfished species, habitat damage and loss of productive fishing habitats due to intensive fishing is still growing.

- An increasing number of fish in super-markets and fish shops are the products of marine aquaculture, which involves farming popular saltwater fish such as snapper and barramundi. Aquaculture farming is affected by many of the same problems that beset factory farming, discussed earlier in this chapter — cruelty through intensive farming, force feeding, and an increase of disease and pollution.

- People eat much more imported seafood than they think because of the lack of labelling requirements. The AMCS suggests that around 60 per cent of fish eaten in Australia is imported.

The organic vegetarian

So, you want to be a truly ecologically sound vegetarian? Here are some foods that are more likely to help you do so:

- **Non-GM canola, corn and soy:** Scrutinise the label — many companies now proudly identify that they're a non-GM food, particularly Australian organically grown and produced olive oil.
- **Nuts:** Buy locally produced nuts that have been organically grown.
- **Local organic fruit and vegetables:** Make the effort to purchase the produce at your local farmers' markets.
- **Tea and coffee:** Look for locally produced coffee (the north coast of New South Wales is becoming a popular coffee-growing location) that's certified as organic and shade-grown (under the canopy of trees, which is great for maintaining bird life and protecting soil).
- **Dairy:** Organic and biodynamic dairy products are now common in Australia and readily available in specialist as well as large grocery chains.
- **Chocolate:** Seek out chocolate that uses organic cocoa and is locally produced (vegans may prefer to buy organic soy-based chocolate).
- **Organic bread:** An increasing number of bakeries and organic food shops sell organic bread.

The 'green' meat-eater?

If you lust for a lamb shank and pine for a pork chop, the news is not all doom and gloom. Meat can be, and is, produced in the same organic and sustainable way that many fruits and vegetables are farmed.

As a result of increasing organic production, you can become a sustainable meat-eating type. The key is to look for meats that have been *pasture raised* or *grass fed* — indicating that the animals were raised outdoors on pasture and that their diet consisted of grasses and hay, a much more natural and environmentally supportive process.

Some animals (especially chickens and pigs) are supported with some grains to ensure the animals are getting their required nutrients, but the grains themselves should be organically grown.

Some sustainable meat-buying issues to look out for on the label and packaging include

- ✔ **Organic free-range:** Check the labelling or a company's Web site to find out whether the chicken or pig has been raised on pasture or in an enclosed free-range shed (outside cages). With beef, avoid *feedlot* produced meat.

- ✔ **Natural:** Labelling may refer to beef and lamb, in particular, being produced naturally, but this usually only means that no artificial colours, artificial flavours, preservatives or other artificial ingredients were added later. The cow or sheep still may have been raised in an artificial and unsustainable environment.

- ✔ **Lean:** Buying lean meat might be healthier, but it's not any more sustainable than fatty meat. The only difference between lean meat and non-lean meat is that the fat has been cut off.

If you're finding it hard to source organic meat, visit your local butcher's shop or the butcher in the supermarket and ask if you can be supplied with some organic and sustainable options — increased demand increases supply. Your health and the environment will be better off and your local supermarket or butcher will have a guaranteed customer.

Chapter 11

Looking Good in Eco-Fashion

• •

In This Chapter

▶ Understanding where your clothes are made

▶ Choosing the right materials

▶ Feeling cool in vintage clothes

▶ Looking after your wardrobe

• •

*T*he fashion industry revolves around glamour, innovation and change. Trends, which most people follow, change quickly. New clothes can make you look good, boost your self-esteem and change other people's perceptions about you. I don't go shopping for new clothes very often, but when I do, I always check the label to see where the garment was made; this quickly tells me how sustainable the clothing is likely to be.

The manufacturing processes for cheap, mass-produced clothing waste resources and cause pollution. Synthetic materials, such as polyester, are based on fossil fuels. Mass-produced natural materials, like cotton, use large volumes of water and chemicals. Also, most clothes in shops today are made using cheap labour in the developing world in order to keep costs down.

You can be fashionable and sustainable at the same time, though. A growing number of retailers sell fashionable, eco-friendly clothing. In this chapter I provide some online resources so that you can track down clothes made using sustainable materials or that are recycled, and show you how buying eco-friendly clothing can help reduce the negative effects that the global clothing industry has on the environment.

Following the Thread of Where Your Clothes Are Made

Take a look at all the labels on the clothes in your wardrobe. If you group them based on where they were made, you may find that many were produced in countries like the Philippines, Bangladesh, China, Fiji, India, Pakistan, Madagascar, Mexico and Turkey. A large proportion of the clothes manufactured in these countries are made under appalling conditions that exploit local workers.

FairWear (www.fairwear.org.au) estimates that just over 50 per cent of clothes sold in Australia are imported from these overseas countries. A high proportion of the remaining 50 per cent of clothes are made in home-based industries, where the rate of pay is much lower than the legislated minimum.

What's the problem with buying affordable clothes?

Maybe you're thinking that if you buy mass-produced clothes regularly, everyone wins. You get nice cheap clothes, companies maintain their profit margins and new jobs are created in developing countries, where money is desperately needed.

The fact is that many manufacturers are exploiting the workers who live in such economies, especially the women. These people don't get a reasonable wage; their quality of life deteriorates as ours improves. Here's why their working conditions are so poor:

✔ **No legal protection:** Workers in developing economies are not always recognised as workers and, in some countries, the factories they work in are not recognised as workplaces. The workers have no avenue to complain about the fact that they work in an unhealthy and unsafe environment.

✔ **No access to a trade union:** Workers have few opportunities to be represented by a trade union. This may be a result of the worker not being officially recognised or the wages being so low that they cannot afford the union fee.

✔ **Extremely low wages:** Many workers in the global textile industry earn less than the *living wage*. This wage is defined (by the United Nation's OECD) as approximately 15 per cent above the *poverty threshold wage*.

In some countries, workers don't even make the poverty threshold. In Australia, the year 2000 poverty threshold was $375 a week (around $10 an hour). Imagine yourself maintaining a family of four on this income.

✔ **Isolation:** Workers can't access other opportunities because they work such long hours for little pay without recognition. They're trapped.

Buyer beware. Buying a *Made in Australia* item doesn't guarantee that it's been made equitably. Clothing manufacturers in Australia often take advantage of the large migrant population, many of whom have limited options for employment. Unethical companies contract these people as home-based workers to save money on wages and avoid the cost of complying with occupational health and safety regulations. These home-based operations are also known as *sweat shops*.

Because of globalisation and deregulation, manufacturers that produced clothes locally in developed nations have either closed, amalgamated with larger companies or moved their own manufacturing operations overseas. This has resulted in fewer employment opportunities in cities and towns. Many formerly vibrant manufacturing communities have almost completely lost their textile manufacturing base.

Trading fairly

Global campaigns, run by different groups, are pressuring clothing manufacturers to take greater social responsibility for their workers and to add real value to the local economies in which they operate. One strategy involves endorsing manufacturers that do trade fairly — that is, labelling products made by companies that practice ethical trading.

Fair trade labels are similar to the international labelling systems that are well established for food, such as coffee. To find out which companies and products currently participate in regional labelling programs, check out the Australian Fair Trade Association of Australia and New Zealand Web site, at www.fta.org.au.

Some global companies and charities that sell clothes are also registered by the International Fair Trade Association (IFAT), which has its own Fair Trade label, as shown in Figure 11-1. So far, IFAT has members in 70 countries. For more details about IFAT members, visit www.ifat.org.

Figure 11-1:
The
International
Fair Trade
Association
label.

Another label, developed in Australia to address fair trading principles, is the No Sweatshop Label (www.nosweatshoplabel.com). This label, shown in Figure 11-2, evolved from the Homeworkers Code of Practice, an Australian code developed by the Textile Clothing and Footwear Union of Australia (TCFUA) and the clothing and footwear industries.

The basic criterion for attaining No Sweat Shop Label accreditation is that home-based workers must be on at least the same wage and benefits as textile factory workers. To find out which companies proudly wear the No Sweat Shop label, visit the Web site then follow the Accredited Companies link on the site's main page.

Figure 11-2:
The No
Sweat Shop
label.

By comparison FairWear, a coalition of churches, community organisations and unions, runs campaigns and shows you on its Web site (www.fairwear.org.au) how to pressure retailers and the textile industry into treating home industry workers more equitably.

If you're planning to buy clothing or accessories overseas or over the Internet, check out www.cleanclothes.org to find out which companies support fair trade practices and those that you should avoid.

Another Web site to check out is Oxfam (www.oxfam.org.au). This large charity has its headquarters in the United Kingdom, and has shops all over the world, including Australia, and sells products produced in the developing world fairly.

The Material World

The materials used to make your clothes come from two different sources: *Synthetic fibres*, created from a chemical process, and *natural fibres*, sourced from plants and animals. Synthetic fibres are generally cheaper than their natural competitors — and, arguably, not as comfortable to wear.

The two most popular natural fibres are cotton and wool, but the processes used to grow and refine these materials can impact on the environment (see the following section 'Natural does not mean sustainable' for more details).

The most popular of the synthetics are nylon and polyester, which are made from petrochemicals. The processing of petrochemicals into small fibres uses a large amount of energy and emits greenhouse gases and other pollution. The process that creates polyester also uses a large amount of water as part of the cooling process. If you can, try to avoid any clothes that have these types of materials in them, no matter how much of a bargain they may appear to be.

Natural does not mean sustainable

Natural fibres generally come from cotton fields or from a sheep's back. It would be nice to think that this makes them good for the environment.

Unfortunately, cotton is one of the most pesticide-intensive crops on the planet. Chemicals are used because cotton plants can be easily affected by insects and fungus.

Pesticides create health problems for those who work on cotton farms, and contaminate ground and surface water, having a long-term effect on the health of the soil. The Pesticide Action Network of North America (www.panna.org) suggests that pesticide residue stays in the fabric after it has been manufactured, putting your health at risk while you wear it. Cotton also uses vast amounts of water. Cotton farms on the Queensland border capture 90 per cent of the water in the Darling River as it passes through their properties.

Wool is the other natural fibre mass produced for the clothing industry. Wool is obviously natural — it comes straight off the sheep's back. It has been a major contributor to Australia's healthy export status (30 per cent of wool used in the world is from Australia) and for many years was one of the key factors in the country's economic success.

Pesticides are also used to produce wool. Sheep dip, a chemical concoction that sheep are dipped into to kill parasites and maintain the quality of the wool, contains organophosphates, which scientists now know are a major cause of excessive tiredness, headaches, poor concentration and mood changes in humans who are exposed to it. One can only wonder how the sheep feels after being dipped in this stuff.

The process of *mulesing,* which involves carving strips of flesh off the sheep without any painkillers to prevent flies planting eggs in the folds of the sheep's skin, is regarded by the People for the Ethical Treatment of Animals (PETA) as unacceptably cruel. Check out www.peta.org for more details.

Environmental problems extend beyond the farm, however. Synthetic and chemical products, including colour dyes and bleach, are usually added to cotton or wool fabrics during the clothing manufacturing process.

Watch out for poly-cotton products on the market, also referred to as *permanent press, no wrinkle, no ironing needed,* and *crease resistant* products.

To avoid this unhealthy combination of processes, many companies are now producing clothes made from organic cotton, organic wool or from hemp. For more details, see the section 'Finding ethical retailers' later in this chapter.

The great debate — leather versus synthetics

Many environmentalists, especially vegans and vegetarians, boycott buying and wearing clothes made from animal skins. This boycott includes leather, fur and reptile skins. Here's why:

- ✔ Any product made from an animal skin involves the premature death or injury of the animal, so it's inherently cruel. That's a fair call; it's hard to imagine skinning an animal as anything but a cruel process.

- ✔ The global demand for products made from exotic animals is a significant reason for the declining number of wild animals across the world.

- ✔ Modern methods of manufacturing leather consume a large amount of energy. Leather from countries such as Morocco is made traditionally using natural dyes, mineral salts and water, and the skins are dried in the sun. Such leather is promoted as a more sustainable product.

A number of cruelty-free and 'vegetarian' clothing stores sell alternative products made of vinyl, PVC and other chemically produced materials. These products also have major impacts on the environment. Unfortunately, you cannot assume that buying cruelty-free clothing is sustainable.

That being said, vegan and vegetarian retailers lead the demand for sustainable textiles. Many of the synthetic alternatives they offer are made from recycled material to minimise chemical pollution and resource consumption. Waterproof clothing, outdoor gear and some shoes have been developed using recycled polyester, rubber and even car tyres.

On a scale of 1 to 10, considering all aspects of social, economic and environmental sustainability, vegan and vegetarian stores rate very highly. The products they sell are more sustainable than mass-produced leather.

A great Web site from the UK Ethical Consumer Research Association can help you rate the sustainability of clothing companies. It uses an Ethiscore out of 20 to rate clothing and every other consumable you can think of. Located at `www.ethiscore.org`, the site is a subscription and payment-based site with a few free pages that rate sports shoes (trainers) and other products.

Several vegan or vegetarian clothing shops around the globe encourage you to buy non-leather alternatives, such as:

- Glamourpuss, Sydney (`www.glamourpuss.com.au`)
- Vegan Wares, Melbourne (`www.veganwares.com`)
- Vegetarian Shoes UK (`www.vegetarian-shoes.co.uk`)
- Moo Shoes, Vegan Shoes NYC (`www.mooshoes.com`)
- Alternative Outfitters, United States (`www.alternativeoutfitters.com`)
- PETA (People for Ethical Treatment of Animals) Mall (`www.petamall.com`)
- Vegan of Light, United States (`www.cafepress.com/veganoflight`)

Sustainable, organically grown fibres

You may be wondering exactly what sustainable clothing options are left to choose from. Don't worry, a growing industry of sustainable clothing materials is now available. The main alternatives are

- **Hemp.** A highly sustainable crop, industrial hemp is fast growing, productive and resistant to pests, which means it does not require chemicals to maintain its quality. *Note:* Although industrial hemp and marijuana have the same technical name (*Cannabis sativa*), they are different varieties of the same plant. Industrial hemp contains untraceable amounts of THC, the active ingredient in marijuana.
- **Linen.** This strong and versatile fibre is made from flax. Flax is naturally resistant to pests and grows well, at least compared to cotton.
- **Organically grown cotton and wool.** Certified organic cotton is not genetically modified and is grown using natural fertilisers and no pesticides. Organic wool is taken from sheep ranging freely on grass, and raised without chemical feed.

Consumer demand for clothes made from natural, sustainable fibres has encouraged many ethical retailers to open up shop. The next section lists a number of them.

Finding ethical retailers

Whether you're peeved with polyester, sick of synthetics in general, or want to leave leather behind, there's a retailer out there waiting to dress you sustainably.

Here's what to look for when you're shopping for clothes and accessories:

✔ Has the product been produced locally? (Locally made products are good for the economy and cut transport costs.)

✔ Has the product been manufactured and produced by an ethical company?

✔ Has the product been made using sustainable materials?

If you can answer yes to all three, you've found a 'winner': You'd be buying some of the most sustainable clothes on the planet. To start building your sustainable wardrobe, check out these retailers' Web sites:

✔ **Benbellen Alpaca Products** (www.benbellen.com.au): A farm that makes and sells clothes made from organic alpaca wool.

✔ **Just Jussi** (www.justjussi.com.au): A Sydney-based company that sells babies' clothes made from organic wool, silk and cotton.

✔ **Just Site** (www.justsite.com.au): A great Australian site that sells local and international clothes, shoes and accessories (such as belts made from recycled bike tyres, organic cotton caps, and bags made from recycled billboards and car seat straps).

✔ **No Sweat** (www.nosweatstuff.com.au): This label carries clothing and footwear made from organically grown materials like hemp and cotton by union-represented manufacturers.

✔ **Blessed Earth** (www.blessedearth.com.au): This company sells a wide range of organic cotton clothing, produced in Australia. The Web site also has some good links to the anti-sweatshop movement around the world.

✔ **Organic Cotton Advantage (OCA)** (http://chooseoca.com.au): Both a supplier and a retailer, the OCA shop specialises in Australian organic cotton t-shirts. Also sells caps and canvas tote bags hand-sewn in the United States.

✔ **Margaret River Hemp Co** (www.hempco.net.au): This Western Australian company sells clothes and accessories made from hemp.

✔ **Sienna Organics** (www.siennaorganics.com.au): An organic fibre specialist offering a range of basic and designer clothes.

✔ **The Organic Trading Company** (www.organictradingco.com): Lots of organic and hemp clothes (and accessories) for women and babies.

Some Australian companies are really on the mark. For example, Trash Bags (www.trashbags.com.au) sets up shop in an Asian country to help disadvantaged communities make products from sustainable materials. Similarly, Taylor & Khoo (www.taylorandkhoo.com) make fashion and homewares in Cambodia. All profits are used to feed and care for children in a local orphanage. Check out the Web site for more details, or visit one of the shops in Sydney, Brisbane, Melbourne, or in Bangalow, New South Wales.

If you can sew, knit or crochet, make your own clothes from eco-friendly yarns (and fabrics). You can use organic marino wool, bamboo fibre, corn fibre, organic cotton, soysilk, and organic alpaca wool. (Soysilk, you ask? Soysilk is the yarn made from the residue of soybeans in tofu manufacturing and contains no chemicals or additives and is completely biodegradable. Corn fibre is similar, but is feels more like cotton than silk.) You can get all these products from the Ecoyarn Web site at www.ecoyarn.com.au.

Some international retailers and Web sites are also worth checking out, even though the shipping and transport involved makes them less preferable to your local company:

- **American Apparel** (www.americanapparel.net): One of the few American clothing companies that ships to Australia, this company promotes itself as paying the highest wages in the United States garment industry, as well as selling several *sustainable edition* lines that are made from organic cotton.

- **Patagonia** (www.patagonia.com): A global sports apparel company that offers organic cotton products as well as fleeces made from recycled plastics.

- **Nike Considered** (www.nike.com/nikebiz/nikeconsidered): This site showcases Nike's new range of sustainably made footwear.

- **Ecomall** (www.ecomall.com): An extensive online directory of sustainable retailers in the United States. Click on 'clothing' to get to the . . . well, you know, online clothing stores.

Old Is Cool: The Attraction of Vintage Clothes

Wearing secondhand clothes saves the environment in two ways: It reduces waste and the consumption of resources. By shopping at secondhand stores and markets, you can create your own unique style. Even if the vintage clothes are made from unsustainable materials — say nylon or polyester cotton blends — they reduce waste and consumption by staying in circulation.

What the cool people are wearing

Don't be shy. The coolest people don't conform to the latest fashions. They set out to be different by creating their own look from a broad range of styles.

Anyone looking inside my wardrobe will quickly attest that I am no fashion guru. So I had to ask the coolest person I know — my partner, Justine — to tell me all about vintage clothes (she wears them, and so do her friends).

Here is her list of what to look for in the vintage clothes line:

✔ Long-sleeved, slim-fit dresses made from a cotton blend.

✔ Chinese cheongsams for formal occasions.

✔ Moroccan style, loose, long-sleeved cotton tops.

By the way, a *cheongsam* is one of those long straight dresses that has a small standup collar and a long slit in the side of the skirt.

Most blokes are more comfortable wearing the following garments (even if the women in their lives want to borrow them from time to time):

✔ Low-cut jeans that sit on the waist and look well-worn.

✔ Slim-fit cotton shirts.

✔ Distressed cotton or wool-blend blazers.

✔ Bowling shirts.

Well, they sound like good ideas to me.

Some of the nicest clothes in Justine's wardrobe are the ones handed down through her family from generations past. To keep these clothes relevant, especially in the size department, it's useful to be handy with a needle and thread. Being able to mend a seam, alter a hem and re-style a shirt or dress not only saves you money, but allows you to keep old clothes in fashion and in circulation.

To maintain your current clothes in reasonable condition, see the section 'Keeping old favourites alive' later in this chapter.

Where to find clothing classics

Lots of online vintage clothes retailers are online. If your mission is to dress in a sustainable fashion, be aware that some sell authentic used clothes and some sell new clothes in older styles.

In consultation with my expert, here is a list of some retailers of authentic used clothes. Go to these places, hand in some old clothes and treat yourself to some new ones. Give yourself a sustainable brownie point and a new look.

- **Hunter Gatherer** (www.huntergatherer.com.au): Operated by the Brothers of St Laurence, the Hunter Gatherer stores in Melbourne sell vintage clothes, as well as their own line of new No Sweat Shop-accredited clothing.

- **eBay** (www.ebay.com.au): Thousands of people sell (and auction off) vintage and used clothes on eBay each day. It's unbelievable.

- **Blue Spinach** (www.bluespinach.com.au): A Sydney company that buys and sells top-end designer clothing.

- **Belinda** (www.belinda.com.au): This business has shops in Sydney and Melbourne where you can exchange or buy used clothes.

- **Salvos Stores** (salvosstores.salvos.org.au): The most well known of the charity shops has a great range of used and vintage clothes.

- **St Vincent de Paul** (www.vinnies.org.au): Lots of clothing and other merchandise. Refer to Chapter 9 for more details.

DIY Clothing Tips

Natural fibres, like fossil fuels and water, are in short supply; the planet can't produce enough to meet demand. One way to reduce demand is to keep your clothes in circulation as long as possible. Hand them on to other people or charities, trade them over the Internet, or keep them for yourself. As long as someone is wearing them, you have taken one small step towards a sustainable future.

Keeping old favourites alive

The old adage 'A stitch in time, saves nine' is literally true. Repair a torn thread or small hole in your clothes as soon as you notice it. If you don't fix it straight away you may have to throw the garment out.

Check your local phone book to find who makes and mends clothes in your area.

If you don't know the difference between a sewing machine and a tailor, here are some tips on how to salvage or care for clothing:

✔ Avoid using a clothes dryer and dry naturally — constantly drying clothes in a machine shrinks the clothes and wears them out very quickly.

✔ Wash thick clothes like socks and pullovers inside out — apparently, this revitalises them.

✔ Lay woollen garments flat on a towel after washing. This helps maintain their shape as they dry.

✔ Use lukewarm or cold water in your wash to help retain the shape and colour of your clothes, especially those made from cotton. It also uses less energy.

✔ When you spill something that could stain your clothes, pre-treat it immediately to make it easier for the stain to come out in the wash. Rub some normal hand soap on the stain, grab a corner of the same garment and scrub the stain with that.

✔ Spills that contain protein — like eggs, gravy and blood — need to be gently removed with cold water before putting them in hot water. Warm water binds the protein to the fabric, creating a stain.

✔ Rub marks from clothes with a damp sponge, instead of throwing them into the wash. Many marks are small and easily removed with soap and water directly on the spot.

More tips like this are available from the About.com Web site in the Frugal Living section. Check out `frugalliving.about.com/od/caringforclothing` for more details.

Revamping your wardrobe

You can make old clothes new again, or turn them into something else. Try reactivating these tried and true practices that have fallen out of favour in the modern, throwaway world:

✔ Long pants can be easily made into shorts (especially for kids who get holes in the knees) by cutting off the legs just above the knee and sewing a hem.

- If you start getting holes in your clothes, use patches either on top or behind the hole to keep the garment together for longer. Sewing patches on is much more effective than using iron-on patches.

- If it becomes too embarrassing to wear those clothes that are just too far gone, rejig them to use as cooking aprons, cleaning cloths, washers, dusting rags or shoe polishers. Make sure you save any buttons, zippers, elastic or trims for use in repairing other clothes.

- Dying old clothes can give them a new lease of life. Commercial dyes are quite expensive and often made from hideous chemicals. Explore organic dyes and dyes you can make at home from vegetables like beetroot, onion skins and household chemicals.

Well-made clothes, cut from long-lasting materials, are easier to repair and look after. Funnily enough, one of the best sources of affordable quality clothing is the secondhand store. After all, it was of good enough quality to survive its first owner.

Do-it-yourself dry cleaning

Dry cleaning is a marvellous invention that cleans delicate textiles that would otherwise shrink or fall apart if washed in water. Unfortunately, dry cleaning is a chemical process that harms the people who work with it, as well as the environment.

You can reduce your dependence on dry cleaning without giving up delicate fabrics by trying these methods:

- To remove most food spills, and marks from brushing against dirty objects, use a damp cloth (not a wet one) on the area.

- To lift oily marks, sprinkle talcum powder on the area, leave it for a few hours then brush the powder off. (You may repeat this process several times for it to work.)

- To remove chewing gum, body fluids, shoe polish and other stubborn stains on most fabrics, add a few drops of eucalyptus oil to a damp cloth. Be careful with delicate synthetics, though, because the eucalyptus oil can dissolve them.

Chapter 12

Homeware Shopping at the Eco Mall

In This Chapter

▶ Homing in on the highest-rating appliances

▶ Shopping for home stuff and hardware products

▶ Sourcing 'natural' garden supplies

Consider this chapter your sustainable yellow pages, where you can let your fingers do the walking — well, at least do the typing — when you're in the mood for a little homeware shopping.

In this chapter, I help you find electrical appliances. I list the companies that make energy-efficient models and the brands they manufacture. I also track down some sustainable homeware products, building materials and gardening supplies.

Many of these products can be found in some of the larger hardware stores, but when you shop at stores that only sell sustainable products, you send a message to the market that you want more stores that do the same.

Browsing the online eco malls

The best way to track down great products, or to find out where to buy them, is to visit the online eco malls. These Web sites bring together resources and articles about 'living green' and are portals to many suppliers and independent shops.

Probably the most well-known in Australia is the EcoShop (www.ecoshop.com.au). The EcoShop has two parts to its Web site: An EcoShop, where you can actually buy a limited range of environmentally friendly products in a variety of categories; and the very helpful Eco-Directory, which I have referred to in this chapter. It provides hundreds of links to companies and retailers selling environmentally friendly goods.

Another online resource is the Planet Ark shop (www.planetarkdirect.com.au). Although this site doesn't sell as many products as similar eco-friendly sites, Planet Ark offers a range of household products to reduce your ecological impact.

One of the best Web sites in the United States for all things environmental and sustainable is the Eco Mall (www.ecomall.com). Coordinated by Ecology America, this site has thousands of links (seriously!) to companies, products, agencies, activists and just about anything that has to do with living a sustainable life.

Last but not least, don't forget to check out eBay (www.ebay.com.au). On eBay you can find lots of used or recycled products for auction, as well as new items that you can buy directly — without bidding on them.

By the way, keeping furniture and homewares in circulation by purchasing through eBay will reduce not only the pressure on waste disposal systems but also the demand for natural products used in making furniture and other homeware items. For more about shopping on eBay, refer to Chapter 9.

Buying Energy-Efficient Appliances

Throughout this book I encourage you to equip your home in a way that reduces your reliance on electrical appliances. But when you do need to buy an electrical appliance or two, why not make them energy-efficient appliances?

You can substantially reduce your electrical energy use at home by ensuring that your appliances are energy efficient. You don't need to work out the energy efficiency for most appliances, though — the Australian Appliance Energy Rating Scheme (ERS) does it for you (http://search.energyrating.gov.au). Appliances that currently carry the ERS label are refrigerators and freezers, air-conditioners, clothes dryers, washing machines and dishwashers.

You should determine the size or capacity and the features of the appliance you need and then compare the efficiency ratings of the appropriate models for each of the brand names listed.

In Chapter 4, I explain how the ERS label system works, and what it means. In this chapter, I provide information about the manufacturers that make appliances with high ERS scores. A six out of six is the best an appliance can rate.

I also include the country of manufacture because importing appliances from overseas adds to transport energy costs, which are not included in the rating system. It is definitely worth adding a few ticks for those appliances made in Australia.

Refrigerators

The manufacturers of refrigerators listed in Table 12-1 make some of the most energy-efficient brands on the market.

Combined refrigerators and freezers don't score a high energy-efficiency rating. This is because large freezers can churn up a large amount of electrical energy. And don't forget that refrigerators are a major source of ozone-depleting gases (refer to Chapter 5 for more information). Electrolux, Liebherr, Miele and Vestfrost sell *greenfreeze* fridges in other parts of the world (refer to Chapter 4 for more about greenfreeze) and may start stocking them in Australia if demand increases for them. Check the companies' Web sites for further information.

Table 12-1		Energy-Efficient Refrigerators	
Brand	*Made*	*Web Address*	*Best ERS Score*
Liebherr	Germany	www.andico.com.au	6
Miele	Germany	www.miele.com.au	6
Fisher and Paykel	Australia	www.fisherpaykel.com.au	6
Conia	China	www.conia.com.au	5.5
Westinghouse	Australia	www.westinghouse.com.au	5
Electrolux	Australia	www.electrolux.com.au	5
Smeg	Slovenia	www.omegasmeg.com.au	5
Vestfrost	Denmark	www.vestfrost.com	5
LG	China	http://au.lge.com	5

Source: www.energyrating.gov.au

Dishwashers

Clearly, the most energy-efficient dishwasher on the market is you. The next most energy-efficient dishwasher available in Australia rates a four (see Table 12-2), which is well short of the maximum of six that other appliances not available here achieve. Of the Australian-manufactured dishwashers, the Electrolux and Dishlex brands, the best models only carry ratings of 3.5.

Dishwashers also carry the water-efficiency rating label, which you should also take into account when buying a dishwasher. To find out more about water ratings, refer to Chapter 5.

Table 12-2		Energy-Efficient Dishwashers	
Brand	**Made**	**Web Address**	**Best ERS Score**
ASKO	Sweden	www.asko.com.au	4
Bosch	Germany	www.bosch.com.au	4
Brandt	France	www.kleenmaid.com.au	4
De Dietrich	France	www.kleenmaid.com.au	4
Kleenmaid	France	www.kleenmaid.com.au	4
Siemens	Germany	www.siemens-homeappliances.com	4
Electrolux	Australia	www.electrolux.com.au	3.5
Dishlex	Australia	www.dishlex.com.au	3.5

Source: www.energyrating.gov.au

Air-conditioners

Two types of ratings apply to air-conditioners:

- A blue band of stars rating units that cool.
- A double set of stars for reverse-cycle air-conditioners that can be switched between heating and cooling.

When the air-conditioner is used for heating as part of its reverse-cycle function, the heating cycle usually carries a lower energy-efficient rating. Reverse-cycle air-conditioners may not be the most efficient form of heating.

The Appliance Energy Rating Scheme Web site, at `www.energyrating.gov.au/acl.html`, also helps you determine the size of air-conditioner you need. This is because an air-conditioner larger than necessary will waste energy every time you switch it on.

Air-conditioners can be installed directly in the wall of the room they are to cool, or can be installed away from the living area with ducts to carry the air to and from the rooms to be cooled. Calculating the efficiency of the two systems is complex because it involves the efficiency of the actual unit, and its effectiveness in cooling the house. Seek expert advice, or get a second opinion.

Newer air-conditioning units use an inverter to alter the amount of power consumed at different settings. Although these units are generally less efficient when run at full bore, they save electricity if run at lower settings.

No Australian-made air-conditioners make the high ratings shown in Table 12-3. Also, note that most air-conditioners are made in south-east Asia.

Table 12-3		Energy-Efficient Air-Conditioners	
Brand	*Made*	*Web Address*	*Best ERS Score*
Daikin	Thailand	www.daikin.com.au	6
Fujitsu	China	www.fujitsugeneral.com.au	6
Sanyo	China	www.sanyo.com.au	5.5
Electrolux	China	www.electrolux.com.au	5.5
Mitsubishi	Thailand	www.mhi.net.au	5.5
Carrier	China	http://carrieraircon.com.au	5.5
Midea	China	www.mideaaircon.com	5.5
Panasonic	Malaysia	www.panasonic.com.au	5
Airwell	China	www.airwell.com.au	5
Dimplex	China	www.dimplex-australia.com	5
Tecoair	China	www.teco.com.au	5
TCL	China	www.tclaircon.com	5

Source: www.energyrating.gov.au

Washing machines

No washing machine currently on the market gains a six out of six rating. In fact, only one reaches five, as shown in Table 12-4. Note that the following ratings are based on a warm wash — you're likely to achieve even better energy savings if you wash your clothes in cold water. Also note that all the energy-efficient machines are front loaders — the highest rating that a top-loading non-drum washing machine (Fisher and Paykel) can garner is three and a half, with most rating under this.

By the way, the Australian-manufactured machines rate quite low. Fisher and Paykel produce a front-loader that rates the highest.

Table 12-4	Energy-Efficient Front-Loading Washing Machines		
Brand	**Made**	**Web Address**	**Best ERS Score**
Kleenmaid	Slovenia	www.kleenmaid.com.au	5
Omega	Slovenia	www.omegasmeg.com.au	4.5
Ariston	Italy	www.aristonchannel.com	4.5
Miele	Germany	www.miele.com.au	4.5
Asko	Sweden	www.asko.com.au	4.5
AEG	German	www.andico.com.au	4.5
Westinghouse	South Korea	www.westinghouse.com.au	4.5
Bosch	Germany	www.bosch.com.au	4.5
LG	South Korea	au.lge.com	4.5

Source: www.energyrating.gov.au

Clothes dryers

Compared to other appliances, clothes dryers struggle when it comes to energy efficiency. The highest rating any machine can get is three and a half out of six. The highest raters have autosensor timing functions, thereby reducing the amount of energy expended when the clothes are actually dry. All the manufacturers listed in Table 12-5 make an autosensing model. The most efficient models condense the water rather than blowing it out into the room (vented).

The best ovens?

Ovens and other cooking appliances aren't covered by the energy efficiency rating system. Although I mention in Chapter 4 that cooking with natural gas emits fewer greenhouse gases than using electricity, natural gas appliances can struggle to compete from an energy efficiency perspective. This is because some models are poorly insulated and allow the heat to escape with the exhaust gases.

You'll find a variety of AGL-recommended shops that sell gas ovens and cooktops on the AGL website (www.agl.com.au). AGL provides electrical and gas energy supplies to NSW, Victoria, South Australia and the ACT. It has won international awards for its promotion of sustainable energy and is one of the better sources for buying energy-efficient gas ovens.

Table 12-5	Energy-Efficient Clothes Dryers		
Brand	**Made**	**Web Address**	**Best ERS Score**
Miele	Germany	www.miele.com.au	3.5
LG	South Korea	http://au.lge.com	3.5
LG	South Korea	http://au.lge.com	3
Indesit	Italy	www.aristonchannel.com	3
Kleenmaid	Slovenia	www.kleenmaid.com.au	3

Source: www.energyrating.gov.au

Entertainment systems

Although there are no energy-rating labels for entertainment systems, you can buy Energy Star products to ensure you are at least saving energy when you are not using each respective unit (see Chapter 4 for a more detailed explanation).

Energy Star Australia (www.energystar.gov.au) provides a list of TV and entertainment system brands that are Energy Star partners. These appliances are about 25 per cent more energy efficient than those which are not rated. Most of the big name electronics manufacturers are listed.

Energy Star Australia also recommends buying these products at retailers who support the Energy Star brand. These include Retravision (www.retravision.com.au) and Harvey Norman (www.harveynorman.com.au).

Homeware and Furniture

When shopping for homewares like linen, towels, manchester or furniture, you'll be wanting to find products that have been made from organic non-toxic products, are obtained from renewable sources (or at least from recycled materials), are reusable or recyclable, and have been manufactured using fair trade principles.

Here are some resources that I tracked down:

- **Biome Living** (www.biome.com.au): At Biome Living, household and outdoor products made from eco-friendly materials and produced under fair trade principles.
- **Blessed Earth** (www.blessedearth.com.au): This site specialises in organic clothing and household furnishing materials.
- **Ecoathome** (www.ecoathome.com.au): A Sydney-based shop that sells a variety of indoor and outdoor environmentally friendly products.
- **Healthy Habitat** (www.healthyhabitat.com.au): You can find a variety of home products that are either organic or naturally made that are healthy alternatives to the everyday products available in shops.
- **Neco** (www.neco.com.au): Neco is an eco hardware store. The company specialises in selling energy-efficient and environmentally friendly indoor and outdoor products.
- **The Eco Collection** (www.ecocollection.com.au): This store's specialty is furniture made from ecologically sensitive and healthy materials.
- **The Environment Shop** (www.environmentshop.com.au): This Melbourne-based shop has a large range of indoor and outdoor products to help you live more sustainably.
- **The Natural Floorcovering Centre** (www.naturalfloor.com.au): You can find a selection of natural fibre floor coverings.
- **The Organic Lifestyle Trading Company** (www.organictradingco.com): This Sydney-based store specialises in eco-friendly and organic products that enable you to create a healthy home.
- **The Sustainable Design Company** (http://sustainabledesign.com.au): This company offers a range of healthy and environmentally responsible indoor and outdoor products and services.

✔ **Aussie Sheet House** (www.sheethouse.com.au): Visit this site for bamboo-fibre bed sheets, which offer all the advantages of Egyptian cotton.

✔ **Wharington International's Sustainable Furniture** (www.sustainablefurniture.com.au): This company specialises in using recycled materials in their furniture.

DIG (Do-it-Green)

Do-it-yourself hardware stores have been a runaway retail success. Some people just love renovating and fixing things themselves and an armada of hardware and home renovation stores has emerged to tickle that fancy.

Most leading hardware stores have a smattering of sustainable products scattered across the endless aisles. Some native plants here, some water-saving products there. These shops are so big, however, that you have to search through the mass of timber cut from old-growth forests, the aisles of dangerous chemicals and a plethora of plastic products to find what you need.

To help you cut to the chase, I direct you to companies that sell sustainable hardware products online. In this way, you can be confident that you can do-it-green.

Hardware helpers

More and more Australian companies now specialise in supplying building materials made from natural or recycled products (for more about building or renovating sustainably, refer to Chapter 3). Some of the companies you can buy building materials from include

✔ **Australian Architectural Hardwoods** (www.aahardwoods.com.au): Located in Kempsey, New South Wales, this company collects timber from disused buildings, cleans it up and sells it.

✔ **Bamboo Australia** (www.bamboo-oz.com.au): All things bamboo are here, including poles, flooring, fencing, handicrafts — even seeds, so that you can grow your own.

✔ **Durra Building Systems** (www.ortech.com.au): This company builds and sells construction panels made from disused wheat and rice straw fibre for walls, ceilings and cladding.

- **Make it Mudbricks** (www.makeitmudbricks.com.au): Naturally made mudbricks, for external and internal walls are available. You can choose between two types of mudbricks — puddled mudbricks or the pressed variety.

- **The Second Hand Building Centre** (http://shbc.com.au): This Sydney company rescues and restores timber materials, old cabinetry, windows frames, doors and more.

- **The Woolmen** (www.thewoolmen.com.au): The company sells wool insulation, polyester insulation, ventilation systems and more.

- **Timber Zoo** (www.timberzoo.com.au): This company specialises in recycled timber posts, beams, remilled flooring and other timber products.

- **Urban Salvage** (www.urbansalvage.com.au): You'll find secondhand timber for flooring and furniture.

- **XSSTOCK** (www.xsstock.com.au): This is an online trading directory for buying and selling excess building products, new and used.

If you want someone else to find sustainable building material products for you, or at least design your renovation and building using these materials, go to www.ecoshop.com.au/ecodirectory/building.htm to find an architect, designer or builder who can do it all for you.

Paints without poisons

For your health, if nothing else, it is wise to search out those companies that sell non-toxic paints made with as many natural ingredients as possible (refer to Chapter 3 to find out why). These sources can help you with your painting needs:

- **Bauwerk Paints** (www.bauwerk.com.au): This company makes lime paints coloured with mineral pigments; it also sells environmentally friendly painting equipment.

- **The Natural Paint Place** (www.energyandwatersolutions.com.au): This company sells BIO Paint (refer to Chapter 3) and other non-toxic paints made from plant extracts. It also sells natural cleaners, recycling tools and pest control products.

- **Painted Earth** (www.house-paint.com.au): This online retailer, based in Byron Bay, New South Wales, sells a range of non-toxic, environmentally responsible house paints and wood finishes.

Gardening and Outdoor Goods

For your outdoor garden needs, check out these resources:

- **Amgrow Garden King** (www.amgrowgardenking.com.au): Supplies organic and eco-friendly gardening products, including potting mixes, soil and natural fertilisers.

- **Biolytix** (www.biolytix.com): Sells domestic wastewater treatment and recycling systems that use no chemicals.

- **Daley's Fruit Tree Nursery** (www.daleysfruit.com.au): Sells native fruit trees and plants for your garden.

- **Eco Organics** (www.eco-organics.com.au): Sells composting products.

- **Elite Pool Covers** (www.poolcovers.com.au): Makes solar blankets and custom-made swimming pool covers.

- **Enviromower** (www.enviromower.com.au): Sells rechargeable and battery-operated lawnmowers and other gardening accessories.

- **Green Harvest** (www.greenharvest.com.au): Sells organic garden supplies, including vegetable seeds, gardening tools and pest-control products, as well as hand-powered food processing products.

- **Greentech Compost Shop** (www.greentech.com.au): Sells compost bins and worm farms — everything you need to make your compost work.

- **Lifestyleclotheslines** (www.lifestyleclotheslines.com): Deals in all types of clotheslines for naturally drying your clothes.

- **Native Seeds** (www.nativeseeds.com.au): Grows and sells Australian native grass seeds.

- **Nylex** (www.nylex.com.au): Sells garden water supply and greywater diversion systems.

- **One Stop Green Shop** (www.onestopgreenshop.com.au): Makes and sells worm farms and water-treatment systems.

- **Water Tube** (www.watertube.com.au): Sells self-watering kits for plants and gardens.

By the way, if you need a plumber, check out the GreenPlumbers site (www.greenplumber.com.au).

Part V
Working More Sustainably

Glenn Lumsden

'Here's that report on reducing
office paper consumption.'

In this part . . .

Making a profit has been the only consideration for many companies for decades, no matter what the consequences. No wonder the planet is just about out of natural resources!

But the times are a-changing. Whether you run one or work in one, you'll know that offices can do plenty to minimise their impact on the planet. The paperless office, the development of new energy-efficient office buildings and more flexible working arrangements are three examples of successful practices being adopted by the corporate world, but much more is on the horizon.

An increasing number of shining lights in the corporate world are now operating with a triple bottom-line philosophy. These responsible companies cost in the financial, social and environmental factors before making decisions.

Chapter 13

The Sustainable Workplace

1 magine arriving at work, relaxed after a stroll from the railway station, opening a window to let in fresh air and sunshine, then sitting down in the naturally lit room, surrounded by oxygen-breathing plants, for your first meeting. If that doesn't sound like your regular start to the day, you're not alone, but you can take heart that eco-friendly office buildings are now hot property, so to speak, and more and more office buildings are being renovated or constructed to be more eco-friendly.

Your work environment is important for your health, and an important component of your ecological footprint — the impact you have on the planet. According to the Australian Bureau of Statistics, more than 30 per cent of employees work longer than 50 hours per week. That means millions of people spend close to half their 24/7 getting ready for work, going to work, working, then getting home again. Because you spend so much time on the job, it's worthwhile thinking about how sustainable your workplace can be.

You may feel that you don't have much control over the way your workplace is run, but in this chapter I discuss ways that you can make a difference. First of all, I focus on the environmental problems in the workplace and their solutions, then I show you some ways that you can engage your company to implement changes. I also look at energy efficiency in commercial office buildings, plus working from home as a telecommuter — by setting up a home office and persuading your company to allow you to work remotely.

The Energy-Efficient Office Building

The challenges of using energy more efficiently at work are similar to those at home, as I discuss in Chapters 4 and 5. Of course, you probably have more influence over how your home is renovated and run than you do at your workplace. Later in this chapter, I outline how to audit the energy consumption and waste in your workplace, so that you can raise any concerns with your colleagues or managers.

Identifying problematic buildings

You may consider going to work every day a real drain. Well, that's nothing compared to the resources that your workplace may be draining from the planet. Consider these facts:

- Almost 9 per cent of all Australian greenhouse gas emissions are produced by the commercial property sector. This sector's rate of greenhouse gas emissions is growing faster than any other.

- Cooling, ventilation and heating systems contribute to the majority of greenhouse gas emissions generated by offices, largely because poor design results in the overuse of air-conditioning.

- Office buildings have an insatiable appetite for electricity. The main culprits are air-conditioning, lighting, computers, printers and photocopiers. Many companies leave electrical equipment (especially lights) switched on 24-hours-a-day, seven-days-a-week. If you don't believe me, take a look at a city skyline at night!

- Offices waste paper. Even though many offices use recycled paper, large amounts of paper waste still go to landfill sites (or into incinerators).

- Most furniture and fittings in offices are made from synthetic materials — chairs, computers, desks, carpets — which poison the air with volatile organic compounds (VOCs). (Refer to Chapter 3 for more details about volatile organic compounds.)

- Computers and other IT equipment contain many heavy metals and other toxins. Regularly upgrading this equipment creates a remarkable mountain of IT waste.

- Traffic congestion is at its worst during *peak hour*, when most people are trying to get to office buildings (or home again).

The good news is that not all offices are bad for your health and the environment. Eco-aware architects and developers have designed stunning workplaces and office buildings that deal with many of these problems. See the section 'Ratings in the workplace' later in this chapter for more details.

Designing for energy efficiency

The classic glass-skinned office block, with central lift wells and ventilation shafts, and windows that don't open, dominates most city skylines. These buildings are the most difficult to make energy efficient, and are gradually being replaced by new or refurbished office buildings.

Sustainable design standards are now in force across Australia, which apply to the construction or refurbishment of any office building. These standards ensure that new buildings are energy efficient and improve the overall sustainability of the commercial property.

One hurdle that property developers face when constructing new buildings is sourcing sustainable building materials. Steel and concrete have high levels of embodied energy, which means that these products use a lot of energy to manufacture (refer to Chapter 3 for more information about embodied energy in building materials). One way property developers can reduce the environmental impact of these materials is to design and construct high-quality buildings that can last a long time.

Another aspect of building or refurbishing an office block is the internal design. The latest standards strive to ensure that office buildings

- ✔ Use recycled products and materials that have low levels of embodied energy.
- ✔ Capture natural light to reduce the need for strong artificial lighting.
- ✔ Employ good ventilation, insulation and shading to allow air-conditioning to operate only when the weather is extreme and the building is fully occupied.
- ✔ Utilise renewable sources of energy, such as solar power, generated by the building itself, as well as sourced from the power grid.
- ✔ Use energy-efficient appliances and equipment.

These types of design elements made Lend Lease's The Bond building in Hickson Road, Sydney (completed in 2004), the first five-star-rated building in Australia. The five-star design features of The Bond building include:

✔ An innovative manual shading system that protects offices from the afternoon summer sun but captures the warmth of the winter sun.

✔ Naturally ventilated and lit sunrooms that reduce the electricity consumed by air-conditioning and lighting, and make the rooms pleasant environments to work in.

✔ External, covered terraces, which can be used for meetings and social occasions in all but extreme weather.

✔ Chilled water running through beams in the ceiling, which carry away the heat generated within the office. This greatly reduces the artificial cooling and heating required.

✔ A roof-top garden with a rainwater irrigation system. This provides a pleasant outdoor environment and helps reduce unwanted heat from the sun.

Ratings in the workplace

Three rating systems in Australia encourage the sustainable construction and operation of workplaces.

✔ **The Australian Building Greenhouse Rating Scheme (ABGRS):** This scheme rates each building on its energy efficiency and greenhouse gas emissions. This rating is used by real estate agents as a major selling point to attract new tenants. To find out more, check the organisation's Web site at www.abgr.com.au.

Buildings rated five-star by the AGBRS employ the principles outlined in the preceding section 'Designing for energy efficiency'.

✔ **The National Australian Built Environment Rating System (NABERS):** This rating system measures the overall environmental performance of a building that's occupied.

The NABERS rating system (www.nabers.com.au) assesses not only energy efficiency but other factors, such as the amount and type of refrigerants used in cooling systems, water usage, stormwater run-off, sewage disposal, landscape diversity, transport patterns, indoor air quality, occupant satisfaction and waste-disposal systems.

✔ **The Green Star Environmental Rating System:** The Green Star rating system combines elements of both the ABGR and NABERS rating systems. This new, voluntary national rating system developed by the Green Building Council of Australia (www.gbcaus.org) evaluates the environmental initiatives of projects based on eight environmental impact categories: Management, energy efficiency, water efficiency, indoor environment quality, transport, material selection, land use and ecology, and emissions.

The Green Star system also rates buildings up to six stars, which is one way to convince buildings to register with its rating system — six stars are better than five! Buildings that achieve a six-star rating, such as the new Council House 2 building in Melbourne (the first six-star-rated office designed in Australia) and 40 Albert Road in South Melbourne, are rated world leaders in sustainable design.

Convincing your company to change its ways

You may have no direct control over the design and management of the building in which you work. So how on earth can you make it more efficient?

Armed with a checklist, you can pick up whether a building is energy efficient (within the limits of its design). And by taking this checklist to your office or building manager to discuss where you think energy is being wasted, you may end up saving your company a heap of money on energy bills.

You can develop your own checklist by starting with the following questions:

✔ Are the air-conditioners, lights and electrical office equipment on when the first person gets to work? (You'll have to be the first to work one day, to find out!) If so, there's a good chance that everything has been left on all night.

✔ Are the electrical appliances in the kitchen or production areas rated highly for energy efficiency?

✔ Are the computers, printers and photocopiers Energy Star-equipped? (Refer to Chapter 4 for more about the Energy Star rating.)

✔ Are there blinds or curtains or outdoor shades on the windows and, if so, do they have much effect on the temperature or the amount of light in the office?

✔ Is anyone using an electric fan to better circulate air in their part of the office? If so, the air-conditioning is faulty and wasting energy.

✔ Are employees regularly ill? If so, the building's air circulation may be poor.

Don't be afraid to present your checklist to one of your managers. Companies are willing to address these types of issues because they know that by doing so, they achieve savings in energy costs and greater productivity from their staff. If you need help in persuading them, download information about energy-efficient buildings from the Web or show them this chapter.

Refurbishing an old building for energy efficiency

Retrofitting old buildings to become energy efficient is a growth industry. Many companies care about energy consumption because managers, staff and shareholders are concerned about climate change, and because saving energy also saves the company money.

Managers or owners of office buildings can achieve a high Green Star rating by doing the following:

- Outfitting the office with highly-rated, energy-efficient appliances and Energy Smart computers and audio-visual equipment (refer to Chapter 4 for more about energy-efficient appliances and computers).

- Ensuring that the building's air-conditioning system is regularly maintained and has timers fitted, so that it's used only when people are in the office.

- Installing water-saving taps and showerheads in the kitchens and bathrooms, as well as dual-flush toilets in the bathrooms.

- Installing sensors that turn on lights only when people are in the office.

- Setting up an easy-to-use waste recycling system, especially for reusing paper (for more information about paper, see the section 'Going Paperless' later in this chapter).

- Changing the fluorescent lighting to a more modern energy-saving type of globe. For example, T-12 lamps are less efficient than the smaller T-8 and even T-5 lamps.

- Installing bike parking and showering facilities to encourage staff to cycle and walk to work.

- Installing screens and shutters on windows to block out direct sun during summer and let sunlight in during winter — this measure enables the air-conditioning to operate effectively at a lower setting.

- Investing in furniture and fittings made from natural or recycled materials, and painting the office with non-toxic paints.

The Melbourne Central Tower in Elizabeth Street, Melbourne, is a shining example of applied thinking to save energy and money. Originally built in 1991, the Central Tower is a 52-storey building that was rated two stars by the ABGRS. As it turned out, though, the building was originally designed to achieve a much higher rating, but was not being run to take advantage of its design features.

An investigation showed that the air-conditioning was running 24-hours-a-day and, during summer, was permanently set to cope with outside temperatures of 40-degrees Celsius. Addressing this simple management oversight resulted in an instant upgrade to a three-star rating and massive savings in energy consumption and the tenant's energy bill.

The Australian Energy Performance Contracting Association (AEPCA) represents a growing number of contractors who perform energy-efficient audits on buildings, and can advise companies how to improve their energy performance. For a list of contractors and government agencies who perform these audits, visit www.aepca.asn.au.

Going Paperless

Back in the 1970s, everyone got excited about technology delivering the 'office of the future' and using less paper. By the 1990s, most companies were still no closer to the paperless office, although hope was rekindled with the introduction of the Internet and email.

Despite such hopes, paper still seems to be everywhere you turn — sitting on the printer, being bound into reports, stored in filing cabinets, scattered on desks, overflowing from recycling bins or being stacked in readiness at the shredder. The more information technology businesses employ, the more demand there seems to be for paper.

For a variety of reasons, people prefer paper. Many people argue that paper is still popular because it's easier to read something on a page than on the screen of a computer, portable organiser or mobile phone. People who read newspapers, for example, tell me they don't like reading the same paper on the Internet — it's just not the same.

Many people print off a report for review, so they can mark it up with a pen. Important emails are printed off and filed as a permanent record. And it's often easier to get something signed by a manager if you leave a printed copy on the manager's desk.

The decline in paper use may not be too far away, though. Since 2004, for example, sales of plain white office paper in the United States have dropped by about half a per cent each year, despite a growing economy, according to InfoTrends/CAP Ventures, a market research firm in the United States. I'm not surprised that the paperless office has been so slow in coming, however. A new generation of workers is often required to integrate new technology into existing work habits.

Defining steps on the path to a paperless future

Computer technology can be used to record and manage information in place of paper-based systems. Reducing your reliance on paper contributes to a sustainable future because paper is produced from a declining natural resource — trees. And, of course, a lot of paper ends up as waste and isn't recycled. (Check out Chapter 3 to find out more about timber resources, and look into Chapter 8 for paper recycling techniques.)

Computer giants, such as Microsoft, enthusiastically promote the concept of the paperless office — less paper means more investment in Microsoft products, right? To provide examples, Microsoft lists on its Web site companies and agencies that have successfully converted to paperless offices. These include the Victorian Department of Education, Employment and Training; the Queensland Department of Public Works; and Goulburn Valley Water in Victoria. Other technology companies that sell paperless solutions also publish case studies about businesses that use their products instead of paper-based systems. Similarly, computer magazines and the IT sections in newspapers regularly run stories about businesses that are putting technology to work to reduce their paper overheads.

For more information about the hardware and software solutions that offices can adopt to reduce paper in the workplace, see the section 'Getting off the paper treadmill (upgrading your IT systems)' later in this chapter.

The IT system I use in my paperless office

I run a home office that's as close to paperless as I think I can get — my printer has been pushed to the back of the desk along with all those diskettes I don't use any more. Here's how I work electronically:

- ✔ I email all my consulting reports in *pdf* (published document format) created using Adobe Acrobat software.
- ✔ The content for this book was typed in Microsoft Word and emailed to my editor and publisher, who provided comments by typing them in the document itself and emailing it back.
- ✔ I carry a Pocket PC with me to meetings, which contains my diary and other valuable information.
- ✔ I take notes in meetings using my Pocket PC.
- ✔ My invoices are sent via email.
- ✔ I encourage my clients to pay electronically.

✔ My accounting is maintained in Microsoft Excel.

✔ All my correspondence is sent via email.

The main paperwork that I handle is bills — which makes them easy to ignore. Only a small number of companies currently offer an electronic billing service, even though the major banks make it possible to integrate electronic bills into online banking.

The software I use each day to achieve this reduction in paper is Microsoft's Office Suite, which bundles Outlook, Word, Excel and Powerpoint software. (Some people use the Open Source equivalent, called Open Office.) The other part of the equation is the Adobe Acrobat software, which enables me to publish professional-looking documents in an easy-to-read format. This means I hardly ever have to use my printer. In fact, reading documents in *pdf* format overcomes some of the issues people have about reading stuff on a computer screen — it presents information onscreen in a format that looks similar to a newspaper or published report.

Getting off the paper treadmill (upgrading your IT systems)

Most offices are larger and more complex than mine, in which case they require additional hardware and software to reduce their paper overheads. Here's a list of the most common tools used in place of paper:

✔ **Email and Internet access — these days, a necessity.** Recent advances in technology enable email to be combined with fax, text messages and voice mail.

✔ **Portable devices, including mobile PCs, laptops and handheld computers.** These are great for carrying documents to read and work on away from the office, and for recording sales, or collecting data, in the field.

✔ **Scanners.** These devices make it easy to bring handwritten or printed documents into a computer so they can be exchanged electronically and copied into reports.

✔ **Online storage systems.** These centralise and organise information so it can be easily searched and accessed by everyone in the company.

✔ **Secure, remote access to the company network.** A *network* links many computers together so they can share information. This allows staff to log in and work from home (or the other side of the world) without lugging about a heap of documents.

✔ **Duplex printers (that can print on both sides of a sheet).** These reduce paper use even further when documents really must be printed.

Telecommuting Instead of Polluting

Do you hate the daily commute in traffic but don't want to give up that well-paid job? Maybe your workplace offers telecommuting?

Telecommuting is working from home via a connection to the office computer network using the Internet or some other system. This reduces the need to 'commute' or travel to work. (Telecommuting is also called teleworking.) Companies usually prefer employees to telecommute on a part-time basis; that way, employees still work in the office at least one or two days a week.

The upside of telecommuting

Here are reasons why employers like telecommuting and allow some employees to work from home:

- ✔ **Reduced costs.** An employer can reduce the number of desks, the size of the office, the amount of stationery, and the amount of parking required if a number of staff telecommute several days a week.

- ✔ **Increased productivity.** Employees working at home can concentrate on a specific task rather than answer phone calls and get distracted by other staff at the workplace.

- ✔ **The feel-good factor.** Telecommuting can build trust between management and staff. By offering staff a choice, and allowing them to work unsupervised, companies can earn the loyalty of their employees. In some cases, telecommuting forms an attractive part of a salary package.

Employees take to telecommuting for a range of reasons, too:

- ✔ **Less travelling.** Telecommuting eliminates travelling time; you don't have to commute to the office. If you normally travel to work by car, telecommuting enables you to help reduce greenhouse gas emissions.

- ✔ **Telecommuting is family-friendly.** Families gain more time to spend together. Even though you have to concentrate when working from home, you can still interact with your family — in the same way you interact socially with your colleagues at the office.

- ✔ **Homes are pleasant environments.** You probably enjoy being at home more than work. Your home is set out just the way you like it.

- ✔ **Flexibility.** Employees who need to spend time at home, for example, to care for family members, can do so without giving up work.

Telecommuting is great for the environment because it reduces the number of peak-hour travellers, and could ease some of the peak-hour traffic congestion and air pollution produced by cars.

At the community level, telecommuting allows people with specific family commitments or individual needs to still access work opportunities. For example, primary caregivers of children and other family members, as well as the physically disabled, can participate more effectively within the workforce. People working from home also spend more money in their community, creating stronger local commerce and diversifying the economy in the region.

As a one-off policy initiative, telecommuting has not yet substantially reduced travel or car trips. Telecommuting needs to be implemented as part of a package of measures to encourage increased public transport, plus walking and cycling to have this effect. For example, workplace travel plans for employees can include not only telecommuting agreements, but also financial incentives to use public transport, car share, and other methods to reduce the amount of people driving cars to work. (For more information about workplace travel plans, see Chapter 15.)

If the shoe fits . . .

Some jobs and some people are simply not suited to telecommuting. Many jobs require face-to-face contact, and some people don't have the discipline and personality to be as productive at home as they would be in a supervised office.

Telecommuting works only if it suits the job, the employee and the organisation, and if all the practical issues are carefully planned. As a result, the proportion of the workforce that can telecommute is lower than many people would hope.

The most suitable candidates for telecommuting are those employees who produce self-contained pieces of work — for example, project work, policy analysis, research, planning and writing.

Setting up a telecommuting office

To telecommute, you need a practical work area. Better yet, set up a home office. Here are some guidelines:

- ✔ **Computing equipment.** Although not essential in some jobs, working from home is much easier when your computer is set up to access files and documents on the company's network, exactly the same way you do when you're at work. For example, get a high-speed Internet connection and run the same software at home that's used at work. You may need someone from your company's IT department to set up your computer to do this. If you can't take your computer to work, an IT person may need to visit your home.

- ✔ **Workspace.** You need to be able to effectively separate your home and work life. A room, dedicated to work, with a desk, an ergonomic chair, good lighting, no outside distractions and space for office equipment (like a phone, fax and scanner) are the minimum requirements.

  An understanding and communication system (such as a 'Working' sign on your home office door) with any family members or housemates who are also at home with you during work hours is also critical. They need to know when it's okay to interrupt and when it isn't.

- ✔ **Telecommuting agreement.** This type of agreement avoids misunderstandings and the trouble they can cause. The agreement can set out whether you have a set working time, whether you need to log on and off the network at certain times, and at what times you must communicate with the office. Also, make sure you establish whether you can claim office expenses (computer and printing costs, paper, coffee and so on). Some companies prefer to formalise these considerations in a special document (preferably online without printing to paper!).

Chapter 14

Responsible Industry Is Profitable Industry

- -

In This Chapter

▶ Investing and trading with ethical companies

▶ Getting to grips with triple bottom-line reporting

▶ Acknowledging those corporations that are changing their ways

- -

*P*ublic distrust of multinational corporations is widespread. Many people believe that global corporations are destroying the planet for short-term profit. What can you do about it? This chapter shows you how you can influence companies to become more sustainable.

You help create a sustainable future for the planet when you're careful about what you buy, and how you use energy and water at home. Although it takes a lot of consumers to sway a multinational corporation, when you start influencing a company's bottom line, they do listen.

On the other hand, if you're investing money, building a new home, or running your own business, you can directly implement or influence sustainable business practices. The best thing about getting involved at this level of the sustainable movement is that you meet lots of genuine people — all working hard to make the world a better place. It's rewarding to do business with people who have the same goals as you.

Some companies now report their environmental and social impacts. These businesses have adopted sustainable business practices because they understand that it can guarantee their long-term profitability. In this chapter, I explain how to invest in sustainable funds, and differentiate between companies that are truly sustainable, and those that are simply window-dressing.

The Business of Sustainable Investment

Put your money where your heart is. If you want to look after the planet, invest your money in sustainable companies. But if you're not an investment expert, you need to ask an investment funds manager, or broker, to invest your money for you.

Sustainable investment funds act like any other funds manager; the big difference is that they invest in companies making efforts to be sustainable. They invest your money in a variety of companies, take economic indicators into account, and manage the risks to make your money grow as much and as safely as possible.

Some companies let you control your investment by choosing between a variety of criteria, so that you're supporting the principles that you believe are most important. For example, you may think fair trade principles are more important than organic farming practices. Or maybe you want a stake in reducing greenhouse gases in the environment.

Sustainable investment funds — which you may have also read about in the financial pages of newspapers — are called *Socially Responsible Investment* (SRI) funds. These funds are now offered by mainstream financial companies such as Westpac, AMP and ING. Superannuation funds are also practising sustainable investment. For example, the Health and Community Services Super fund, HESTA, is the first fund in Australia to offer SRI options.

What gets me excited about SRI funds is that investments in sustainable companies are showing good returns. And this is the reason that major corporations and financial institutions are getting involved.

You can invest in one of three different types of SRI funds. These are:

✔ **Screened portfolios.** The investment company assesses all available stocks against socially responsible criteria. Some companies enable you to select which criteria are most important to you, then they tell you which SRI stocks meet your criteria. Your investment is then spread over a portfolio of various SRI stocks.

✔ **Shareholder actions.** You (as a shareholder) seek out a company that's prepared to work with you, and the other shareholders, on developing agreed socially responsible criteria. Once engaged — the process is also called responsible engagement — the shareholders monitor and work with the company to ensure compliance and to fine-tune the criteria.

> **Cause-based or community investment funds.** This approach involves finding yourself a company that addresses a certain environmental or community issue. The company may specialise in sustainable agriculture, aquaculture and forestry, or affordable housing projects and community facility development. You then invest directly in the company.

It's not difficult to understand why screened portfolios are the most popular of the three options; all the work is done by your investment company and the risk is spread across a portfolio.

Don't forget that when you invest in a screened portfolio, you give the ultimate decision on where your money goes to the investment company. Sure, you may know the criteria for the investment but, to maximise your financial return and to reduce your risk, the investment company will spread your investment across as many funds as possible. Companies may slip into your investment portfolio that you would not personally choose or endorse. So, you need to decide whether to live with the imperfections in your funds manager or, alternatively, go it alone and do all the investment work yourself.

The Ethical Investment Association (EIA) of Australia offers two mechanisms to help you identify companies that may handle your money in ways that do not suit you. A document must be prepared by all investment companies called the *Product Disclosure Statement*, which describes the way investments are selected, retained and sold. The EIA suggests you read this document very carefully.

The EIA also introduced a new labelling system in 2005 to help you identify whether a fund is truly an SRI fund. Of course, that is according to EIA's criteria, which the organisation says takes into consideration labour standards, environmental impacts, social impacts and ethical viewpoints. However, this doesn't automatically give you specific details about the companies you're investing in when you select an SRI fund, so you still need to do your research before you proceed.

To check out the SRI label, go to the EIA's Web site at www.eia.org.au. To research sustainable companies, follow the links to the list of member financial advisers, managed funds and superannuation funds.

I also list some SRI-endorsed companies in Table 14-1, selecting those that provide easy-to-access information. Note that the Bendigo Bank is the manager of Oxfam's Ethical Investment Trust portfolio.

Table 14-1	Companies with Ethical Investment Credentials
Company	*Web Address*
AMP Socially Responsible Investments	www.ampcapital.com.au/advisers/multimanager/ril/ril_funds.asp
Ausbil Dexia Australia	www.ausbil.com.au/products/dexia-sustainable-global-equity-fund.asp
Australian Ethical Investment	www.austethical.com.au
Bendigo Bank	www.bendigobank.com.au/public/community/ethical_investment_fund.asp
BT Financial Group	www.westpac.com.au/internet/publish.nsf/Content/CBIV+Socially+responsible+investments
CVC Sustainable Investments	www.cvc.com.au/sustainable/sustainable_investments.html
Ethinvest	www.ethinvest.com.au
Forester's ANA	www.forestersana.com.au
Grameen Foundation Australia	www.grameen.org.au
Hunter Hall	www.hunterhall.com.au
Perennial Investment Partners	www.perennial.net.au/inves.asp
Sustainable Asset Management Group	www.sam-group.com/htmle/australia/products.cfm
Sustain Tech	www.sustaintech.com.au

The Triple Bottom Line: Everybody Profits

For many, the term 'economic growth' conjures images of exploitation, destruction of natural resources, greed and manipulation. Gordon Gekko, in the movie *Wall Street*, portrayed this approach to business, crystallised in the line, 'Greed is good'. Now there's a new mantra for achieving profitability and longevity: 'Green is good!'

To measure business activities that don't exploit the environment, companies use a financial approach called *triple bottom-line reporting*. This new catch phrase is derived from the term *bottom line*, which refers to the profit left over after all expenses have been deducted from the income. This line is always at the bottom of financial reports. The emphasis that companies place on the bottom line suggests that there's only one thing to consider when making a decision: What impact will the decision have on profit?

In triple bottom-line reporting, environmental and social profits and losses are also calculated and included on the company's financial statements. The lines reporting on environmental and social profits are negative if the overall activity of the company has had a negative sustainability impact. A paper mill that consumes timber from old growth forests, for example, would have to measure and report on the environmental cost of destroying the forest.

Traditional accounting treats any costs that don't affect profit as 'external' — they're defined as somebody else's problem. A triple bottom-line report makes it obvious if a company is exploiting a community or the environment to cut costs and make more money for its shareholders. To get its triple bottom-line position 'in the black', a company has to show an investment in the environmental and social lines, as well as in the financial one.

Measuring the benefits

If you're preparing a triple bottom-line report, you need to be able to measure the impact you have on the community and the environment. The easiest way to measure the environmental cost, or social cost, is to calculate how much it costs the community to resolve the impact. Money invested by the company that results in a positive effect shows up as an environmental or social benefit.

For example, a logging company needs to factor in an environmental cost for chopping down an existing forest, but can offset this 'debit' with an environmental benefit if the company also plants trees in previously deforested areas.

Social benefits may not seem directly related to environmental benefits, but the two are closely tied. Companies who help sustain local communities are helping promote a generally sustainable social structure. Here are some activities that can be considered social benefits:

- New local employment opportunities that the company has created.
- Employment opportunities provided to segments of the community that are considered disadvantaged.
- Contributions the company has made to a healthy workplace.
- Investment the company has made in employee training, education, mentorship and other professional development activities.
- Contributions the company has made to the local community (for example, funding community health-care or child-care facilities, community events, or youth groups).
- The savings that accrue in the community by reducing a negative impact of the company's products on the health and safety of people.
- The support the company provides to encourage sustainable activities in the workplace and community (for example, subsidising public transport fares or providing recycling facilities).

Similarly, here are activities that a company can chalk up as environmental benefits:

- Reductions in pollution from choosing materials with low waste and emission components.
- Investments that minimise the company's greenhouse gas emissions.
- Savings to resource use derived from manufacturing products that can be recycled after use.
- Energy and greenhouse gas savings made by manufacturing products that require low levels of energy.
- Savings in indirect energy costs related to transport (fuel) and packaging (manufacturing plastics).
- Benefits to the environment from choosing to operate in locations that have minimal impacts on natural ecosystems.
- Energy savings from creating an energy-efficient workplace.
- Savings from reducing the amount of water used in production and operations.
- Subsidies for staff travel on public transport, walking and cycling (to reduce car travel).

As you can imagine, the rules for performing triple bottom-line calculations are the subject of fierce debate. But the United Nations (UN) has done a lot of work on triple bottom-line reporting and developed guidelines to help companies around the world to apply them. These guidelines include standard rates of measurement, which companies can use to calculate the financial cost of their environmental and social impacts. For more details, go to the UN supported Global Reporting Initiative Web site at www.globalreporting.org.

Greenwashing: Being seen to be sustainable

Many companies sell sustainable products that easily meet triple bottom-line objectives. Wind and solar energy companies, or fair trade food distributors, are typical examples. These companies show profits in the environmental and social bottom lines because their products clearly have a positive impact.

An increasing number of mining, oil and car manufacturing companies are embracing triple bottom-line reporting. Big multinationals like BP, Shell and BHP Billiton, for example, now report their (quite large) investments in sustainable energy. Similarly, car companies such as Toyota and Honda are keen to promote their alternative fuel-powered motoring alternatives.

But does triple bottom-line reporting mean that companies are becoming more sustainable? Perhaps they *are* worried about the decline of fossil fuel reserves or they're reacting to consumer concerns about fossil fuels. Or maybe they want to be seen to be investing in things such as land rehabilitation programs or community building projects to offset the negativity surrounding their mining businesses.

This exercise of boasting about green credentials without making a serious commitment to becoming a sustainable business is called *greenwashing*. Corporations that deserve this term spend a lot of money promoting their sustainable credentials without changing their basically unsustainable business operations one little bit.

Another problem with greenwashing is that companies can be honest but remain uncommitted. No penalties apply to a company that keeps on reporting a triple bottom-line loss but makes a bottom-line profit. The honesty displayed may be admirable but, if nothing is done to improve the environmental and social benefits, such reporting could be perceived as a hollow marketing exercise.

In the long run, though, I think triple bottom-line reporting is a good thing, even if the company greenwashes its position. Whatever their reason for reporting this way, these companies are taking a step in the right direction. Over time, the reporting will translate into real environmental and social benefits and, hopefully, companies will start to value the positive contribution they make to the community and environment as a result of measuring it. Thankfully, many major companies put their money where their mouth is and don't greenwash at all.

Checking out company report cards

If you can cope with the massive amount of detail in company reports, you can gain a much deeper understanding of how sustainability reporting works.

The following Australian companies received awards from the Association of Chartered Certified Accountants (www.acca.co.uk) for the best sustainability reporting in Australia and New Zealand for 2005:

- ✔ **Members and Education Credit Union** (www.mecu.com.au): A market leader in financial services. This company's report emphasises its role in community and social services.

- ✔ **Australian Ethical Investments** (www.austethical.com.au): Reports comprehensively, displaying trends in environmental impacts. See the section 'Leading the way from downunder' later in this chapter for more details.

- ✔ **BHP Billiton** (http://sustainability.bhpbilliton.com): Very good at providing publicly accessible reporting via the Internet, with transparent warts-and-all information regarding performance. Case studies are provided.

Turning Business Around (Well, Sort of)

Don't forget that multinational corporations are more likely to get in on the sustainability act if doing so improves their bottom line. Well, the stats are starting to suggest that it does.

In his 1999 book, *Cool Companies* (published by Island Press), Joseph Romm provided figures showing that environmentally proactive companies performed better than environmentally inactive ones. The proactive companies returned 4 per cent more money to investors, sales increased by 9 per cent more, and their cash holdings grew 17 per cent faster.

Being sustainable can positively impact the good, old-fashioned bottom line as well as the triple bottom line.

The global advocacy group, Business for Social Responsibility (BSR, online at www.bsr.org), agrees with these principles. BSR reports that several benefits flow to responsible companies. These include:

- ✔ Attracting investors and financiers who support their long-term plans.
- ✔ Greater productivity and, in many cases, greater profits.
- ✔ Attracting customers who support their principles.
- ✔ Enhanced integrity, image and market share.
- ✔ Reduced costs — not just energy and waste costs, but legal and regulatory costs as well.
- ✔ A positive attitude by staff that spurs innovation and proactive decision-making within the company.

It can be difficult measuring the good work that a company does. Triple bottom-line reporting goes some way but, some companies cheat, as explained in the section 'Greenwashing: Being seen to be sustainable' earlier in this chapter. The trick is to figure out which companies actually make a genuine effort.

Two popular rating systems (some people reckon they should be called greenwash ratings) can help measure corporate commitment to a sustainable future. These are the Global 100 Most Sustainable Corporations in the World list (see the following section for more details) and the 100 Best Corporate Citizens list. You can find out more about the 100 Best Corporate Citizens list online by visiting the Business Ethics Magazine Web site at www.business-ethics.com/whats_new/100best.html.

The Global 100 Most Sustainable Corporations

The Global 100 Most Sustainable Corporations in the World list is developed yearly by Canadian company Corporate Knights. Announced at the annual World Economic Forum — also known as the Davos summit — the Global 100 list is considered highly credible by financial commentators.

Environmentalists are less impressed, pointing out that most companies on the list are also involved in unsustainable industries (such as some companies in the textile and clothing industries that are also listed by The Clean Clothes Campaign as companies that compromise fair trade principles).

REAL-LIFE STORY

From mean to green

A widely publicised big business that totally restructured itself to become truly sustainable is the American floor-covering company Interface.

Interface claims to be the largest commercial carpet manufacturer in the world. It started in 1973 and, until the mid-1990s, produced carpet like any other carpet manufacturer — converting petrochemicals into textiles. By 1993, it produced over one million kilograms of synthetic carpet and fabric every day in 26 factories around the world. You can only begin to imagine how many pollutants and waste products that created, not to mention the amount of non-renewable resources consumed to make the carpets.

In 1994, though, company president Ray Anderson had an epiphany. He realised that most companies *pillage*: they consume resources as fast and as cheaply as possible, for private gain. He decided his company could be different and developed a concept that he called *industrial ecology* — outlined on Interface's Web site at www.interfaceinc.com. Ray's grand plan encompasses the following vision:

⤳ Eliminate waste.

⤳ Eliminate negative or toxic waste emissions.

⤳ Use renewable energy by substituting existing non-renewable resources with renewable sources.

⤳ Redesign processes and products to create cyclical material flows (reusing and recycling).

⤳ Use resource-efficient transportation to reduce traditional means of transporting products. This includes plant location, logistics, information technology, video-conferencing, email and telecommuting.

⤳ Create a community within and around Interface that understands the functioning of natural systems and their impact on them.

⤳ Influence and redefine commerce to focus on the delivery of service and value instead of the delivery of material.

Although the company admits that it has a long way to go before it reaches these lofty ambitions, Interface has put processes in place to achieve them as fast as practical. The following changes show that the company is making a genuine effort and real progress:

⤳ The company has introduced a range of carpets and tiles made from biodegradable and recycled materials. The percentage of recycled or bio-based content in products has increased from 0.5 per cent in 1996 to 15.9 per cent in 2005.

⤳ Interface has reduced its waste to such an extent that the company has saved US$299 million. Total manufacturing waste diverted from landfills has decreased by 63 per cent since 1996, with recycling and converting waste to energy both reducing overall waste.

⤳ Total energy used at Interface factories is down 41 per cent since 1996 through better management of existing non-renewable power sources and increase in renewable power sources.

⤳ Greenhouse gas emissions have been reduced by 35 per cent due to improved efficiency and direct renewable energy purchases. (The company's emissions have always been low in Europe, where it had always purchased power from green sources.)

⤳ Water intake per square metre of carpet is down 81 per cent in modular carpet facilities, due to changes in the production process that use water more efficiently.

⤳ The company has made substantial increases in workforce and local community program funding.

The other problem is that only huge corporations make the list — selected from the Morgan Stanley Capital International (MSCI) Index — which means they're heavily involved in activities that make money by consuming resources that are not replaced. Many far more sustainable companies, by their relatively small size, simply cannot make it onto the Global 100 list.

So who's on this controversial list? To find out, go to the Global 100 Web site at www.global100.org. On this Web site you can also find details about the Innovest methodology used to calculate the top 100. By the way, two Australian-owned companies make the list: IAG insurance and Westpac.

Here's an idea. Use the Global 100 list to select corporations when you need to buy global products, such as fuel. For all your other commercial transactions, focus on smaller companies dedicated to creating a better world.

Leading the way from downunder

The annual Australian Sustainability Awards identifies leading sustainable companies and not-for-profit organisations covering different aspects of sustainability. Organised by the Ethical Investor journal (www.ethicalinvestor.com.au), these awards, like the SRI labelling system I referred to earlier in this chapter, don't make clear all the criteria used to measure who wins. However, the Ethical Investor journal looks for companies and organisations that show 'excellence in sustainability across the environmental, social and corporate governance spheres'.

The winners of the Australian Sustainability Awards in 2005 were:

- ✔ **Sustainable Company of the Year:** Westpac Banking Group (www.westpac.com) for social and community enhancement within the company.

- ✔ **Sustainable Small Company of the Year:** Geodynamics (www.geodynamics.com.au), a producer of geothermal energy, considered to be an alternative fuel that produces no greenhouse gases.

- ✔ **Merit Award for Environment:** Origin Energy (www.originenergy.com.au), supplier of power from green sources.

- ✔ **Merit Award for Community/Social Services:** Bendigo Bank (www.bendigobank.com.au) for its commitment to regional communities.

- ✔ **Merit Award for Corporate Governance:** Insurance Australia Group (www.iag.com.au) for equitable management.

Other nominated companies included So Natural Foods, BHP Billiton, Woodside Petroleum, David Jones, Healthscope, Pharmaxis, Macquarie Office Trust, CO2 Australia, Wesfarmers, CSL, Oxiana, AGL, GRD, Investa Property Group, Ramsey Health Care, ANZ Banking Group, Crane Group, McPhersons, Flight Centre and Waste Management NZ.

Part VI
Travelling the Sustainable Way

Glenn Lumsden

'He gave up the company limo for the sake of the environment, but he couldn't completely give up the status.'

In this part . . .

The earth is choking, thanks to the increase in motor vehicle use over the last 50 years. Cars are a major contributor to the drying up of fossil fuel supplies, the degradation of air quality, global warming and increasing obesity within the population. Your choice of transport can't be underestimated.

Unfortunately, urban areas have developed in a way that makes it difficult to get around without a car. You do have options, though, such as using public transport services, riding a bike or just simply walking. And even if you need to drive, you can still share a lift with other people. All these actions have the positive impact of reducing the amount of cars on the road.

This part also shows you the innovations being made in developing alternative fuel cars. These new greener cars should eventually improve air quality and reduce greenhouse gas emissions, not to mention taking pressure off fossil fuel supplies.

Finally, I take you on a different type of trip that doesn't include a car — the eco-holiday. I help you develop an itinerary so that, as a tourist, you'll make a minimal environmental and social impact on the places you visit. I finish by naming my pick of the best eco-tourism places and those companies that have sustainability in mind when catering to your holiday needs.

Chapter 15

Wheels, Pedals and Heels: Getting Around

*W*hen I was growing up, I dreamed of the day I would own my first car. A car that would give me the independence I yearned for — to visit friends or new places, or to just get away from it all. Other kids wanted a brand spanking new set of wheels to turn heads and to show people that they were as cool and important as the next person. Looking back, not too many of my friends grew up craving to catch the bus or train, or planned to upgrade their push bikes. At the time, neither did I.

Cars provided independence and status, and they've had as much influence on the style and development of our urban areas as the dream to live in a large house with plenty of space. Cars gave people the freedom to live in nice homes in new suburbs, far from jobs, shops, schools, friends — even families.

Unfortunately, urban sprawl and high car use go hand in hand. Cities and large towns have *evolved* into large, poorly serviced urban areas because people can travel far and wide in their cars. But high levels of car use have become synonymous with other unsustainable characteristics: Air pollution, traffic jams, road accidents, reduced health and fitness, and poor public transport access.

So what gives? Can you maintain your travelling freedom by owning and using a car, and do something about living more sustainably? The answer is yes, if you're willing to balance your car use with other forms of transport. This chapter shows you how, by looking at the impact cars have on the environment, and explains some of the more sustainable transport options that you can use to get through your day.

The Benefits of Relying Less on Your Car

You may be wondering how you can reduce your driving time. Whether you live in an urban or rural area, you probably rely on a car to get to work, go shopping, or to drop off the kids at school or childcare. But do you need to use your car for every trip, every day?

If fewer cars were on the road and more people used other transport options, our cities and towns would be much more 'liveable'. Imagine places with less roads and more green spaces, better air quality with subsequent reductions in diseases like asthma, fewer traffic accidents and safer walking spaces. Sounds great, doesn't it?

Before I talk more about using a car less often to benefit the environment and your health, have a think about different ways you could get around without reaching for your car keys.

Here are some practical methods to consider:

- ✔ **Leave your car at home for a day.** Use your car to drive to work only four times a week rather than every day of the week — consider using public transport instead.

- ✔ **Share a lift.** Reduce the amount of time you drive alone by organising to drive to and from work with a workmate. (For more on this topic, see 'Sharing the driving — and the car' later in this chapter.)

- ✔ **Free up some space in the garage.** Sell the second family car and organise to share the driving with other family members.

- ✔ **Telecommute.** Ask your workplace whether you could work from home one day a week.

- ✔ **Plan your travel.** If you drive to the shops, consolidate your shopping into one big trip rather than lots of smaller trips.

I don't own a car, and my wife and I agree that selling our vehicle years ago was the best thing we ever did. Working as an urban planner specialising in the development of sustainable transport policies, I realised that if I wanted to be taken seriously, I couldn't turn up to meetings and events in a car.

I needed to practise what I preach. At first, my wife was not so sure; she was used to the idea of driving everywhere in a car. We carefully considered our choices.

We moved to the centre of Sydney and these days travel by train, bus or taxi. The rest of the time, we walk. Where we live is the key: We're close to train lines and bus routes that travel all over Sydney, and walk to shops and restaurants only a stone's throw away. Our stress levels are less, we get to work on time, and we're relaxed — maybe too relaxed. Over the years, we've saved a lot of money, once put aside to run the car.

Owning a car costs a small fortune. You can lose thousands on the value of your vehicle over time and fork out hundreds of dollars each year for registration, insurance and maintenance. At the very least, driving less reduces your weekly fuel bill, as well as wear and tear on your vehicle. For a reality check, see Figure 15-1 and work out how much you're spending on one car each year (and imagine how much families with two or more cars would save!). The costs I quote in this table are the lowest and highest average costs worked out by the NRMA in New South Wales (go to www.mynrma.com.au/ operating_costs.asp for more details).

Table 15-1	Average Annual Cost of Running One Car	
Car Type	*Cheapest Average Annual Whole of Life Costs**	*Most Expensive Average Annual Whole of Life Costs**
Light car (1 to 1.6-litre engine)	$5,889	$7,908
Small car (1.6 to 2-litre engine)	$7,020	$12,446
Medium car (2 to 3-litre engine)	$8,711	$15,696
Large car (3 to 6-litre engine)	$10,274	$20,376
Compact SUV	$8,872	$13,577
Large SUV	$13,103	$19,593

* Whole of Life Costs include capital (loss of car value over time); fixed costs (registration, insurance, car club memberships); and operating costs (fuel, tyres, service and repairs). Source: NRMA, 2006

Hey, the air just got cleaner!

Reducing your car use can go a long way towards helping clear the air and reduce the health effects associated with pollution.

Statistics from the Australian Greenhouse Office (www.greenhouse.gov.au) show that cars are having an alarming impact on the environment:

✔ The Australian transport sector accounted for 79 million tonnes of Australia's total net greenhouse gas emissions in 2002, representing 13 per cent of Australia's total emissions.

✔ About 88 per cent of transport sector greenhouse gas emissions come from road transport, mainly cars and trucks. Cars are the main culprit — they contribute up to 64 per cent of road transport emissions.

✔ Greenhouse gas emissions from the transport sector are growing substantially. Projections indicated that transport sector emissions would rise by 42 per cent between 1990 and 2010. By 2005, levels had already reached 53 per cent above 1990 levels.

The combination of all these emissions contributes greatly to the air we breathe and produces *smog* — that dirty looking horizon you often see in cities. Around the globe, this makes driving a car a typical person's most air-polluting activity.

A number of the contaminants in smog have been linked to causing cancer, birth defects, brain and nerve damage, and long-term injury to lungs and breathing passages. I also talk about contaminants in Chapter 2, but if you take a closer look at what's in the emissions that cars produce, you get the full, unhealthy picture:

✔ **Carbon dioxide:** Considered one of the world's most troublesome greenhouse gases, contributing to global warming. And no wonder: A typical car pumps out about two kilograms of carbon dioxide per litre of petrol used (see Chapter 16 for more details about fuel use in vehicle engines). Higher than normal concentrations of carbon dioxide in the air increase pulse and breathing rates, and at even higher levels lead to clumsiness, severe headaches, dizziness and even death.

✔ **Carbon monoxide:** Reduces oxygen levels in the blood, resulting in headaches and impaired coordination.

✔ **Lead:** Declining since the introduction of unleaded fuel. Can retard learning in children and development of nervous system. Affects every organ in the body.

✔ **Hydrocarbons:** Produced when fuel molecules in the engine burn only partially (for example, when you start a vehicle or the engine is idling). A number of the exhaust hydrocarbons are of particular concern because they can cause coughing and chest pains, along with the potential to cause cancer. Some components can damage plants.

✔ **Nitrogen dioxide:** Known to cause breathing disorders and contributes to acid rain and damage to the globe's protective outer ozone layer.

✔ **Ozone:** Produced when nitrogen dioxide mixes with sunlight and hydrocarbons. Causes eye irritation and affects the lining of the lung and respiratory tract. (*Note:* The earth's outer ozone layer is a good thing that helps reflect the sun's harmful rays, but when ozone is present at the ground level, it's toxic.)

✔ **Particle matter (soot):** Damages lung tissue and is a factor in breathing disorders. Also contributes to heart disease.

Car emissions are especially unhealthy for the increasing number of asthma sufferers. Emissions from cars that cause smog and soot have been proven to worsen asthma and trigger attacks. And evidence also suggests that ozone actually causes asthma in some people.

The fitness factor

As well as the toxic emissions your car is spewing into the environment, sitting in your car all the time has an adverse effect on your health. This over-reliance on car travel encourages a lazy lifestyle. Why walk when you can drive, right? Well, if you've noticed that your midriff is expanding, think about how many times you could have walked or cycled during the last week, instead of using your car. Many urban car trips — trips to the local park, school or shops — may actually be within easy walking or cycling range, and walking is one of the best ways you can get your circulation going and lose that 'spare tyre' round your middle.

The car can be defined as *non-active transport.* By comparison, *active transport* choices, such as walking and cycling or combining longer journeys with buses, trains, trams and ferries, can have extremely positive benefits for your health. For example, if you walk some of the way as part of your commute to and from work, you're not only adding value to the time you need for daily exercise, but you're also doing your bit to reduce the cost of maintaining the health system.

Every time you decide not to use your car, you increase your physical activity, which can go a long way towards preventing cardiovascular disease and reducing your risk of obesity, adult-onset diabetes and osteoporosis. In fact, I think that the recent spate of *road rage* incidents, caused by impatient drivers on busy roads, suggests that less driving time could potentially have psychological benefits as well.

Sitting in a car, instead of spending some time walking, cycling and so on, particularly impacts on kids and may encourage them to develop a lazy lifestyle. Children who grow up inactive are more likely to be overweight. According to a recent Deakin University study, the proportion of Australian children who are now overweight is reaching approximately 25 per cent.

Apart from the negative health aspect of physical inactivity, children who are accustomed to being driven to school and related activities every day are missing out on some important life skills. Here's why:

- ✔ Kids who are 'ferried' everywhere may be less motivated to get out and find their own way around.

- ✔ When kids are driven everywhere, day in, day out, they're more likely to be unaccustomed to navigating and being comfortable in public places.

- ✔ Kids who travel only in cars usually have less experience in personal road safety.

If safety concerns are holding you back from allowing your kids to catch the bus or train to school, how about walking them to the bus stop or train station and travelling with them on your way to work. If work commitments make this impossible, take turns with family or friends, or organise a parents group to escort some neighbouring kids to and from school on public transport. There are financial benefits in this for you, too — school kids can take advantage of very cheap or free bus passes (and in some cases, train passes) offered by most schools. Check with the school, or your local bus or train operator, for further information.

Sidestepping the energy crisis

Less cars on the road would lower the pressure that exists on mining for and using fossil fuels. Some commentators argue that fossil fuel reserves have already peaked and the world is now into the second half of using the remaining stores.

As fossil fuel stores dwindle, fuel prices — like those we're experiencing now — will continue to rise. This is simple primary-school economics. Oil and gas, like most things that are mined or harvested from the earth, are *finite resources* that need to be managed much more effectively before they run out.

Most of this oil and gas is used for transport, so it's a no-brainer to suggest that if you can cut back on your car travel time, you'll use less oil and gasoline, and play a part in decreasing the pressure on ever-dwindling resources.

Alternative fuel cars are one option, but these are currently expensive to buy — or to convert fuel tanks over to in standard vehicles (see Chapter 16 for more information about hybrid cars and alternative fuels). Rather than wait for more affordable alternative-fuel cars to arrive in car sale lots, by which time oil and gas reserves will have dwindled further, throttling your addiction to your car use and choosing more sustainable transport choices is the way to go.

Sustainable Transport Options

In the preceding section, I explain why a continued high level of car use is unsustainable. However, walking and cycling, which require only the energy your legs can exert, are very sustainable. But what about public transport? Buses and ferries run on diesel — why are they more sustainable? And trains and trams use a lot of electrical energy — what makes them so sustainable?

The answer is all in the numbers. For example, buses and trains fit many more people in the one vehicle or carriage than cars do. Cars can take only up to four people, although they regularly carry only one or two. By comparison, buses take approximately 60 passengers and a train carriage can fit close to 200 passengers (an average eight-car Sydney train can carry up to 1,600 people).

It's not hard to work out that 60 pollution-emitting cars are going to have a greater impact on the environment than one bus carrying 60 passengers, not to mention the comparative benefits of a 1,600-person train. Also, queuing for traffic lights half the morning and evening is a waste of time and money — if you travel more often in buses, trains, ferries and trams, you avoid (and help ease) traffic congestion.

Now for the crux of the matter: You may agree that it would be nice to reduce your car use, but you can't realistically see your way clear to changing your travelling habits. You don't have to go the whole hog. Switching to more sustainable options for some trips may be easier than you think.

Getting to work the stress-free way

The most obvious trip that can be converted from car to other forms of transport is the journey-to-work trip. If you don't need a car as part of your job, look into changing to public transport. And if you work regular hours, you're travelling at a time of day (the morning and afternoon peak-hour periods) when public transport runs regularly and efficiently.

If your office or workplace provides showering and changing facilities, walking or cycling to work is much more appealing (and less smelly) than walking and cycling the same distance for other errands. If your workplace currently doesn't have any showering facilities, what would be the harm in asking whether it would be possible to add them? In fact, showering and change facilities are becoming compulsory in new developments in many urban areas across Australia.

If you change your travel-to-work habits, you not only do something positive for the environment, but also your peace of mind. How many times have you spent an inordinate amount of time in peak-hour traffic and got to work feeling wrung out? Compare your experience with someone who catches the train and has a chance to read the morning paper while listening to some soothing music on an mp3 player, and who arrives at work ready, willing and able. (This same person probably squeezes in a snooze as part of the journey home, or opens a laptop or a good book.)

The relative cost savings to your wallet are also substantial. A non-car user who combines public transport and taxis over the year, with the odd hire car thrown in, is likely to incur fewer costs than those who buy and operate a car, and pay the substantial registration, insurance, fuel and maintenance costs (refer to Table 15-1 earlier in this chapter for more details).

Some companies even offer subsidised public transport travel or provide company Cabcharge dockets if you give up your car parking space (or turn down a company car offer). If your employer doesn't, try lobbying the personnel department for these things. For more details, see 'Workplace travel plans are making a big difference' later in this chapter.

These legs were made for walking (and pedalling)

The reality is that many people live too far from their work to walk all the way. Or do they? The trend in many cities around the world is that more people are living closer to their workplaces and social attractions, and they walk to work via the many shops and services in their urban areas.

Even if the walk to work is too far, walking to a nearby train or bus stop and then catching the service the rest of the way is much healthier and less expensive than driving.

Cycling is also becoming an increasingly popular transport option, mainly because many cities and towns are investing in good, safe and direct cycling paths that do not compete with other traffic. In some cases, using a bicycle to get to work may be quicker than dealing with traffic congestion.

The key to cycling to and from work is planning and being prepared. The following checklist can help you get underway:

✔ **Stowage:** Make sure your workplace has good bike parking and locker facilities. This provides you with peace of mind that no-one is going to cycle off with your treasured transport investment.

> ✔ **Freshening up:** Ask about accessible showering and change facilities at your workplace. (As I mentioned in the preceding section, including these services in new commercial buildings is becoming compulsory in many Australian urban centres.)
>
> ✔ **Research the route to work:** Look for roads or paths that are well surfaced and wide enough to avoid conflicts with other vehicles. (Okay, admittedly flat is easier than hilly as well.)
>
> ✔ **Invest in the right gear:** You need to be safe — and comfortable. Make sure your bike is in top shape, buy a well-fitting helmet and small backpack, and get some reflective and protective gear. Don't forget to carry water and a kit to fix a flat tyre.

If you work flexible hours, you can even combine riding your bike part of the way to a train station, then take your bike along for the ride. Make sure your travel times avoid peak services, though; public transport authorities allow bikes to accompany commuters, but your bike must not obstruct the way for other passengers. In some states, you can travel with a bike any time you want, but you need to buy an additional ticket for your bike in peak periods. Check with your local rail agency for further information.

In some regions, such as the Australian Capital Territory and some cities in the United States, you can take your bike with you on your local bus. These public buses have bike racks on the front so bikes get carried safely out of the way of passengers.

Training yourself to use public transport

People cite various reasons for refusing to use public transport; others give just as many reasons why they love it. Those against trains and buses, in particular, refer to safety and security concerns, unreliable services or lack of options near where they live. Those for public transport usually say they feel more relaxed after the trip, and talk about the relative low costs and the support they receive from the public transport system.

Yet another group isn't exactly sure how to use public transport. These people grew up not using buses or trains, and find getting started a bit daunting. Never fear: In the age of the Internet, it's much easier than you think.

Most public transport providers in cities and towns offer excellent Web sites that can help you plan your journey. You can find timetable information, maps to show you each route, fare information, ticketing options and destination information.

Some of the Web sites run by larger transport agencies can provide you with a trip planner that tells you what to do after you leave your home. On these sites, you simply enter your home address, the address of your destination and the time you want to leave. You're then provided with the quickest transport options, route information, what bus stops or train stations to get off at, and even walking routes and distances to your selected destination. See Table 15-2 to check out the public transport services and schedules available in your state.

Table 15-2	Public Transport in Australia, State by State	
State	**Type**	**Web Address**
NSW	CityRail	www.cityrail.nsw.gov.au
	SydneyBuses	www.sydneybuses.nsw.gov.au
	NSW Transport Info	www.131500.com.au
Victoria	Trains, Trams and Buses	www.metlinkmelbourne.com.au
	Victoria Transport Info	www.viclink.com.au
Queensland	Queensland Transport Info	www.transinfo.qld.gov.au
Western Australia	Transperth	www.transperth.wa.gov.au
South Australia	Adelaide Metro	www.adelaidemetro.com.au
Tasmania	Metro Tasmania	www.metrotas.com.au

If you're a public transport novice and find a service that you'd like to try, develop a timetable for yourself that reminds you how much time you need to get up in the morning to walk to your bus stop or train station in time for your service. Do a similar thing for the way home.

When you start using public transport, you'll find that many interesting people are along for the ride — in large numbers at some key peak periods of the day — and in most cases the term *safety in numbers* rings true when you're travelling with many other commuters. The comfort and ease that you eventually experience getting to and from work this way may even encourage you to use public transport at other times: Before long you may find yourself hopping on a bus or train on the weekend because you know you'll get to your destination more cheaply, with fewer traffic hassles and parking problems.

Sharing the driving — and the car

If public transport is out of your reach, or not practical for you, you can still make a sustainable difference to the way you travel: Try car sharing or ride sharing. Although car sharing is not yet big in Australia, it has become very popular in the United States and in some European cities that limit car access but do not have quality public transport alternatives. The great thing about *car sharing* and *ride sharing* (also called *car pooling*) is that it reduces the number of single-vehicle trips on the road, therefore cutting back the number of cars on the road.

You can ride share with workmates, or sign up to share a car with local residents — to use socially and on the weekends. Here's how the two different models work:

✔ **A group of employees regularly share a ride to and from work.** The car used each day is provided by the person whose turn it is to drive. Car sharing companies such as Go Get (visit www.goget.com.au) can assist companies to organise ride-sharing groups based on where people live and what time they wish to arrive and leave from work. In some cases, workplaces actually donate the car to the group for sharing the ride to work.

✔ **A group of residents share a centrally located car.** This is a sort of communal car system. A company, such as Go Get, provides several cars in centrally located residential areas that people can book to use by the hour for a very reasonable price. This is a little bit like a hire-car system, except you have to share the car only with the small number of residents that live near you, which means that the car is more than likely to be available at the times you request it.

The TravelSmart Web site at www.travelsmart.gov.au (see the sidebar 'Get travel smart' for more details) provides information about government-sponsored community transport initiatives, including a links page that lists car-sharing Web sites.

Workplace travel plans are making a big difference

If you want to use public transport, it helps if you live near a reliable and direct public transport service, and that your workplace is located near one as well. Even better, your company may also offer *workplace travel plans* to subsidise your new sustainable transport choices, and make it easier for you to leave your car at home.

Get travel smart

TravelSmart Australia (www.travelsmart.gov.au) encourages communities and workplaces to think more about their travel choices. Funded by the Commonwealth, state and territory governments, the community-based TravelSmart program sets up site offices in suburbs and shows people how to make voluntary changes to their travel choices. Everyone is encouraged to use other more sustainable ways of getting around, rather than driving alone in a car.

The TravelSmart project seems to be working, because after the visit, more people in a community use buses, trains and ferries when they're shown a better route, get timetable information or are given financial incentives. This means that existing transport systems are more likely to be better used. TravelSmart programs also help coordinate car-pooling programs and encourage families to share car trips and to replace their short car journeys with walking and cycling.

Fortunately, many employers are becoming more interested in offering their employees subsidised public transport fares and passes, and other sustainable transport incentives. This is cheaper for the company, as well as for the employees who choose public transport over driving cars to work each day. Many companies have become burdened by employees expecting cars in their salary packages. And all that floor space allocated for car parking could be used for more productive purposes.

The types of workplace travel plans that companies provide may include:

- Public transport fare subsidies and passes
- Personalised travel information and marketing material
- Better bus stop facilities at the workplace
- Carpark space allocation that favours car sharers
- Flexitime and teleworking arrangements
- Local area cycling and walking route information
- Car share mileage clubs rewarding those with reduced car use
- A pool of bikes that employees can use to cycle to and from work
- Low emission vehicles for staff
- Public transport service announcements and other real-time information
- Public transport, walking and cycling events (such as breakfasts, lunches, seminars and so on)
- Timetables and links to interactive trip planners

If your company doesn't yet offer a workplace travel plan, ask some of your colleagues if they would be interested in joining you to lobby for one. When you gather some support, go to your manager with a report or some Internet material that outlines the benefits for the company if it develops a travel plan. Hey, you could even take along a copy of this book and show your boss this chapter!

Provide your company with information that promotes the positive benefits of developing a workplace travel plan. The following outcomes would be music to most employers' ears:

✔ Fosters improved relationships between staff and management.

✔ Helps retain and attract staff.

✔ Gives the company a better image in the community.

✔ Saves money — subsidising public transport is cheaper than providing employees with cars or car parking.

Shop 'til You Drop — From Home

Nothing on the Internet has made as big an impact on transport as the ability to shop online. For example, if you make most shopping trips in your car — to buy groceries, hardware items and things that can fit in your car boot — you can avoid the hassle of finding a car space in a humungous shopping centre. Instead, you simply park yourself in front of your computer and use the Internet to buy the things that you don't need to see, touch or try on.

Here are some online shopping categories that can help you reduce your individual car trips:

✔ **Books, music, DVDs, electronics and more.** Many retailers, such as Angus & Robertson (www.angusandroberston.com.au) and Sanity (www.sanity.com.au), operate Web sites for shoppers who know exactly what they want. Rather than drive to the store, you visit the company's Web site and search the vast online catalogue. The best part about shopping this way is that you're more likely to find what you're after: You get a better selection online compared to what's in stock at the nearest store.

✔ **Perishable foods.** Large supermarkets, such as Woolworths (www.homeshop.com.au) and Coles (www.coles.com.au), and specialist organic food stores (refer to Chapter 10 for more details), offer online shopping and home delivery to Internet-savvy shoppers who have set shopping lists and don't need to visit the store to see what they're buying.

- ✔ **Fine dining, delivered to your door.** Instead of driving to a restaurant and struggling to find a parking space, why not get a gourmet meal delivered? Many good restaurants in cities and large regional areas run Web sites and allow you to order online. Other companies, such as Cuisine Courier (www.cuisinecourier.com.au), let you select from the tasty and culturally varied menus of many well-known local restaurants.

- ✔ **Furniture and appliances.** Most national retailers in this category have glossy online catalogues that encourage you to order and have your big, bulky purchase delivered to your door without you having to lift a finger. Saves you from driving to the store as well, right? (Refer to Chapter 12 for lots of homeware shopping resources.)

- ✔ **Specialty products and services.** The Internet gives you access to products and services that may not be in your area at all. You can use a search engine such as Google (www.google.com.au) to find products then purchase what you want without driving for miles (or standing in queues). For example, you can compare competing contents insurance policies, purchase a holiday or track down a great 'green' cleaning product sold by a small business in another state.

- ✔ **Auctions and secondhand resellers.** Sites like eBay (www.eBay.com.au) and other places where you can buy or sell pre-loved goods basically enable people to trade with each other no matter where they are. These sites are famous for broadening shoppers' horizons beyond local newspapers and having to trade with local secondhand stores or pawnbrokers. (For more details about eBay, refer to Chapter 9.)

Some commentators worry about an increase in online shopping, especially the negative impacts it could have on the economic and social sustainability of our urban centres and towns. For example, small businesses in town and suburban centres could suffer if consumers buy more products from national online retailers.

Similarly, the amount of commercial deliveries made by planes, trains and couriers may increase as online shopping becomes more popular, although this is offset by the fewer individual car trips people make to shopping centres to purchase and pick up goods.

So far, the impacts of online shopping appear to have been minimal. Most town and suburban retail centres continue to survive because of the social role they play: They provide places where people can interact and relax. Many retailers now have two avenues to a thriving business: The traditional shopfront (which people visit to physically browse for the things they want), and the Internet (where people log on to find what they're ready to buy).

Many products you're likely to buy from online companies can be delivered by Australia Post, or some other postal service, that already goes past your door, every day. To find out how, see the sidebar 'Wheeling a virual shopping cart to the checkout (and other ways to pay)'.

TECHNICAL STUFF

Wheeling a virtual shopping cart to the checkout (and other ways to pay)

Most retailers run interactive Web sites that provide picturesque catalogues of their goods and services that you can browse through to your heart's content. As you scroll through the catalogue, you can place products in the virtual shopping cart, where they're stored until you proceed to the virtual checkout.

The virtual checkout steps you through several pages that total the products you've selected along with additional taxes and the delivery costs to give you an invoice total. These pages are usually *encrypted* so that your personal information and payment details are secure: To confirm this, make sure a little padlock appears at the bottom of your browser's window.

To progress through the checkout, you need to provide your personal details and a shipping address, and then select a shipping method. At this point you can usually click on a button to choose Australia Post (the cheapest method), unless you're buying perishable goods or a bulky item. You then reach the payment pages and add your credit card details to pay for your purchase. Shortly afterwards you receive an email that confirms the goods you bought, how much it cost and when your purchase will be delivered.

Some Web sites, especially many run by smaller businesses, don't offer virtual checkouts and provide you with other ways to buy. Instead, you order by email or call the listed telephone number to talk to a real live person. You can then arrange to pay by COD, cheque, money order, credit card or, if you're set up for Internet banking, make a direct deposit into the business's bank account.

Two warnings, though: Don't ever email your credit card details to pay for an order. Emails can be intercepted. And if you use online banking to deposit the money into the business's bank account, double check that you correctly type the recipient's BSB and account number and that you've included an invoice number or your name to identify the payment as coming from you.

For more details about shopping online securely, check out *Internet For Dummies*, 2nd Australian Edition (published by Wiley Publishing Australia).

Chapter 16

The Green Car Evolution

In This Chapter

▶ Moving on from the internal combustion engine

▶ Using fuels that reduce emissions

▶ Comparing alternative fuel prices

▶ Designing the green car of the future

1 don't own a car. I don't like driving them and I don't like the fact that they harm the planet. For a start, cars spew greenhouse gases and other emissions out of their tailpipes. Traffic congestion, traffic accidents, sprawling urban development and more sedentary lifestyles are also synonymous with car travel. On the other hand, it's hard to imagine living entirely without cars. They provide unmatched mobility and freedom, and are an integral part of modern life. You may be able to help the planet by using your car less often, but the reality is cars won't become extinct any time soon.

Because a car is probably an important part of your life, this chapter concentrates on ways you can reduce the environmental damage caused by owning and driving one. In this chapter, I focus on renewable, cleaner energy sources, and explain some of advances in car technology that use alternative fuel. In fact, so many options are on the horizon, that I think I can see the beginning of a green car revolution.

The Green Car — Myth or Reality?

The car of the future will use less energy to make, less energy to run, and will be able to run on energy that's renewable. This is already a reality. Years of research has produced options for powering cars with renewable, clean or energy-efficient fuel (for more details, see 'Fuelling interest in alternatives' later in this chapter). And an increasing range of alternative-fuel cars are zipping along Australian roads.

Alternative-fuel sources and technological innovations are unlikely to convert the car into a sustainable mode of transport. Cars will always consume energy to produce, and a car-based lifestyle can lead to a number of social and health-related problems (refer to Chapter 15 to find out how). Governments spend a lot more money on car-related infrastructures — motorways, roads and parking stations — than on public transport, walking and cycling infrastructures. Unfortunately, this disadvantages a lot of people like myself, who prefer not to drive.

Evaluating the environmental performance of cars

As well as consuming fossil fuels (petrol and gas) that produce greenhouse gas emissions, the metal, rubber and plastics used to make and maintain vehicles are largely non-renewable and polluting. Of these problems, the build-up of greenhouse gas emissions and pollution created by cars, trucks and other vehicles on the road are foremost in everyone's mind. Therefore, I'm not going to mince words here:

- Australia creates approximately 565 million tonnes of greenhouse gas emissions each year.
- Transport produces over 76 million tonnes of greenhouse gases.
- The rate of greenhouse gas emissions emanating from transport has increased by 23 per cent over the last 10 years.

The simple explanation for the growth in transport-related emissions is that you probably drive farther than you did ten years ago. Over the last decade, the pattern of where people live, work and socialise in Australian cities has expanded widely.

Some people I know commute over two hours each way, every day, just to get to work. Long car trips like this, made by thousands of people in cities every day, quickly add up to a major environmental problem.

Driving a car is not an efficient use of energy. Only a tiny portion of the fuel that you put in your car is actually used to move you along. The following statistics show just how wasteful the car engine is:

- A litre of petrol contains 34 megajoules of energy.

- 62 per cent (of that available energy) is lost due to the inefficiency in the engine.

- A further 8 per cent is lost running engine accessories, such as charging the battery and cooling the engine.

- 17 per cent is used while the car is idling.

- In total, 87 per cent of the fuel burned by a car is wasted. Only 13 per cent is used to actually move the vehicle; very little is used to actually move you around.

My point is this: Even after you take into account the inefficiency of car engines, people are using energy just to drive a 1.5-tonne vehicle around. Because you weigh much less than 1.5 tonnes, most of the energy is wasted on the car, not on getting you (and other occupants in the car) from place to place.

Some engines are more efficient than others, as are some car designs. The car you drive today — with an internal combustion engine under the bonnet, two seats in the front, room for three in the back, a chassis to protect yourself and your passengers, all sitting atop four rubber tyres — has changed very little for nigh on 100 years. This is not the most efficient design.

You're probably now wondering why car owners have put up with such inefficient and polluting cars for so long, right? One answer is that the oil producers and engine makers profit from producing cars with inefficient combustion engines. These cars have been subsidised, well promoted and remain an affordable motoring alternative. Imported four-wheel drives, for example, attract a government subsidy in Australia that makes them 10 per cent less expensive than a small car that costs the same amount to manufacture.

Extending your petrol dollar

As fuel prices rise, consumers are beginning to consider fuel efficiency as a major buying point for new cars. That's a good start, but you can easily cut your fuel bill by 20 per cent or more without radically changing the way you live. Most of the advice I offer in this section shows you how to use less fuel.

Time for some driver training and car management tips. Here goes:

- ✔ Ensure that your car is regularly tuned and serviced. A badly tuned car does not burn fuel properly, wasting your money and poisoning your friends and neighbours.

- ✔ Reduce your speed and avoid heavy braking and accelerating. Driving more slowly and smoothly reduces fuel consumption. For city driving, the most fuel-efficient speed range is 50 to 60 kilometres per hour.

- ✔ Travel lightly and remove unnecessary items from your car to reduce weight. This simple step can improve your fuel consumption a little and reduce emissions.

- ✔ Make sure your tyres are inflated to the correct pressure. Soft tyres increase fuel consumption by up to 5 per cent.

- ✔ Use your air-conditioner only when you need to. An air-conditioner can use up to 10 per cent more fuel than driving around with the windows open (at speeds less than 100 kilometres per hour).

- ✔ Avoid peak-hour traffic (you're burning fuel when you're sitting in the traffic going nowhere).

- ✔ Consider buying a motorbike or powered scooter to commute to work. These smaller vehicles use less fuel. (For more about two-wheeled wonders, see the section 'Two wheels are better than four' later in this chapter.)

- ✔ Adopt some of the recommendations I make in Chapter 15: Use public transport, walk, ride a bicycle and consider car pooling.

Gauging fuel consumption

If you're in the market for a new car but can't afford a green car, check out the Australian Greenhouse Office Fuel Guide (www.greenhouse.gov.au/fuelguide), which offers a guide to fuel consumption rates for various models of vehicles on the road. For example, a powerful 5.4-litre 2003 Ford Falcon V8 consumes 15 litres of fuel every 100 kilometres when driven on city streets compared to the smaller 1.3 litre Hyundai Getz, which consumes only

7.8 litres every 100 kilometres under the same conditions. The V8 will cost you approximately double the fuel and produce double the emissions to travel the same distance.

To make things a little easier when browsing for a new car, the Australian federal government introduced a mandatory fuel consumption labelling system in 2004 to be displayed on all new vehicles for sale. These fuel consumption labels (see Figure 16-1) display the fuel type if the vehicle doesn't run on petrol, a carbon dioxide emissions value, and comparative fuel consumption telling you how many litres of fuel the vehicle would use to travel 100 kilometres. Check out the Greenhouse Office Web page to get more details: www.greenhouse.gov.au/fuelguide/label.html.

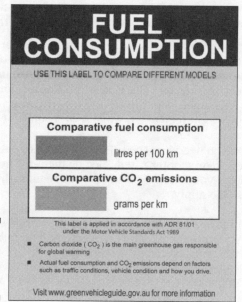

Figure 16-1:
The Fuel
Consumption
label.

Two wheels are better than four

Size does matter. For a variety of reasons, smaller vehicles are gentler on the environment. The main reason is that fuel consumption increases with weight — a car that weighs two tonnes uses about twice as much fuel to travel the same distance as a car that weighs one tonne. Because most cars carry the same load, regardless of how big the car is — usually one or two people and a few kilograms of goods — the extra fuel used by a heavier vehicle is completely wasted.

Small vehicles also take up less room on the road, so they cause less traffic congestion. They spend less time stuck in traffic and wasting fuel. The following list looks more closely at two-wheeled options:

- Motorcycles are much more fuel efficient than cars. They're lighter and smaller, so they use less fuel when they are moving, and spend less time stopped in the traffic. Motorcycles range in size, and those with small-capacity engines are more efficient than those with larger engines.

- Motor scooters travel at lower speeds than motorcycles, and are easier to ride and park. In towns and cities, motor scooters are becoming increasingly popular. The Italian Vespa brand of scooter is almost a fashion accessory in some suburbs.

- Motor-assisted pedal cycles, or mopeds, use fuel only when you engage the motor, say to travel up a hill. They can be powered by electricity or petrol. Electric bicycles are becoming the more popular of the two.

You can ride an electric bicycle (as long as the motor's output is no more than 200 watts) without registering the vehicle or having a driver's or rider's licence. Of course, helmets are still mandatory. A number of companies make electric bicycles. The PowerPed Raptor, for example, has a top speed of 30-kilometres-per-hour and can travel up to 50 kilometres after being charged at a normal powerpoint for four hours.

In most states in Australia you need a special rider's licence to get around on a petrol-powered motorcycle or scooter rated 50cc or higher: The exception is Queensland, which allows you to zip around on your regular driver's licence. Registration fees also apply.

Given their popularity in Europe and Asia, most small motorbikes, scooters, mopeds and electric bicycles are manufactured overseas. The following Web sites are resources for these small vehicles in Australia:

- Scootersales Australia: www.scootersales.com.au
- My Scooter: www.myscooter.com.au
- The Electric Bike Company: www.electricbike.com.au
- Electric Vehicles: www.currietech.com.au

Fuelling Interest in Alternatives

Petrol prices regularly go through the roof, and are likely to keep creeping up. Many car owners, especially those who own large, petrol-chugging, four-wheel drives, are spending well over $100 each time they fill their tanks. As a result, small car sales are on the rise again.

Rising fuel prices have also sparked interest in alternative fuels. Even George W Bush, the President of the United States — a modern day prophet of fossil fuel consumption — has said that Americans need to overcome their 'addiction to oil'.

On a recent trip to the United States, I observed the frenzied exposure given to hydrogen, ethanol, electricity and even solar power as possible fuels for the car of the future. Hollywood is also getting in on the act — the gossip columns reckon that every cool person in Los Angeles owns a half-electricity, half-gasoline-powered Toyota Prius hybrid car.

Although new electric cars are getting a lot of media attention, what the industry really needs is a powerful fuel that can realistically drive the millions of cars that are already on the road. Among the less polluting, more energy-efficient fuels that may keep the wheels of society turning without killing the planet, are:

- Ultra-low and low-sulfur diesel.
- Unleaded petrol mixed with ethanol.
- Biodiesel made from vegetable crops such canola, soy, tallow and waste cooking oil.
- Gaseous fuels, including hydrogen, compressed natural gas (CNG), liquefied natural gas (LNG), and liquefied petroleum gas (LPG).
- Ethanol-based fuels, including Diesohol (15 per cent ethanol and low-sulfur diesel) and hydrated ethanol.

Some of these alternative fuels can be mixed with traditional gasoline and diesel. These mixed fuels are easy to switch to because they work in existing cars and can be delivered through existing service stations. Even though they still produce emissions, these are much reduced — at least it's a start.

Biofuels, such as biodiesel, are made from plants and have a striking advantage in terms of global warming. The plants used to make them capture carbon dioxide from the air. This means that they're not pumping new greenhouse gases into the atmosphere, but recycling it. For more details about these alternative fuels, see the sections 'Ethanol blends' and 'Biodiesel' later in this chapter.

The simplicity of hydrogen

Hydrogen is the cleanest and most energy efficient of the alternative fuels, according to the United States Department of Energy. Not only that, hydrogen is everywhere. Water is just hydrogen and oxygen — H_2O, don't you know? And, of course, water is found in the oceans and in all plants and animals.

Hydrogen is not a source of energy. It must be separated from substances before it can be used as a fuel. And the process of creating hydrogen fuel can consume energy. You can think of hydrogen as a way of storing energy, rather than a source of energy. The energy used to separate the hydrogen may be solar electricity, for example, which makes it a renewable fuel.

For hydrogen to power a car, it must be mixed with oxygen in a fuel cell. Hydrogen-powered fuel cells can be used in conjunction with gasoline and existing internal combustion engine cars.

For hydrogen to be adapted for widespread use in cars, however, the following issues need to be resolved:

✔ Manufacturers need to produce hydrogen fuel-cell vehicles for sale to the general public.

✔ Manufacturers need to produce hydrogen fuel in large quantities.

✔ Hydrogen fuel storage problems need to be addressed. For example, gasoline provides up to five times more energy per litre than a hydrogen fuel cell. This means you would have to refuel five times more often, or have five times the storage capacity, to go the same distance using current hydrogen fuel cells.

✔ New hydrogen fuel stations would need to be built.

The United States government has conservatively estimated that it could be anywhere between 10 to 20 years before hydrogen vehicles become standard and the infrastructure to support them becomes widely available. Maybe so, but well-known Japanese car makers are developing new hydrogen-powered vehicles already. Within the next five years, you may be able to buy a hydrogen fuel-cell vehicle from a showroom.

Becoming electric

Electric vehicles promise to lower greenhouse gas emissions. If the electricity is sourced from a renewable power source, such as wind or solar, you have a form of transport that's almost free of greenhouse emissions. However, if the electricity is generated by burning coal, then greenhouse gas emissions are still being produced.

The cost of running and maintaining electrically powered vehicles is also low. They have fewer moving parts to service and replace, although the batteries that store the electrical power need to be replaced every three to six years. Also, the batteries tend to be heavy and are usually made from toxic materials such as lead, metal hydrides or lithium.

Also, electric cars cannot yet travel long distances without recharging, nor can most reach speeds greater than 60 kilometres per hour. For more information on the pros and cons of electric vehicles, go to the United Kingdom's Environmental Transport Association Web site at www.eta.co.uk.

Gas is great (CNG and LPG, that is)

Compressed natural gas (CNG) is better than gasoline, or petrol, because it produces fewer harmful emissions. Because of the relatively strong market for natural gas cars in the United States, the gas can be purchased at many refuelling stations. CNG is not yet widely available in Australia.

CNG's energy output per litre is not as good as petrol/gasoline (petrol provides up to three times more energy per litre than a CNG), but it's better than hydrogen. Another downside is that CNG is a fossil fuel. Like most fossil fuels, global demand is outstripping supply. Half of Canada's annual natural gas production is exported to the United States. And Australia is shipping natural gas to the United States and China at such a rate that local supplies may run out in 40 years if that export rate continues.

The good news about CNG is that it's basically methane. *Methane* is a byproduct of rotting plant matter and can be captured from the treatment of sewage and other waste. Of course, it may be difficult making enough methane from these sources to supply growing demands.

The other popular gas option, especially in Australia, is *liquid petroleum gas* (LPG). LPG used in cars contains propane and butane and is available at most fuelling stations. LPG is produced as a by-product of natural gas processing and petroleum refining. It's therefore not as natural as CNG sourced from wells in the ground, but has similar clean air benefits.

The Australian government began offering rebates for car owners converting to natural gas at the end of 2006. People buying a new LPG-powered car receive a subsidy of $1,000; those converting a normal petrol tank to LPG receive $2,000. This policy initiative occurred during the height of the massive price hike in petrol costs in October 2006 and the rebates will be available for eight years. They apply only to cars used privately. For more information on how to take advantage of this subsidy, check out www.ausindustry.gov.au and click on LPG Vehicle Scheme link.

Ethanol blends

Ethanol is the alcohol you drink in wine, beer and spirits. It's produced by fermenting and distilling sugar or starch from sugar cane, corn, barley and wheat, to name a few plants commonly used to produce ethanol for fuel. Like all biofuels, using ethanol reduces greenhouse gas emissions because the plants used to make it capture greenhouse gas from the air. Ethanol also burns cleanly, producing water and carbon dioxide, so it produces less pollution than petrol.

To use ethanol, though, you'll need a car that is branded as a flexible fuel vehicle (FFV). These cars are not uncommon, especially among newer models. If you're buying a car, check that the engine is branded FFV.

Ethanol is generally mixed with petrol for use in combustion engine motor vehicles. The most popular mix is 85 per cent ethanol to 15 per cent gasoline (or petrol). Called E85, this ethanol mix reduces greenhouse gas and pollution emissions from the car, as well as in the refining and processing. Because it can be used in standard vehicles and offers greenhouse benefits, the E85 ethanol mix is the favoured alternative fuel at the moment.

The E85 ethanol mix is only a compromise, however. The land, water and energy required to grow the crops to make the ethanol is currently used to grow food. To feed the world's population *and* supply large quantities of ethanol fuel, the world would need to cultivate more arable land.

Biodiesel

Biodiesel is the preferred compromise fuel for diesel engines. Biodiesel outlets are common in Europe and are opening across Australia.

Biodiesel is generally manufactured from recycled vegetable oil, or from new oils extracted from plants. Recycled oil has a lower environmental impact, because no extra energy, land or water is required to create the raw material. Most of the sources of recycled oil in Australia have now been contracted to the major biodiesel companies.

Until recently, most biodiesel was made by small operators, often operating in their backyards, and supplies varied greatly in quality. As a result, biodiesel earned a reputation for causing damage to engines, and was generally mixed with regular diesel (usually 20 per cent biodiesel) to avoid this.

Driving in a haze of fish and chips

Owners of diesel vehicles in northern New South Wales can buy biodiesel at the pump through North Coast Biodiesel. The company encourages people to switch from regular diesel, which it calls 'dino-diesel'. Initially, many customers who switched to biodiesel reported that their fuel filters had clogged up after the first two or three tanks. The reason was that the biodiesel was actually dissolving the build up of glassy substances present in dino-diesel. When customers changed their fuel filter, though, their engines ran cleaner and more smoothly than they had previously when using the fossil fuel diesel.

Cars and trucks running on biodiesel have a distinctive vegetable oil smell, which is much more pleasant than dino-diesel fumes. Locals know it as 'mobile fish and chips'.

Now that most biodiesel is created commercially, these problems have disappeared. In fact, most biodiesel suppliers claim their fuel improves engine performance and reduces wear and tear.

Fill 'er Up, Thanks!

Comparing fuels based on their impact on the planet is one thing, but many consumers will continue to make the decision about which fuel to use based on price rather than environmental impact. You'll be happy to know that it won't be long before you can defend your sustainable fuel choice based on price as well and convert friends and family through the powerful persuasion of the purse.

In Table 16.1, I compare the relative price of alternative fuels currently available in Australia and the United States. After you get over the shock of how cheap unleaded petrol is in the United States, you'll note that the gaseous fuels are also cheaper than the liquid alternatives.

This table shows price per litre, but you may be more interested in how far your dollar can drive you. Because liquid fuels tend to get more miles per gallon, to use the US measures, they offer slightly better value than this table indicates. Even taking this into account, if you eventually convert to alternative fuels, you may well end up in front. Ford Motors in Australia, for example, estimates a 45 per cent cost saving for its eGas model vehicles.

Table 16-1	Average Fuel Price Comparison	
Fuel	**Australian Price Per Litre (US$)**	**US Price Per Litre A$ (In US$)**
Petrol/Gasoline (Unleaded)	$1.33 ($0.99)	$0.78 ($0.58)
Diesel	$1.38 ($1.02)	$0.91 ($0.68)
Natural Gas		$0.71 ($0.53)
LPG	$0.44 ($0.33)	
Ethanol E85		$0.71 ($0.53)
Propane		$0.70 ($0.52)
Biodiesel B20		$0.94 ($0.70)
Biodiesel B100		$1.14 ($0.85)

Adapted from US Department of Energy Clean Cities Alternative Fuel Report, Feb 2006, for national averages and `http://motormouth.com.au` *prices for Sydney in June 2006. Note that US prices are quoted in the US Department of Energy Report as per gallon. This table converts from gallons to litres.*

The Future Is So Bright You'll Have to Wear Shades

Buying a new, alternative-fuel car from a large car maker does not come cheap in Australia. Unfortunately, you'll likely have to wait until sales of green cars reach significant volumes before the prices even out. Innovative alternative-energy cars are selling well overseas, which makes it realistic to hope that a range of alternative-fuel cars will be available at comparable prices in the not-too-distant future.

The two main alternative-fuel vehicles available to Australian motorists right now are hybrids that combine a combustion engine with an electric motor, and LPG vehicles.

Hybrid hysteria

What are these hybrids that everyone is talking about? I'll give you a hint: They're not roses, or a breed of dog.

A *hybrid car* combines the everyday combustion engine you probably have in your car with an electric engine. The car switches from petrol mode to electric mode when idling or travelling at low speeds to reduce petrol consumption and emissions. One selling point of the hybrid is that the battery does not need to be refuelled via an electrical socket on the wall; you charge the electric battery every time you press the brakes.

Hybrid cars have been available in the United States and Europe for some years now, but have only recently been introduced to the Australian market. The best known of the hybrids is the Toyota Prius (`http://prius.toyota.com.au`), which retails at approximately $37,000 in Australia. The Honda Civic Hybrid (`www.honda.com.au`) is the only competition to the Prius in Australia and retails for approximately $32,000.

LPG-ready vehicles

Ford and Mitsubishi recently released dedicated LPG vehicles in Australia. Buses and taxis have been running on LPG in Australia for some time now. Some people have also been using LPG in their private vehicles for many years, but these vehicles had to be custom-modified to run on the fuel. New LPG cars come fully modified, and these may become more popular now that subsidies are available (refer to the section 'Gas is great (CNG and LPG, that is)' earlier in this chapter for more details).

The Ford Falcon E-Gas (using LPG) is the first LPG powered car to roll off the mainstream production line. The Ford Web site (`www.ford.com.au/landing/egas`) describes sedan, wagon and utility models that will set you back at least $37,000.

What the future holds

Taking a look at what's available around the world provides a picture of how quickly these new technologies are emerging. One obvious trend is that the major car manufacturers are focused on liquid fuels in their mainstream releases. Independent newcomers, like Tesla Motors in California, have released innovative electrical cars, but these vehicles are far from mainstream.

In the United States, the following alternative fuel cars were on the market in 2006:

- Honda — four alternative fuel models: A CNG-only powered Honda Civic and three electric/gasoline hybrids (a Honda Accord, a Honda Civic and a Honda Insight).

- Ford — five alternative fuel models: One electric/gasoline hybrid and four E85 Ethanol-powered cars.

- General Motors — six alternative fuel models: One electric/gasoline hybrid, one CNG-only powered engine; one CNG/gasoline bi-fuel utility; and four E85 Ethanol models.

- Nissan — one E85 ethanol model: The Titan.

- Toyota — two electric/gasoline hybrids: A Highlander SUV and the Prius.

- Daimler Chrysler — four E85 ethanol models. The Stratus, Sebring and Caravan sedans, and the Durango SUV.

These types of alternative fuel vehicles are also available in other parts of the world, including Europe and Asia.

Electric cars are also becoming popular in other parts of the world. In London, for example, a great example shows what can be done when innovation and government support come together. GoingGreen (www.goingreen.co.uk) sells the electric-powered G-Wiz, a 2-door hatchback with a top speed of approximately 60 kilometres an hour, which is considered adequate for London driving conditions and speed limits. It also has a range of up to 60 kilometres before it needs to be recharged.

With government help, recharging ports have been set up around London. This makes the vehicle a serious option only for Londoners, but the big attraction is that this vehicle has no radiator, clutch, gears, exhaust, oil filters, spark plugs or many of the parts that wear out. And it produces no emissions.

Holding out for hydrogen

Most of the world's major car makers are racing each other to get the first fully fledged hydrogen car on the road. These days, every car show seems to showcase a new hydrogen fuel-cell car developed by a major manufacturer.

Honda first introduced its FCX fuel-cell car in 1999, but still does not have the vehicle ready for the market. (For more about how hydrogen fuel-cell cars work, refer to the section 'The simplicity of hydrogen' earlier in this chapter.) One of the issues Honda has had to resolve before bringing the car to market is developing a small yet powerful hydrogen tank to fit within the relatively tiny car-frame that Honda is famous for.

Honda has also developed a prototype hydrogen refuelling station and a home-based energy station that generates hydrogen from natural gas (because it'll be impossible to sell hydrogen cars widely in the market without an infrastructure to support them).

General Motors, Ford, Toyota and Mercedes-Benz are also in the process of developing fuel-cell prototypes using hydrogen.

Chapter 17

Committing to Acts of Eco-Tourism

• •

In This Chapter

▶ Defining eco-tourism and choosing an eco-friendly holiday

▶ Planning your holiday itinerary

▶ Understanding eco-tourism do's and don'ts

• •

You've worked hard to save the world, so now you deserve a holiday. Of course, to keep your impact on the environment to a minimum, you'd naturally choose an eco-friendly holiday. No, you don't have to camp in your backyard — you can arrange a green getaway.

This chapter helps you find a great place to go, plan your holiday to enjoy the area you visit without damaging it, and support those tourist operators that do the most for the local community and the environment. Sounds good, but some factors can easily trip up budding eco-travellers.

First trap! Holidays generally involve travel, and travel consumes fossil fuels. In this chapter I look at ways you can neutralise the carbon dioxide emissions that result from jumping on a plane or driving long distances. Second trap! There's confusion, even in the travel industry, over eco-friendly travel terms. Many businesses that offer tours, accommodation or services in natural locations — such as national parks, wildlife areas, beaches, lakes and even remote islands — claim to be eco-friendly, even though they're not.

Understanding the new accreditation systems I also cover in this chapter can help you choose the best eco-tour service for your dream vacation. New definitions, such as *sustainable*, *responsible* and even *ethical* tourism, attempt to clarify environmentally-responsible tourism in cities and towns, as well as areas of natural beauty. But enough of the bad news, already. Your intention is to get out there and enjoy the world, sustainably. You're not alone — can I come, too?

'I'm Dreaming of an Eco-Friendly Getaway'

Here is the fun bit (for me anyway): Planning your sustainable holiday. There's so much in the world to experience, it can be tough choosing where to visit. The most environmentally-friendly option is to stay home on the sofa and read a book, so clearly you'll use other criteria as well if you want to see more of the world. (See 'Keeping your focus local' in this chapter for cool holidays that minimise your travel.)

The experience you want is probably the most important influence on where you go. You may want to enjoy natural beauty, a great cultural heritage, an exciting experience or immerse yourself in a different culture. You may be influenced by friends who have had a great time in a particular place. Your first step is to choose your destination and the type of experience you want, then apply the hints I offer later in this chapter to make your holiday as sustainable as possible.

'Where in the world shall I go?'

Internationally, a number of countries and regions have become popular eco-tourism destinations. These eco-tourism hot spots include:

- **Africa:** Kenya and Swaziland are blessed with national parks, deserts and forests. Each region offers rich wildlife and traditional culture (think the Kenyan Masai warriors). This combination makes them extremely popular places to visit.

- **South-East Asia:** Indonesia and Thailand remain Australians' most popular destinations, with their rainforests and mountain ranges contrasting with stunning beaches. An increasing number of eco-tourists visit the relatively untouched countries of Cambodia, Laos and Nepal.

- **Caribbean and Central America:** Some of the fastest growing eco-tourism spots in the world are popping up in pristine beach and rainforest areas found in small countries like the Dominican Republic, Belize and Costa Rica. In fact, Costa Rica has become one of the most popular eco-tourism destinations in the Americas due to its government support for tourism and its unmatched variety of rainforests, volcanoes, mountain ranges and beaches.

- **South America:** Ecuador, Peru and Brazil continue to top the eco-tourism lists. The Amazon region in Brazil, the snow-capped volcano mountains and indigenous populations of Ecuador and the Andes in Peru pervade many eco-tourist's dreams.

- **North America:** The beautiful, extensive national park systems on this continent continue to woo people, but if you want the relative wilderness visit the sub-Arctic regions in Alaska and Canada.

Guide books, such as the Frommer's travel series, explore all the attractions in these natural parts of the world, and can give you all the information you need before heading off on a holiday. For more information about the labelling systems that the tourism industry uses, see the section 'Eco-tourism or eco-trash' later in this chapter. Similarly, the international tour group coordinator Intrepid (www.intrepidtravel.com) provides one of the most responsible adventure and eco-travel services available.

Keeping your focus local

The most environmentally-friendly holiday is the one you take close to home. By travelling locally, you can save on the massive greenhouse impact of international flights. Becoming familiar with your own environment can also inspire you to look after it better.

In Australia, Ecotourism Australia is a useful place to start your search for a local adventure. To give you a feel for the type of attractions and services that meet its eco-certified standards, check out the organisation's Web site, at www.ecotourism.org.au. For more details about Ecotourism Australia, see the following sections in this chapter.

Australian eco-tourism attractions

The following Australian destinations are covered by Ecotourism Australia's Advanced Ecotourism certification.

- ✔ Alice Springs Desert Park, Northern Territory
- ✔ Banrock Station Wine and Wetland Centre, South Australia
- ✔ Birds Australia Gluepot Reserve, South Australia
- ✔ Blue Mountains Scenic World, New South Wales
- ✔ Brisbane Forest Park, Queensland
- ✔ Cooper Creek Wilderness, South Australia
- ✔ Couran Cove Island Resort, Queensland
- ✔ Daintree Discovery Centre, Queensland
- ✔ Daintree Rainforest River Train, Queensland
- ✔ Forestry Tasmania Centre, Tasmania
- ✔ Marine Discovery Centre, Victoria
- ✔ Mount Buffalo National Park, Victoria
- ✔ Naracoorte Caves, South Australia
- ✔ Phillip Island Nature Park, Victoria
- ✔ The Rainforest Habitat Wildlife Sanctuary, Queensland
- ✔ Skyrail, Queensland
- ✔ Tilligerry Habitat Reserve and Centre, New South Wales

Exploring the Eco-Tourism Phenomenon

The principles behind eco-tourism relate to any holiday you take, whether you visit areas of natural beauty or major cities and towns. The eco-tourism label, though, has usually been applied only to natural areas.

The International Ecotourism Society (TIES) defines eco-tourism as responsible travel to natural areas that conserves the environment and improves the wellbeing of local people. According to TIES (www.ecotourism.org), businesses that implement eco-travel services, and the people who participate in eco-tourism activities, should follow these principles:

- ✔ Minimise environmental impact.
- ✔ Build environmental and cultural awareness and respect.
- ✔ Provide positive experiences for both visitors and hosts.
- ✔ Provide direct financial benefits for conservation.
- ✔ Provide financial benefits and empowerment for local people.
- ✔ Raise sensitivity to host countries' political, environmental and social climate.
- ✔ Support international human rights and labour agreements.

What does all of this actually mean? Does it mean that eco-tourism takes place only when you experience natural areas? And how do you measure whether a company is providing positive experiences and raising sensitivity to local political, social and environmental issues?

The problem with such woolly definitions is that you can't just take the word of a self-proclaimed eco-tourism company. For example, the eco-travel Web site Planeta (www.planeta.com) warns that in the age of the Web, eco-tourism means whatever you pay the ads to display.

To help would-be travellers, tourism organisations have adopted a range of definitions to cover different aspects of tourism. Most of the widely accepted definitions try to achieve the same end: Promote tourism that minimises environmental, cultural and economic harm.

Three of the most popular descriptions now being used to guide the rest of the tourism industry are:

- **Sustainable tourism:** Use environmental resources sparingly to maintain essential ecological processes and conserve natural heritage and biodiversity.

- **Ethical tourism:** Respect host communities, conserve cultural heritage and traditional values, and act to increase understanding and tolerance.

- **Responsible tourism:** Ensure viable, long-term economic operations that benefit host communities and share the profits fairly.

Looking after the locals

Once upon a time, the closest many people could get to the world's natural wonders was flicking through an old National Geographic magazine in a dentist's waiting room. When I was a child, for example, I didn't fathom that one day I would be able to get up-close and personal with elephants and lions on a safari in Africa or hike to the Mount Everest base camp, if I wanted to.

Travel is much more accessible these days — ironically, due to cheap energy from fossil fuels. Today, you can visit any number of far-flung natural wonderlands, no matter how remote they are.

The impact on the environment and local communities from at-one-with-nature holidays has been significant, though. The World Wildlife Fund (www.wwf.org) lists the damage caused by tourism in once remote parts of the world. The problems include:

- **The destruction of eco-systems on formerly pristine coastal areas.** Major breeding grounds of marine life and birds disappear when estuaries are drained to create holiday playgrounds.

- **Over-use of local water supplies.** Hotels, swimming pools and golf courses all use large amounts of water, reducing the water available for local populations, especially in arid regions.

- **Interruption to wildlife.** Highways and sprawling development inhibits the nesting and migration patterns of bird, sea and animal life.

- **Exporting of wealth.** Much of the income generated by tourism in the developing world is not distributed back to the local population, sometimes leaving them worse off than they were before.

Eco-tourism or eco-trash?

Sure, it can be difficult to know what you're buying when you're researching a travel destination from afar, but you can rely on different eco-tourism labels around the world to help make sound travel choices. Two of the best known and trusted international labels to look out for are:

- **The Blue Flag Label** (www.blueflag.org)**:** This label covers companies operating at beaches and marinas around the world that meet strict criteria relating to water quality, environmental management, education and information, and safety. Unfortunately, Australia isn't included in this program.

- **Green Globe 21** (www.greenglobe21.com)**:** Based on the UN's Agenda 21 sustainability principles, the Green Globe label provides certification under four sustainability standards, but it's not limited to just eco-tour companies. Tourism in both cities and natural areas is covered.

Australia has its own advanced labelling program for eco-tourism, managed by Ecotourism Australia (www.ecotourism.org.au). In fact, Green Globe 21's ecotourism standards are based on those developed by Ecotourism Australia.

Ecotourism Australia's labelling accredits products not companies: Tours, attractions and accommodation. To be eligible for accreditation, Ecotourism Australia requires operators or businesses to meet certain economic, environmental and social sustainability principles. These include:

- **Economic sustainability.** The business or operator, and all its personnel, adopts and follows ethical business practices, and focuses on allowing people to directly and personally experience nature.

- **Environmental sustainability.** The business or operator positively contributes to the conservation of natural areas.

- **Social sustainability.** The business or operator exhibits sensitivity to the value of interpretation and involves different cultures, particularly indigenous culture.

Travel products that meet Ecotourism Australia's accreditation process display the Eco-certified label, as shown in Figure 17-1.

Figure 17-1:
Ecotourism
Australia's
Eco-Certified
label.

Creating a Sustainable Holiday Itinerary

After you have a clear idea of where you want to go, talk to a tourist agent or do your research online to put together an itinerary that incorporates eco-friendly tourist operators.

Some key questions to ask, or to look for online, when you're developing your travel itinerary are:

✔ Can you travel independently and make your own sustainable choices?

✔ Is the travel, or tour package, provided by a trusted and certified company? Refer to the preceding sections in this chapter for more details.

✔ Does the destination offer accommodation that's rated as green? For example, if you choose to stay in an apartment, does the accommodation offer energy-efficient appliances?

✔ Can you 'live' sustainably where you're going — just like you would at home?

Getting there and back

Travel has major energy impacts because it consumes fossil fuel and creates greenhouse gases. The most sustainable travel options are those that reduce your flying and driving mileage. Of course, local holidays are best from this point of view, especially if you can use trains, buses or bicycles to get you there.

For many holiday options, especially from Australia, flying is unavoidable. The trick is to reduce the amount of flying you do. Unfortunately, the domestic hub-and-spoke system adopted by most airlines around the world means you will end up flying indirect, consuming extra time and fuel. For example, getting a direct Qantas flight from Adelaide to Darwin might require you to get off in Sydney, Brisbane or Alice Springs and hop on another plane.

Usually, the cheaper the international flight, the more indirect (and time and fuel-consuming) it is likely to be. I know someone who recently flew return from Sydney to London and ended up flying via Tokyo, Moscow and Paris, which took well over a day to complete in each direction. This person chose the cheapest fare available.

Using the Internet, you can calculate the greenhouse gases emitted flying from one destination to another. The Climate Care Web site at www.climatecare.org in the United Kingdom, for example, enables you to enter your proposed departure and arrival airports and then calculates how many tonnes of carbon dioxide are emitted. For example, each person flying Sydney to San Francisco is directly responsible for the emission of 3.62 tonnes.

The beauty of sites like this one is that you can offset these emissions by contributing money to fund alternative-energy projects. Climate Friendly in Australia (www.climatefriendly.com.au) offers a similar service.

Of course, the best way to reduce your impact is to not fly at all, but these carbon trading schemes, at least, neutralise the impact you do have.

Your home away from home

Whether you decide to spend your holiday in the world's great cities or in a remote mountain eco-lodge, the place that you rest your head has its own environmental footprint.

If you choose a place that's a member of an eco-tourism or green hotel alliance, you save yourself the trouble of working out how environmentally sensitive each place is. The section 'Eco-tourism or eco-trash?' earlier in this chapter discusses these rating schemes in detail. Table 17-1 lists Web sites that can help you select accommodation that has been audited for sustainability.

Table 17-1	Environmentally Audited Accommodation
Ecotourism Australia	www.ecotourism.org
Green Hotels Association	www.greenhotels.com
Sustainable Travel International	www.sustainabletravel international.org
Responsible Travel	www.responsibletravel.com
The European VISIT (Voluntary Initiative for Sustainability in Tourism) initiative	www.yourvisit.info
Green Globe	www.greenglobe.org
Eco Club	www.ecoclub.com

If the place you want to stay in is not part of an association or alliance, the next best option is to choose self-service apartments or lodges that enable you to live as you would at home.

I know a lot of people don't like cooking, cleaning or even washing on a holiday, but by doing these things yourself you reduce the energy required to service your daily needs (for example, changing and washing your sheets and towels). Table 17-2 lists sites that I have used to find self-serviced accommodation.

Table 17-2	Self-Serviced Accommodation Chains
Homelink Home Exchange	www.homelink.com.au
Hostelling International	www.hihostels.com
Biz-Stay Short and Long Stay Apartment Directory	www.biz-stay.com
Saco Apartments	www.sacoapartments.co.uk
Hotel Club	www.hotelclub.com.au
Hotel Hero	www.hotelhero.com
Wotif	www.wotif.com

When you find a place you'd like to stay in, check out the accommodation's sustainability credentials. Here are some things to ask for:

- A copy of their environmental policy, especially with regard to waste and water use.
- Their suggestions for minimising damage to the local environment — their response will give you some idea of their degree of concern.
- Their suggestions for supporting the local community and how best to assist/contribute to the local economy.
- Evidence that the company employs local people.
- Evidence that the company makes use of local produce, materials and other services.

Another option is to exchange homes with another traveller from overseas. Not only does this reduce your accommodation costs to almost nothing, it considerably reduces the resources consumed to provide your accommodation. A number of online home-exchange networks make this approach a snap. Home Exchange Vacation, at www.homexchangevacation.com, is just one. Do a Google search to find more.

If you're planning to exchange homes with someone else, your questions can be less formal and specific than those you would ask an accommodation house. Nevertheless, to establish rapport with the owners, let them know that you care about their local environment.

Staying Sustainable While You're Away

Planning a holiday that's environmentally friendly is one side of the equation; the way you behave while you're on holiday is the other. Not only do your actions have an effect on the environment, they also provide an example for other tourists, and for locals who provide the services you purchase with your powerful tourist dollars.

Getting around

The most sustainable accommodation places make it easy for you to walk, cycle and catch public transport when you get there. It could be a lodge at the bottom of a hiking track or a centrally located apartment, or hotel in your favourite city or town. Whatever the case, make sure you get hold of a map and check that you're within walking or public transport distance of the attractions you're keen to see.

Most regions provide lots of local maps to help you get around. The Internet is also a great source for maps. To get started, check out these sites:

- Google Maps, `maps.google.com` (add a country extension to the Google Web address, such as 'au' for Australia or 'uk' for the United Kingdom, to get maps outside of the United States).
- MapQuest, `www.mapquest.com`.
- National Geographic Maps, `www.nationalgeographic.com/maps`.
- Online Maps to Everywhere, `www.multimap.com`.

If you really do need to drive when you're on holiday, hire one of those new alternative-fuel hybrid cars I discuss in Chapter 16.

Take only photos, leave only footprints

Whether you're trekking into the wild, or simply plan to visit a deserted beach, the following principles, developed by Leave No Trace (the Center for Outdoor Ethics in the United States, `www.lnt.org`), outline how to treat the environment when you visit natural areas:

- **Plan ahead and prepare:** Schedule your trip to avoid times of high use, visit only in small groups, and package your food and drink to minimise waste. Check regional tourist bureau information or heed signs for details about what activities you can or cannot do in areas.
- **Travel and camp on durable surfaces:** Choose ready-made camp sites, don't alter a site to suit your purposes, and stick to existing trails. Avoid camping in places where you can see that overuse is degrading an area.
- **Dispose of your waste properly:** If you bring it in, take it out. If you're camping, use biodegradable products for washing and cleaning.
- **Leave what you find:** Don't take any rocks, plants or other artifacts with you as you go.
- **Minimise damage from camp fires:** Light a camp fire only if permitted and try to use established fireplaces. Burn everything to ash to reduce the likelihood of your fire flaring up after you leave. Some people pour a bucket of water on a camp fire to ensure that it's out, but a more resourceful solution is to bury the fire. Get out your portable shovel and start digging.
- **Respect wildlife:** Don't feed the animals or other wildlife, or chase them around — you could alter their natural behaviour. Just view them quietly from a distance.
- **Be considerate of others:** Respect others visiting the same region. Excessive noise, unleashed pets and damaged surroundings take away from everyone's experience.

When in Rome . . .

The onus is on sustainable travellers to learn from and contribute to the cultures and communities they visit. This means you need to strike a balance between enjoying your privileges as a holiday maker and tourist, and immersing yourself as much as possible in the local culture.

There's little point travelling to remote areas inhabited by indigenous or traditional communities if you stay in a five-star resort that offers little or no interaction with the people you have gone to see. Cultural environments are sensitive. It's important that you support local businesses and communities when you visit. Buy locally produced goods, donate to local causes and learn about the traditions and culture of the local population.

Regardless of whether you're visiting a remote location or one of the world's biggest cities, use these simple guidelines to ensure that your tourism dollars support local businesses and that you learn as much as you can about the local culture:

✔ Choose accommodation that integrates with the local community and employs locals.

✔ Use local guides and assistants from the local community if you need help getting around.

✔ Buy locally-made crafts and products. For example, avoid large tourist shops that make cheap copies or are imported from elsewhere. Visit local marketplaces instead.

✔ Try to learn a little of the local language before you go. If you do, you'll get better results and much more pleasure from your interactions with the local population.

✔ Be respectful of the local culture by dressing appropriately. These days, most guide books suggest what to wear.

✔ Understand the local environment of the place you're visiting and, if required, conserve your consumption of water, food and energy. This is particularly important in many remote developing parts of the world.

Travel is all about broadening your horizons by discovering and understanding other people and places. The idea behind *responsible tourism* is to make sure that you enrich the places you visit (see the section 'Exporing the Eco-Tourism Phenomenon' earlier in this chapter). There's no point getting out into the local culture if you're going to be disrespectful and complain that things are different to what you expect at home.

When I stay in other cities and towns, I love to immerse myself in the place by trying to do what other locals do. Here are some things that you can do to experience the local community:

- If possible, rent an apartment, then buy food from markets and shops to cook at home — even better if the apartment you choose to stay in is green-rated and has energy-efficient appliances. This gives you the chance to mix with locals at the market and to try local foods. Your run-of-the-mill hotels don't encourage you to do this — they prefer you to order room service. For more information about staying in apartments, refer to the section 'Your home away from home' earlier in this chapter.

- Walk everywhere! Not only can you mix more with local people (remember, the only people you mix with on tour buses are other tourists), you can stay fit and healthy, and be pleasantly surprised by the many interesting things you see on your walks.

- Visit the local cafés for coffee or tea and observe life going past on the streets.

- If you can, read the local newspaper, tune in to some local radio and TV. You may find this hard to believe but, even if you don't understand a word of what is being said, the images and sounds can give you an appreciation for what makes the locals tick.

- Catch public transport. In some of the busiest cities in the world, you can get up-close and personal with the locals on a packed train or bus, as well as visit interesting areas that are outside walking distance and off the beaten tourist track.

Part VII

The Part of Tens

Glenn Lumsden

Christmas Past

Christmas Future

In this part . . .

1 once disliked writing lists; I didn't want my life to be so organised and structured. Now that I'm older and wiser I write lists all the time, and I find they help me get more things done.

This part of the book consists solely of lists. I offer lists about stuff you absolutely have to do, lists about Web sites that pick up on the themes I cover in this book, and lists of shining examples to help inspire and transform the way you live. Most important of all, I include a list for the most precious of beings — your kids. After all, they're the ones we hand this planet to.

Chapter 18

Ten Simple Ways to Start Living Sustainably

1 admit that living a sustainable life requires some planning, preparation and persistence. But you can start doing many simple things straight away, which instantaneously takes the pressure off the planet. Here's my top ten suggestions.

Catch a Train or Bus

Many people are hooked on travelling in cars, which spew greenhouse-forming gases and polluting particulates into the environment. Driving an alternative-fuel car is one way you can reduce your tailpipe emissions, but these vehicles are expensive to buy.

A cheaper and more effective solution is to leave your car in the garage and use public transport. Sure, public transport also produces pollution, but it's got nothing on cars. Many more people fit into one train or bus (or tram or ferry), compared to one car, so per person, pollution rates are much reduced (refer to Chapter 15 for more details).

Start by catching the train or bus to work one day a week. If you live too far away to walk to public transport, get a lift with someone else — or ride your bike to the bus depot or train station.

Walk or Ride Your Bike to the Shops

Before car travel became the norm, people regularly got their daily exercise by walking to shops and essential services. Back then, health officials didn't have to issue warnings to populations in cities and towns about the inherent dangers in becoming increasingly unfit and obese.

The next time you need to go shopping, why not give walking or riding a bike a go. Walking or cycling is even better than taking public transport because it generates no greenhouse gas emissions. If you're really fit (or want to be), start riding or walking to and from work; your workplace probably has showering facilities designed for this very purpose.

Note: Make walking or riding a part of your routine. Take a stroll every day and chat to neighbours along the way — you'll soon make new friends as well.

Convert Your Energy Supply to a Green Power Source

Converting to green power is easy: All you need to do is ask your local energy provider, or an independent company like Climate Friendly (www.climatefriendly.com.au), to change your supply from the normal electrical energy source — usually produced by burning coal — to a green power source. The company then purchases the equivalent amount of electricity from renewable energy sources, such as solar and wind.

Most energy suppliers now provide this option, for a few extra cents per day (refer to Chapter 4). All it takes is one phone call — you don't have to upgrade your electrical equipment and you'll see absolutely no difference in the quality or amount of electricity supplied. In fact, your local energy supplier may already have sent you some literature in the mail offering this service. If not, check the company's Web site.

Go for Green Cleaning Products

Most well-known commercial cleaning products are based on toxic chemical ingredients. When these are rinsed down the drain, they enter ecosystems, damaging waterways and contributing to outbreaks of algae blooms in rivers and streams.

The next time you're shopping, look for cleaning products that are made from more natural ingredients, such as baking soda, lemon and natural oils. Make sure the products you buy are biodegradable and don't contain phosphates. To find out more about green cleaning products, or to discover how to make your own natural cleaning products, refer to Chapter 5.

Slow Down

Slowing down may be the key to living sustainably, especially if you're hooked on buying the latest and greatest products on the market. Called *affluenza*, this addiction to consumption inflicts many people in the developed world, and is a primary reason why natural resources are in short supply today.

So, sit down and think whether you really need to buy that big, petrol-chugging 4WD. If you must buy a new vehicle, consider getting an alternative-fuel car, like a Toyota Prius. Ponder why you need to buy a big plasma TV, when a smaller, energy-smart, 51-centimetre TV shows the same pictures. Or whether you need to buy all those new clothes every time the season changes. Or . . . well, I think you get the picture.

Sort Out Your Clothes

Mass-produced fashion labels made from synthetic materials and sold in trendy fashion stores pressure you and your kids to dress a certain way. You can push back by simply not buying new clothes so often.

Start by recycling your clothes. That way, you'll save money and help keep clothes in circulation until they literally fall apart. Sort through your wardrobe and pick out the ones worth keeping, then set aside, in individual piles, the items that can be mended, passed on to a charity, or ready to be used as rags around the home. When you're done, take the clothes you can recycle to your favourite charity, and while you're there, browse through the racks. You never know, you might find a pair of 20-year-old mustard-coloured flares that are suddenly hip again (which only cost you a couple of dollars to buy).

I offer more simple tips to make your clothes last longer in Chapter 11.

Buy Organic Food

Buying organic food not only goes a long way towards living a healthy life, but ensuring the health of the planet as well. It also tells businesses that you want your food made and produced in the most natural way possible.

Thankfully, the market for organic food has increased substantially over the last five years, giving you access to a whole range of organic produce, even in big supermarkets. Check out Chapter 10 to find out what to look for when buying organic foodstuffs.

Support Sustainable Industries

These days, more and more companies claim that they're 'sustainable'. This is admirable, but to be classified as truly sustainable, a company needs to be involved in a sustainable industry. This means playing a part in manufacturing products that add value to the planet, rather than making or creating things that take something away from the earth.

Besides working for and choosing products made by companies and businesses involved in sustainable industries, you can invest in them as well. Ethical investment companies and Socially Responsible Investment (SRI) funds make serious commitments to three things: The environment, social justice and equitable economic development (refer to Chapter 14 for more details).

Investing your money in sustainable industries may be the most powerful tool you have to convince companies that sustainability is the way to go. Similar to converting your electricity supply to green power, getting in contact with an ethical investment broker is simple: Just source a good one online then pick up the phone.

Turn Off Appliances at the Power Point

Even if your home gets its electricity from green power sources, you still want to reduce how much you use.

The simplest way you can cut back on your electrical energy use — no matter how it's provided — is to turn off most of your electrical appliances at the wall before you go to bed. Yes, most of your appliances are still drawing power when you switch them off or when they enter sleep mode. Before you turn in for the night, go around the house and turn off appliances at the power point (except the fridge and freezer of course!). Needless to say, leaving on appliances like air-conditioning and heaters all night is a big no-no. For more information about managing the appliances in your home, refer to Chapter 5.

Turn Off the Tap

Government campaigns encouraging people to use less water around the home appear to be working. However, most people still use more water than they need to, and pray for the day when water restrictions will be lifted. But gone are the days of plentiful water supplies. Rainfalls are expected to continue to decline — which just puts more pressure on everyone to use even less, especially in urban areas.

The simplest step you can take to use less water is to reduce the amount of time you leave taps on. Whether you're cleaning your teeth, watering the garden or washing the dishes, count the seconds every time you're running a tap. This simple but effective step can help take the pressure off water supplies.

Chapter 19

Ten Informative and Fun Web sites

T he Internet is a goldmine of information about sustainable living. The following Web sites are my favourite places to visit when I want more eco-friendly information.

Australian Certified Organic

www.australianorganic.com.au

To find out where good food comes from, check out the Australian Certified Organic (ACO) Web site, produced by the Biological Farmers of Australia (BFA). BFA is Australia's largest certifier of organic and biodynamic produce and has more than 1,500 operators on its books. The Web site explains how organic food is produced and includes an online database listing every company that has been certified by the BFA.

Ecodirectory

www.ecodirectory.com.au

The Ecodirectory and its online shopping site, the Ecoshop, provide you with comprehensive links to Australian companies involved in the promotion of sustainable living. The Ecoshop is not as comprehensive as other online shopping sites, but nothing beats the Ecodirectory if you're looking for information on sustainable services in Australia.

Ecological Footprint Quiz

www.myfootprint.org

According to the Earth Day Network, the average person's ecological footprint is bigger than the planet can handle. At this interactive Web site you can calculate your footprint — that is, work out the amount of land area required to support your consumption habits (refer to Chapter 2 to find out more). Go on, take the quiz. Discover how many hectares of earth you're using.

The Eco-Sustainable Hub

www.ecosustainable.com.au/links.htm

This online hub contains one of the most comprehensive lists of global sustainability Web sites that I've come across. It brings together resources from around the world. Just about everything and anything sustainable is covered here.

Freecycle

http://freecycle.org

Freecycle is a unique, not-for-profit Web site that promotes free community exchange of secondhand or unwanted goods. The Freecycle Network, sponsored by Yahoo! Groups, is free to join and open to any individual who wants to give something away (or take something off someone's hands). Freecycle groups are moderated by local volunteers who facilitate the exchange of goods within each community. The Freecycle Network started off in Tuscson, Arizona, and has grown to 3,700 communities around the world.

Making the Modern World

www.makingthemodernworld.org.uk

Set up by the British Science Museum, this Web site summarises the development of the modern world and explains the impact (and destruction) humans have had on the planet during this time.

The site provides colourful and easy-to-read stories about how the developed world evolved into a modern industrial society from the 18th century onwards. Even the kids will love it — and learn from it.

Subway Navigator

www.subwaynavigator.com

You can trace the world's railway systems on this Web site. When you're next organising a sustainable holiday, make sure you check this amazingly detailed site to find which railway systems are near the hotels you want to stay in, and which ones you access to reach the tourist attractions you want to visit.

Sustain Lane

```
www.sustainlane.com
```

Sustain Lane is probably the most organised and best illustrated of all the sustainable Web sites on the Internet. A comprehensive guide to sustainable living at home, Sustain Lane focuses on food, health and family matters. This site is based in the United States, so its rankings that highlight the most sustainable US cities to live in and where to shop aren't too helpful unless you're visiting the country. However, the site also provides great advice and articles relating to healthy living.

Sustainable Gardening Australia

```
www.sgaonline.org.au
```

At the Sustainable Gardening Australia site, you can wise up on sustainable garden practices and eco-friendly garden products. You'll find stacks of information on choosing local plants, sustainable gardening techniques, water conservation, mulching and composting, landscaping and design, and more.

The Greenhouse Office (For the Home)

```
www.greenhouse.gov.au/yourhome/index.htm
```

The Australian Greenhouse Office site is both a consumer shopping guide and a technical building guide that aims to help people design, construct and renovate their homes in the most eco-friendly way possible. The site helps you design and build for energy efficiency and water conservation.

Chapter 20

Ten Environmental Innovations

Anyone with a simple grasp of economics knows that entrepreneurs will provide any service if enough consumers demand it. As more people seek eco-friendly products and services, an increasing number of businesses have jumped at the chance to create innovative solutions. In this chapter, I present ten of the best eco-friendly innovations.

Alternative Fuels

Despite media hype to the contrary, car companies have invested a lot of time, effort and money into alternative ways of powering cars with renewable, clean and energy-efficient fuels. Alternative fuels that are less polluting and more energy efficient include low-sulfur diesel, biodiesel made from vegetable crops, gaseous fuels including hydrogen and natural gas, and ethanol-based fuels. You can also add new electric cars to this list. (Refer to Chapter 16 for more information about alternative fuels.)

There's really no reason — other than overcoming the entrenched and economically powerful culture of oil production — why cleaner, alternative-fuel cars aren't being mass produced. But when lots of people begin driving around in alternative-fuel cars, the current level of greenhouse gas emissions will be cut substantially.

At the moment, hydrogen-powered, fuel-cell cars may be the most innovative and eco-friendly of the current alternatives. Most of the world's major car makers are currently racing each other to get the first fully-fledged hydrogen fuel-cell car on the road.

Eco-Design and Construction

Thanks to the following innovations, you now have more ways to design, construct and outfit buildings using sustainable materials:

- Modern architectural, engineering and building techniques that use natural elements to light, heat and cool buildings effectively, creating energy-efficient buildings.
- Natural building materials that carry low levels of embodied energy.
- New products made from natural materials that are both energy efficient and renewable, including cork, some timbers, grasses, straw and mud.
- Designer eco-friendly furniture and flooring products.

These days, many architects and builders constructing new homes and office buildings for clients strive to meet the latest environmental design standards. New commercial buildings lead the way. To find out more about what's happening at the top end of town, check out Chapter 13.

Energy Star

Finding a new TV or computer that's not covered by the Energy Star system to help you save power is a difficult thing to do. These days, most electronic manufacturers use the technology in their products.

Energy Star equipment can be switched to sleep mode or powers down to sleep mode when you stop using it (usually after a few minutes) — greatly reducing the electrical energy that it draws in standby mode. For more details about Energy Star products, refer to Chapter 4.

Green Power

Most Australian energy suppliers can now purchase electricity from renewable energy sources, such as solar and wind, and offer these alternative power supplies to you. As more people sign up for these alternative electrical energy sources, companies can invest more into increasing the amount of alternative energy that's produced and decreasing the amount they obtain from unsustainable sources, such as coal. For lots more information about green power, refer to Chapters 4 and 18.

Internet Retailing

Internet retailing may seem like a strange bedfellow in a list emphasising sustainable innovations. However, the Internet and Internet businesses such as eBay have elevated the status of secondhand trading across the globe. Right now, buying and selling secondhand goods on eBay is trendy; just about everyone I know is reusing and recycling their wares. Even suburban markets, car boot sales and garage sales have been swept up by this trend and have become more popular. The Internet has also encouraged freecycling, which enables people to locally exchange goods they no longer need.

Rating and Labelling Systems

Thanks to organisations auditing and labelling products to ensure they meet various sustainability credentials, people can shop, buy and consume products with confidence. Whether you're shopping for organic food, electrical appliances or want to gauge a product's fuel consumption, these rating and labelling systems support and help drive demand for sustainable products.

Recycling Waste

Once upon a time, all your food waste, empty plastic bottles, soft drink cans, old paper and cardboard boxes went into the same bin and were then burned in one big incinerator or sent to the same landfill site. Sorting these throwaway items and recycling much of the stuff is an innovation that has caught on in most developed countries. In fact, because people have been so willing to sort their own rubbish and waste, companies have been able to invest in new recycling plants and factories, especially in Australia.

Smart Growth (The Urban Vision)

Not so much a product as an innovative policy, *smart growth* promotes sustainable housing and building products. An American concept that promotes sustainable living through urban planning, smart growth applies to most developed nations that experience urban sprawl (refer to Chapter 3 for information about urban sprawl in Australian cities and towns).

Smart growth development is considered innovative but actually harks back to the way cities and towns used to function before the advent of the car. Smart growth is the opposite of urban sprawl and aims for the following outcomes:

✔ More compact building design to minimise space required for new residential development.

✔ A range and mix of housing opportunities and choices.

✔ Walkable neighbourhoods.

✔ Preserved open spaces, farmland and nature reserves.

✔ Integrated communities.

✔ A variety of transportation choices, with a heavy emphasis on public transport, walking and cycling.

The good news is that an increasing number of government agencies are now demanding that new suburban areas be based on smart growth principles.

Triple Bottom-Line Reporting

Many companies now financially factor in their environmental and social position alongside their profit and losses. Called *triple bottom-line reporting*, this innovative accounting practice allows companies to highlight their investment in sustainable initiatives, whether they're making environmental improvements or investing in local communities.

Even mining, oil and car manufacturing companies are now embracing triple bottom-line reporting. Of course, these companies may simply be 'greenwashing' their position for the time being (refer to Chapter 14 for details about triple bottom-line reporting and greenwashing). In the long term, however, I believe that triple bottom-line reporting will encourage these companies to become more sustainable.

Water Recycling

In my opinion, water recycling is the most innovative sustainability initiative of them all. Technology now makes it possible to recycle water that was once washed down the drain and reuse it as drinking water. Amazing! Even at home, you can reuse the greywater from your kitchen sink or your washing machine on your garden. Some homeowners even recycle the greywater to supply water to their toilets.

Every one of these solutions takes pressure off urban and rural water supplies. For more details, check out Chapter 7.

Chapter 21

Ten Things to Teach Your Kids

*H*opefully, your children are learning about the benefits of sustainable living both at home (refer to Chapter 5) and at school. But why stop there? In this chapter I give you some other important messages about the environment that you can share with your kids.

Appreciate Space

In this section, I'm wearing my urban planning hat. One of the major contributors to urban sprawl (and the many social and environmental problems it causes), is people's desire to occupy large areas of private space. Lots of Australians live in big homes with roomy bedrooms, large living areas and play rooms, a backyard, car parking spaces for two cars and space around the property to separate themselves from their neighbours.

Why do Australians desire so much space? One reason is they want their children to grow up as they did, on properties with lots of space around them. But this continues the legacy that contributes to urban sprawl. I sometimes wonder how European, African, South American or Asian parents would respond if an Australian told them that Aussie kids are better off simply because they have rumpus rooms and big backyards to play in!

I encourage Australian kids aged ten and older to:

- Play with friends in public parks and spaces rather than play by themselves in their own backyards.
- Use their bikes and public transport to get around, rather than expect their parents to drive them everywhere.
- Understand that growing up in an apartment or townhouse is not abnormal and that, in fact, most of the world lives this way.
- Walk to their local shops, library and other community facilities.

How Your Garden Grows

Not all backyards are a waste of space; quite the contrary. Many support local ecosystems. A sustainable backyard garden also reuses household greywater, composts food scraps from the kitchen and also puts food on the table, like fruit and vegetables.

To help your kids appreciate recycling, water use and how things grow, get them involved in the garden. Offer them some space to grow their own plants from seeds. If that doesn't hold their attention, try worm farming. Some children are really attracted to worm farms, along with the mulch they provide for the garden and the local bird life they attract. Other kids just love picking fresh fruit and vegetables, especially if they can eat it straight away. If this is the case, help them start a strawberry patch, or grow tomatoes or snow peas.

Where Electricity Comes From

When I was growing up, I took electricity for granted — it was just there in the walls, waiting to be used. I had no idea how it got there, although I figured out that the overhead wires on the street had something to do with it. For a long time, I didn't know that generating electricity to supply most Australian cities and towns relied on burning coal, or that this created environmental problems. Obviously, electricity was not a hot topic in my childhood home.

If you tell your kids from a young age how electricity can be made, how it works, and how much it costs, you'll get them thinking about the environment and the different ways energy can be harnessed (refer to Chapters 2 and 4 if you need a primer). And if you emphasise ways they can minimise how much electricity they use (check out Chapter 5), your kids are more likely to not take electricity for granted as they get older. Hopefully, by that time, clean renewable electrical energy will be the norm.

Keep On Cycling

A youngster's first opportunity to escape their parents happens when they get their first bike and start riding to places they could only get to if someone, usually mum or dad, gave them a lift. A bike is sometimes the first step to independence and freedom!

When you give your kids their first bikes, don't simply discuss the safety facts. Explain the social and environmental benefits of riding a bike as well: For example, bikes don't produce pollution and they *do* provide an inexpensive way to get around.

The trick is encouraging them to keep on riding, even when they're old enough to drive a car. Of course, the best way to encourage them is to lead by example. Ride with your children whenever you can while they're growing up.

Throw Less Stuff Away

I used to empty the contents of the classroom bin without a giving a thought to where the rubbish ended up. No-one ever told me. In this era of recycling, though, most kids are taught at school what can be recycled and what can't, but it shouldn't end there.

Recycling is only one way to reduce waste (refer to Chapter 8). Kids should also be shown how to generate less waste and reuse things more often. To get started teach your kids to think about what they're throwing in the bin. Set up separate bins around the home — for plastics, compost and general waste, for example — to give them control over what happens to waste after it leaves their hands.

Appreciate Water

Kids love swimming and playing in water. But what your kids may not appreciate is how precious water is. For example, do your children do their best to preserve water when they use the hose or the bathroom?

Explaining that water is essential to life, and is in short supply, is not as hard as you may think. Get started by telling them these basic facts:

✔ Everything you drink is mostly water.

✔ Your body is mostly water.

✔ People, animal and plants die without water.

✔ You pay for water — show them the water bill.

✔ A drought happens when not enough rain falls to replenish water supplies — back this up with news stories if a drought is in full swing.

If you discuss these facts with kids, they'll soon start lecturing you, and the neighbours, on using water wisely.

Respect Nature

Most kids love the outdoors. There's no better opportunity to teach your kids the value of the environment than to take them camping and adopt some 'leave no trace' principles (check out Chapter 17).

Follow these guidelines when you take your kids camping:

✔ Minimise waste and dispose of it properly.

✔ Don't alter natural areas to suit your purposes.

✔ Avoid camping in places where you can see that overuse has degraded the area.

✔ Use biodegradable products, especially for washing and cleaning.

✔ Leave what you find where you found it.

✔ Respect wildlife by not feeding animals or other wildlife. Instead, view them from a distance.

As well as adopting these tips, talk about the decisions you make to keep within camping ground or national park rules and discuss how your actions help protect the environment.

Respect Other Cultures

Appreciating how other cultures live and what they value can help kids understand the social aspects of sustainability.

Explain fair trading, globalisation and the importance of a strong local community to your children. Help your kids understand how other cultures live by visiting the areas in your city or region where people from different cultures are visible. Discuss the day-to-day problems that people in other countries have to deal with. Sit down with your children and watch news stories and documentaries about other cultures.

Be Trendy without Buying New Gear

I know, I know. The peer group pressure among kids to buy the latest fashion is stronger than any influence you might hope to have. It's a tough call to encourage your children to recycle or reuse their clothes as they get older. Even so, it's an extremely valuable lesson if you can pull it off.

Taking your kids on shopping expeditions to secondhand shops when they're young is an important first step. So is teaching your kids how to care for their clothes and how to become handy with a needle and thread (refer to Chapter 11 for more tips and hints).

Setting an example, and introducing your children to other people who live by the same principles, is the best way to convince your kids that what you're asking them to do is not unreasonable.

Eat Healthy Food

Of course, you want your kids to grow up consuming less of those unnatural chemicals and other additives that enter the food production process. Make sure your kids get a taste for fresh fruit and vegetables as early as possible, before they get addicted to soft drinks and snacks that come in packets.

Explain some of the food production processes to them. They'll probably be taught some of the basics at school, but you can fill in the blanks by telling them about the mass-market processes that involve food additives, genetic engineering and unnatural farming methods (refer to Chapter 10 for more details). Hopefully, they'll be so disgusted they'll actually request healthier and more sustainable foods as they get older.

Be aware that talking to your children about what goes into the foods they eat will only make sense if the whole family has converted to healthy eating habits.

Index

● O ●

● P ●

Notes

Notes

FOR DUMMIES®

Business

Small Business
1-74031-109-4
$39.95

Superannuation
1-74031-061-6
$39.95

Personal Finance
1-74031-004-7
$39.95

Business Plans
1-74031-124-8
$39.95

Buying & Selling Your Home
1-74031-166-3
$39.95

Investing
1-74031-041-1
$39.95

MYOB Software
0-7314-0541-2
$39.95

GST and BAS
1-74031-033-0
$39.95

Reference   ## Gardening

Superannuation - Choosing a Fund
1-74031-125-6
$29.95

Tracing Your Family History Online
1-74031-071-3
$39.95

Job Hunting
1-74031-030-6
$39.95

Gardening
1-74031-007-1
$39.95

FOR DUMMIES®

Technology

1-74031 086-1
$39.95

1-74031-160-4
$39.95

1-7403-1159-0
$39.95

1-74031-123-X
$39.95

Cooking   ## Pets

1-74031-010-1
$39.95

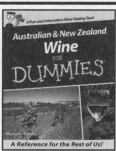

1-74031-008-X
$39.95

1-74031-040-3
$39.95

1-74031-028-4
$39.95

Parenting   ## Health & Fitness

1-74031-103-5
$39.95

1-74031-042-X
$39.95

1-74031-143-4
$39.95

1-74031-140-X
$39.95

FOR DUMMIES®

Health & Fitness Cont.

Football

1-74031-122-1
$39.95

Basketball

1-7403-1135-3
$39.95

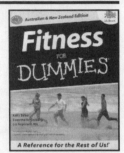

Asthma and Allergies

1-74031-054-3
$39.95

Fitness

1-74031-009-8
$39.95

Golf

1-74031-011-X
$39.95

Cricket

1-7403-1173-6
$39.95

Aussie Rules

1-74031-035-7
$39.95

Fishing

1-74031-006-3
$39.95

Yoga

1-74031-059-4
$39.95

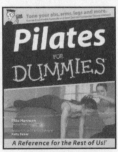

Pilates

1-74031-074-8
$39.95

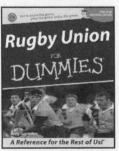

Rugby Union

1-74031-073-X
$39.95

Diabetes

1-74031-094-2
$39.95